DONALD FRASER

Photo, Annan, Glasgow

Yours very sincerely
Donald Fraser

DONALD FRASER

OF LIVINGSTONIA

BY

AGNES R. FRASER, M.B., Ch.B.

AUTHOR OF
"TEACHING HEALTHCRAFT TO AFRICAN WOMEN"

HODDER AND STOUGHTON
LIMITED   LONDON
MCMXXXIV

First Printed, October 1934
Second Impression, November 1934

Made and Printed in Great Britain
by Turnbull & Spears, Edinburgh

FOREWORD

In the world of missions Dr Donald Fraser was an outstanding international figure. Among African missionaries of this century he held a pre-eminent place. Throughout a great part of Nyasaland he was the chief founder of a new civilisation, and the spiritual father of a people. For a whole generation Scotland knew him as the most romantic and captivating of missionary pioneers, and in his later years he became perhaps the most widely beloved of living Scotsmen. Yet more : there were many people for whom he incarnated the authentic essential spirit of the religion he commended ; beyond everything else they felt that he was a great Christian.

Such a life demanded that some record of it should be written. It was with the utmost diffidence that Mrs Fraser yielded to pleading that she should undertake the task. Now that the thing is done, the prescience of those who urged her to it is fully justified. It is not the ordinary official type of biography that she has written, but something more intimate. She has painted for us in the vivid colours of experience the African scene and the realities there of missionary work and endeavour ; and she has succeeded in capturing in what she writes the very spirit of the man whose story she is telling, so that he lives again for those who knew him, in all his lovableness, and even those who did not know him must feel his winsomeness and charm. Her story of the African work is one of the most convincing of apologetics for Christian missions ; but the presentation of a life so profoundly and attractively Christian is much more : it is the best kind of apologetic, as Fraser himself in his lifetime was felt to be, for the Christian faith itself.

MILLAR PATRICK

v

ACKNOWLEDGMENTS

ALTHOUGH I have tried to overcome my reticence and to share my memories of my husband with those who will read this book because they knew and loved him, I am yet acutely conscious of how much I have kept back of the best, and how much I have omitted that might well have been included. Many facts and numerous friends have been left out of the story to allow space for the less familiar tale of the African years, and even in those chapters colleagues and mission history have had to be blocked out to keep this sketch within reasonable limits.

It is impossible to mention all whom I would fain thank for their help in sending letters and reminiscences that have filled up the gaps in my personal knowledge; but I must record my indebtedness to Miss Hunter for copying letters, to Miss Genner for typing services and for compiling the index, and to my mother, under whose roof I found quietness and leisure to write.

Whether or not I should thank the friends who urged me to undertake this task myself, I must at least acknowledge gratefully the interest they have shown and the encouragement they have given me. The Rev. W. T. Cairns and Dr Millar Patrick not only read the manuscript but revised the proofs, and now Dr Patrick is seeing the volume through the press for me.

AGNES R. FRASER

September 1934

CONTENTS

LIST OF ILLUSTRATIONS

CHAPTER I

DONALD FRASER was born and bred in Argyllshire, and, like all true Highlanders, retained to the end of his life a deep love for his native countryside. Many who have heard him speak must recall his description of his birthplace " lying among the hills, lapped by the waves," and he always felt that the hills on which he had wandered, the fields in which he and his brothers and sisters had played, the loch in which he had bathed and sailed, were all part of him. On one of the last days of his life he must have been " seeing with love most passionate " these scenes of his boyhood, for when, on noticing him place his hands together and then raise them, I asked if he wanted anything, his reply was, " Oh, for a plunge into Lochfyne ! " He was always seeing " the long drab ebb when the tide was out, and the sweet loch shining in the sun, or lashed by the winds when the tide was in, with the brown-sailed fishing skiffs racing in long procession as they came home on the Saturday mornings." He could always recall the smell of the barking of the nets, the crowded excitement of the feeing markets, the silent somnolence of the streets till they wakened up at noon, when the buses went to Ardrishaig to meet the steamer, and came back an hour later laden with passengers. Always he was hearing " the clattering of the Sabbath bells, the slow singing in the church, the cadences of his father's voice in the pulpit."

His father, the Free Church minister at Lochgilphead, had come from the Fraser country about Beauly. An old

1

diary with faded writing found after his death contained all that the family knew of his early history. They had met no relations on the paternal side, though they remembered that twice when in the North their father had vainly tried to trace any members of his family. One of the times was when Donald accompanied his father to the Free Church Assembly, in the year when it met at Inverness.

William Fraser's father—Donald's grandfather—had belonged to Killearnan in the Black Isle, and lived in the Muir of Tarradale ; his mother was Mary Bisset from Knockbain. The father was a crofter and weaver, and married twice, William being the youngest of three sons by the second wife. Before his birth in 1824 the family had moved to Inverness. While the boy was still very young both his parents went down at the same time with some fever of which the father died, the mother recovering to find herself a helpless widow with three boys. All William could remember of his father was his saying, " Poor Willie, what will become of you ? "

As soon as he was strong enough the boy had to go to work, and became apprentice in a painter's shop. He records that he was " without Christ till about the year of the Disruption, when he and some other young men became anxious about their souls and by God's grace were enabled to give themselves to the Lord Jesus Christ." At this time a great desire possessed him to become a minister of the Free Church of Scotland, and he took every available opportunity of educating himself by attending night classes. When he was thirty he went to Glasgow to work at his trade and find better opportunities of continuing his education. Getting an appointment as a city missionary he began to attend the University, and afterwards the Free Church Theological Hall, which he was one of the first batch of students to enter after it was opened in 1856.

Finishing his course in 1860 he went as assistant to Mr Mackenzie, the minister at Lochgilphead, arriving with all he possessed in the world—three shillings—in his pocket. "But," he adds, "I trust I had greater treasure than money." He was very kindly received by the minister and his family, was ordained the following year, and, until at the age of sixty-eight he passed away suddenly and peacefully, as his younger daughter bent to kiss him good-night while he lay on the sofa, he knew no other home.

To that Manse on the hillside he took his bride, and in it a family of six boys and two girls were brought up. They kept two maids, at least in the early years, had a cow to supply the necessary milk, and the incredible number of loaves that went up the hill to satisfy the healthy appetites of the household was something the baker's wife talked about to her daughter in her old age.

Donald, born in 1870, came fourth in the family, and, if the possibly partial evidence of his nurse, still alive, is to be credited, he was "the darlingest baby." Mrs Fraser's time was not so entirely engrossed with the family that she was unable to take an interest in other affairs. She was keenly interested in the Zenana Mission of the Free Church, and had a regular work-party for the women of the congregation; and each year a box was sent to India, occasioning a purdah party out there which was a great joy to the Indian ladies for whom such a social event was an unwonted treat. This bit of work was the outcome of an invitation to Mrs Morrison of Bengal to come and address a Ladies' Meeting. She stayed at the Manse, greatly enjoying the visit with its happy friendliness, and remembers being taken round the garden by her hostess on the following day and coming across a very neat little shanty compactly built of branches, straw, etc. An iron spike had been driven into the wall, and from it a three-legged pot was suspended. "This is what Donaldie has been doing," said his mother; "he has made this all by himself." "That is grand training for Africa," said the visitor, little thinking how true the chance forecast was.

Dr Duff was another of their missionary visitors, and that the parents' interest was real was proved by the fact that, when Donald told his father of his intention to be a missionary, he learned from him for the first time that he had been dedicated by his parents to this service.

It also happened that Donald's first hero was a missionary—a lad from his own district. In later life he more than once talked to boys about Chalmers of New Guinea—the great big man bubbling with energy who sailed about the islands of Polynesia and New Guinea facing wild savages, hurricanes and tumults of angry men, the pepper and salt of his life being danger. He heard Chalmers speak at a meeting at Inveraray to an audience which included the Duke and Duchess of Argyll, seated in semi-regal state, before he went back for what was to prove his last term. No wonder he was not afraid of the element of romance in trying to interest boys in the missionary adventure of the Church! Had not R. L. Stevenson, so attracted to this man, the biggest human he had met, reflected how different his life might have been had he met him earlier?

Another interest—unusual at that time—in the Highland Manse seems to have been Temperance. In those days Lochgilphead boasted of a big fishing fleet, and drunkenness was not uncommon, so Mr Fraser started a Temperance Society and got many of the men to promise that they would not drink more than one glass of whisky a day. But he forgot to reckon that while they were out in their boats they drank nothing, and so had a good many glasses to their credit when they came ashore! Young Donald appears to have shared his father's zeal. He had a tale of having started a Band of Hope among his school companions. He was elected president, and the first meeting went off successfully; but the second was handicapped by the absence of the chairman, who had been "kept in" at school!

The boys had a boat, rigged with a small sail, on Lochfyne, and grew up accustomed to the sea, being as adventurous and careless of danger as boys are. Their aunt, who lived at Ardrishaig and commanded a view of the loch, used many a time to watch that boat anxiously when the weather was stormy, expecting to see her nephews drown before her very eyes. On one occasion at least even the less timid fishermen grew so concerned about their safety that they put out hastily to the rescue. It was not the only time in his life that Donald was nearly drowned.

They seem to have been pioneer "hikers," too. For a long time Donald and his brother John, having saved up their pocket-money till they were able to buy a quantity of unbleached calico, were at work on a tent, sewed without help from anyone. Their father was so pleased with their handiwork that he readily gave them permission to go off tramping with it. Evidently there was in the district more than one farmer's wife who had once been "the Manse servant," and gave a hospitable welcome to the campers when they pitched their tent in her vicinity.

Many of our summer holidays during furloughs from Africa and in later years were spent in that neighbourhood, and it was during one of the earliest of these, when the family were young, that we got our introduction to the scenes of "Daddy's" boyhood. The old Manse had passed after the Union of 1900 into the hands of the remaining Free Church, and was standing empty, with the garden overgrown and strangely smaller than when he had played in it as a boy ! But, getting in through a window, we went over the house, seeing the shutter in the dining-room behind which the strap used to hang, and hearing of the day when the family somehow got upset and hysterically " giggly " at family prayers, and their father was reduced to laying aside the Bible, getting out the strap (apparently its use was infrequent in the hands of the kindly old man), using it, and then resuming devotions, presumably with a chastened crowd of youngsters. We saw the room in which the boys were quarantined with scarlet fever, and the ridge of the outhouse wing on which, to her horror, their mother discovered her three patients, exit having been made through the bedroom window. We saw where the first family group had been taken by a local photo- grapher who had to be " encouraged." He had brought a suitable background, and setting it up at the back of the house, grouped the parents and children in front. But the large little family spread beyond the bounds of the rural background so that the lake and rustic bridge were flanked by kitchen walls. But that did not detract from the interest of the picture of the bright-eyed little group with a strong family resemblance.

We went down the brae where they used to toboggan in winter, and saw the cross-roads where the Lochgilphead boys used to meet their Ardrishaig rivals and faction fights took place. So keen was the feeling between the two places that their boy cousins from the latter town, when coming to visit them at the Manse, went by a roundabout road rather than venture through the village. We saw the drinking fountain put up to the memory of his eldest brother Alec, when he died in the Red Sea, by those whom he had attended during a cholera outbreak in India. In Ardrishaig we saw the house where his mother had lived when she was Violet Ferguson, and we heard from those who remembered her how handsome she had been, and how before her marriage she used to drive about in a little pony phaeton. She died, after some years of invalidism, before her husband, and he summed up her character in the words, " a very transparent Christian."

The minister's boys began their education in the village school, and it was Mrs Macalpine, who kept the most hospitable baker's shop that our family had ever known, who told me, to my husband's embarrassment and my delight, that wee Donald had been " a great favourite with the lassies," including herself. " He was that bonny with his beautiful wee curls all over his head that they were fair in love with him." And as she spoke she was recklessly taking down bottle after bottle of the sweeties he had probably bought from her mother in his childhood, and filling up paper bags with which to load his pockets.

We noted too with interest how, still, he was one of themselves. To some of the older people who had held " the minister " in love and reverence and some awe, Donald was just his father's son. He had to suffer comparisons—not always, in their mind, to his advantage. Once when he arrived to preach at some local church, riding his push-bike, the elder at the plate shook his head, sadly remarking, " Your worthy father would never have done that ! " " No," replied the son with a smile, " he would have hired a man and trap."

He used to tell with joy of one old woman who, after scrutinising him carefully, said, " You're no a bit like your faither. *He* was a bonny man." Another, more polite, exclaimed when he introduced himself, " Indeed and I'd have known you anywhere : it is your father's very teeth you have got ! " Her sight was, we hoped and suspected, not acute enough to see his blushes and the suppressed amusement of his wife and family, who knew that terms of

B

five years at a time in Africa, with no dentist nearer than hundreds of miles away, have a habit of hastening the period at which one begins to have one's third set. In reality he bore a strong resemblance to his father. One had only to cover the white beard in a photo which always stood on his son's mantelpiece to see how like Donald's own were the eyes looking out from under shaggy brows and the hair so early white.

It was more especially his contemporaries who were proud of their old schoolfellow, and gleaned all the news they could get of him, and rejoiced in any honours that came to him. They were among the first to wire congratulations when he was elected Moderator, and, not content with that, they presented him with his robes of office, subscriptions being given even by members of the Free Church who had remained aloof when the Union took place; for ecclesiastical divisions never broke any of his friendships. When he arrived for the presentation of these robes the porter met him on the quay with a friendly "Where's your luggage, Donald?" and the letters he received from an old fisherman began with the same friendly use of his Christian name.

Sometimes they felt that it might not be the correct thing to be so familiar. The following conversation between an old woman and an old man is related by one who overheard it:

"You'll no be guessing who I saw in the bus."

"No, no; who was it?"

"Well, when I set eyes on him, 'It'll no' be Donald Fraser,' I says to him without thinking. 'Oh! I beg your pardon, it's the *Rev.* Donald Fraser I should be saying.' '*Donald* Fraser's fine,' says he to me, and it was himself all the way from Africa."

The last summer that he was in that neighbourhood our

English hosts were impressed with the feeling of humiliation he evinced when a polite but somewhat drink-sodden native of the district accosted him and borrowed some cash from him. " He was an old playmate," said Donald, blushing to think of the man's present loss of self-respect. He could never dissociate himself or keep aloof from those he had lived among and known—their shame and degradation were always his, too.

There was much in his boyhood's experience that was training him for his future, and helping him towards an understanding of those other highlanders with whom his life was to be identified in the coming years.

CHAPTER II

GLASGOW DAYS

As the boys grew older they went to board in Glasgow in order to attend the High School there. Those years seem to have been a little drab and depressing on the whole. Perhaps that was to some extent inevitable for one so naturally dependent on his physical environment as Donald, but it was accentuated by the harshness of one of the masters, who did not realise the dispiriting effect of his constant punishments on the shy, sensitive boy. In later life we once travelled with him, and he rather sought out, and was very cordial to, his quondam pupil; but, in the privacy of our cabin, Donald confessed that he found it a little hard to forget and forgive the former unsympathetic attitude which had made him feel so hopeless about his mental powers. Perhaps it was this early experience that taught him to believe as firmly as he did in the power of encouragement. " Blessed is he that saveth a man from self-despisings " was one of his favourite sayings.

Though he was at school with those who became his intimate friends in College days, he seems to have had no real chum except J. M. E. Ross,[1] another shy and rather delicate lad who, though a brilliant scholar, was not able to join much in the school sports. On Sundays the Fraser boys attended Dr Andrew Bonar's church, and there they were brought in touch with the Miller family, at whose home they often spent their Saturdays—preferably, for some mysterious reason, gathering in the laundry—and

---

[1] Later the Editor of the *British Weekly*.

this was the beginning of his friendship with Harry Miller.[1]

The happiest times of those school years were the holidays, with which was associated the excitement of travelling on the *Columba*.[2] In order to do justice to the unstinted meals to be obtained on board the boys used often to start without any breakfast, and to his family in later years he used to dilate, with a reminiscent twinkle in his eye, on the greater variety in the fare and the larger size of the helpings that prevailed in those former days compared with the meals to which he loved to treat his own children on board. Throughout life the joy of a day on the beautiful Clyde estuary never palled. Once, passing through the Kyles of Bute on a lovely summer day, he recalled an incident which happened at that point when he was a young man. Going up to an old minister he had exclaimed enthusiastically, " Isn't this glorious ? What a revelation of God there is in sea and hills and sky ! " " My young friend," said the old man dryly, " beware of Pantheism ! "

To his sisters he was deeply attached. One year, when in Glasgow, he realised with dismay that Mary's birthday was very near and he had not a penny of pocket-money to buy her a present. To let it pass without a gift was so unthinkable that he took the only way he could devise of obtaining money : he went down to the station to see if he could earn something by carrying a bag. The first gentleman he accosted noticed that the boy was not of the usual type and told him kindly to go home—this was no place for him. But he stayed till he had earned the cash, and the birthday present was bought and despatched without his older brothers finding out what he had done.

Before these school years had ended he had had his first

---

[1] Dr Harry Miller of the Pleasance Church and Settlement, Edinburgh.
[2] A well-known Clyde steamer.

definite religious experience in Berkeley Street Church,
now a picture-house, near St Andrew's Halls, which he
once pointed out to me as the place where he was converted.   It was an experience that made him willing, as a
lad in his first or second year at the University, to join
with other students in addressing an evangelistic meeting
in Pollokshields Free Church.   The youthfulness and
the courage of the lad, and the sincerity and straight-
forwardness with which he spoke, made a vivid impression on one of his Divinity Hall friends whose
memory of him starts with this incident.

In 1886, at the age of sixteen, he went up to the University.
Although he always alluded to himself as a hopeless duffer,
an old bundle of class certificates signed by Veitch, Nichol,
Ramsay, Jack, Jebb, Edward Caird and Sir William
Thomson [1] showed that he had acquitted himself credit-
ably in all subjects, and he passed without difficulty the
classical and mathematical parts of his M.A. examination.
He always felt sensitive about having left without his
degree, but the reason was, not that he failed, but that he
did not sit for the examination in Mental Philosophy.   His
friends could not understand why.   To them the study of
Moral Philosophy under Edward Caird had been like an
intellectual new birth, and they could scarcely believe that
Fraser had been untouched by his powerful influence, and
that it failed to force him, as it did others, to examine
and re-fashion his familiar and traditional beliefs.

But, in spite of his friendliness and popularity, for he
seems to have been much more social and happy at College
than at school, there was an unsuspected amount of reserve
in his nature, and his reasons he kept to himself.   His
diffidence about his powers would not by itself have prevented him from sitting his examination, but time and

[1] Afterwards Lord Kelvin.

money had both to be considered. He was tutoring through the summer, and he had his entrance examination for the Free Church Hall to pass ; so, as he could not afford to fail in that, he gave up reluctantly the thought of working for the other. As for his attitude towards Edward Caird's teaching—far from being indifferent, it had shaken him so much that at times he felt little better than an agnostic. It was with a very uncertain faith that he entered his theological course.

He spoke more enthusiastically in later life of Principal John Caird's sermons than of Edward Caird's lectures, recalling the crowds they drew, the eagerness of the students, who had almost to fight their way into the Bute Hall, and the electrifying effect of one of those wonderful perorations of his when, after gathering himself together in the pulpit, he almost leaped out at them, while his audience responded by involuntarily rising in their seats. He also enjoyed, at any rate in retrospect, Lord Kelvin's lectures, with the unfailing ritual of reaction on the students' part, as when for some illustrative reason Lord Kelvin would shoot off some kind of gun in the classroom, and open his eyes after this feat to find an apparently empty room, the students having slid from their benches to crouch beneath them.

He took an active part, too, in the political interests of the University where he was a contemporary of Sir Robert Horne and others who became well known in later years. But his chief interest was the Students' Settlement at Possil Park, in the founding of which he took a share. His friends ascribe it to his enthusiasm that the plan survived a time of difficulty. He was one of the first to live there, and threw himself into all its activities—men's club, evangelistic and temperance meetings, and visiting the houses in the district. A contemporary of his tells how, when they were gathering in off the streets their audience for their temperance meeting, Donald disappeared : but it was to " go one better." He was inside a public house trying to persuade them to come out. For some years he lived at the Settlement along with J. H. Maclean,[1] Andrew Low [2] and others, and these future foreign missionaries certainly did not go abroad because they failed to realise the conditions and needs at home. Two murders in the street were among the incidents of the years Donald spent there.

In 1891, while he was in his first year at the Theological Hall, a lady in his father's congregation handed him a five-pound note and asked him to use it to go to Keswick. More for the interest of a new experience and seeing a new district than for any other reason, he went. Along with him was a senior in the Hall, John Torrance.[3] He tells how Fraser's favourite place in the tent was the back seat at the side of the platform behind the choir, where he spent much of his time filling his notebook with drawings and carica- tures. One day Torrance, sitting beside him, handed his own notebook across to Donald, and he drew in it a portrait of Bishop Tucker of Uganda, one of the most impressive speakers of that year, and a sketch of an evangelist giving a *very* rose-coloured account of mission work, underneath which he wrote, " A howling dervish ! "

But before the week was over Fraser had been greatly impressed, apparently by something said by Eugene Stock. It is a little uncertain whether it was this experience or a later one that he, in writing to Robert E. Wilder, one of the founders of the American Student Volunteer Mission- ary Union, described as the realisation of the wonder of forgiveness. Certainly to him all through life it was God

---

[1] Dr J. H. Maclean of Conjeeveram.
[2] Rev. Andrew R. Low of Rajputana.
[3] Afterwards missionary at Poona, now minister at Rothiemay.

and God's attitude to men that compelled his worship and service. When men tried to make much of their religious experiences and tended to make their religion an egocentric thing, his gentle protest was along the lines of a remark he once made to an ardent " Grouper " : " You are a nice chap, X, but you aren't half as interesting to hear about as Jesus Christ."

At the Saturday morning missionary meeting Wilder, just across from America, clinched the deep impression the missionary element of the Conference had made on Donald, forcing him to realise as never before the opportunity of influencing the student world. At the close of the meeting he stretched out his hand to Torrance saying, " We must do something for the men in our Hall next winter." In the afternoon they went boating on the lake (his companion noticing his skill in handling the canoe) and discussed plans. They interviewed Wilder about coming to Glasgow the following winter.

Torrance, as assistant to the Professor of Hebrew, had opportunities of noticing the burning missionary zeal of the young second-year student, and the effect it had on his fellows. Wilder's visit and its consequences led to the opening of a new chapter in Fraser's life. But one of its most immediate results was that sixteen students of the Free Church Hall sent in their names in the year 1891–92 for foreign work, creating such an *embarras de richesses* that Donald himself was nearly driven to offer his services to the English Presbyterian Church. Of his own year eight became volunteers, and five found their life-work abroad, one in colonial service.

Many " Celestials "—as his year called themselves—have sent reminiscences of his time there, and one of them tells how the following year he induced a number of his fellow-students to attend the Keswick Conference. New College,

Edinburgh, was also represented there with G. H. C. Macgregor as leader. It was his presence that attracted the Scottish students, for, while he was in complete sympathy with the spiritual message of Keswick, he was known to hold what were then advanced views on Old Testament criticism. " The days we spent there," writes the friend referred to, " were a heart-searching experience. If we learned nothing new, we were forced to face honestly the question of what the Christian life ought to be. That was what appealed to Fraser. He was open-minded and ready to accept all the light scholarship had to shed on the Bible ; but his own supreme interest was the Christian life and its expression in Christian Service. . . .

" From there I returned with him to Lochgilphead to help him in a series of evangelistic meetings which he had planned in his native town. His cousin, Roderick Lochhead, was another helper, and we had the co-operation of several Lochgilphead people and two Pilgrim Sisters of the Faith Mission who were on a visit there. It was a sign of Fraser's catholicity that he worked cordially with people of the most diverse views and methods. We had meetings for children in schools, and for all who would listen in the open air. Whatever interest we aroused was due to Fraser's fervour and enthusiasm. To me the experience was memorable because it was the first time I had ventured on open-air speaking, and it was a surprise to find what a happy experience it could be.

" Fraser's father had recently died, but the family was still occupying the Manse, his two young sisters keeping house, for their mother had passed away not long before. It was a typical Free Church manse, plainly but comfortably furnished, and brightened by a sunny outlook as well as by the warm-hearted hospitality within. Soon afterwards the family removed to Glasgow and took a flat in

Garnethill. Here Donald's fellow-students used to drop in at all hours, especially about tea-time. Occasionally, too, he would bring home a waif from his mission district, who was entertained to supper. All were welcomed, cheered and fed. Sometimes a wild rush would have to be made to provide for a sudden arrival, but nothing ever disturbed the good humour of the household."

He held two assistantships during these busy years, the first in the old Briggate Church with its outside pulpit to which he used to point in later years as we passed it in the train. For a while he tried living amongst the people, but felt it prevented him from bringing any freshness of outlook into their midst. Forty years later one of his old Bible Class members still remembers where he stayed, and the meetings he used to have in her granny's house. Not only did he work there, but in summer he delighted to take a band of boys down to a holiday camp on the shores of Lochfyne—a memorable time for the youngsters, many of whom had never been out of Glasgow before.

His second assistantship was in the Wynd Church, Glasgow, with Mr Riddell, to whom he felt he owed much. That he was remembered and loved there was evident from the several gifts—varying greatly in intrinsic value—that came to him at the time of his wedding, and the little crowd of loyal "Wynd" friends who saw us off at the station when sailing to Africa in 1901. His name remained on their roll till he became an elder in Wellington Church.

This outside work, though financially necessary, naturally limited the time he had to spare for study. A class-mate, now the Rev. R. B. Douglas of Alibag, Bombay, remembers a Hebrew examination in which Donald sat immediately behind him. "When the paper was given out I heard a groan, ' I say, I can't make out a word of this ! ' Then, as his eye lighted on a familiar name, there came an exclamation of relief : ' Oh ! Mosheh ! ' " This, of course, is not an indication of the amount of Hebrew Fraser acquired in College. He certainly learned enough to enable him, with diligent use of his grammar and dictionary, to do Bible translation in Africa. A letter to Professor George Adam Smith in which the young African missionary expressed his regret about his lack of application as a student, used to be read to following " years " as an incentive !

His humorous sketches were a source of endless amusement in the Hall. Sometimes they illustrated poems by his friend J. M. E. Ross. He had the rare art of catching a likeness, and could give it a touch of humour without distortion. Even a skeleton sketch was recognisable by some trick of gesture or attitude. The professors did not escape. Professor James S. Candlish, a saint and a scholar whom everyone loved and reverenced, had written an article on pseudepigraphical writings, in which he said that if Ecclesiastes, as he thought there was strong reason for believing, was not written by Solomon, then he could not accept its canonicity. It was the time when Spurgeon was writing about Down Grade Theology. One day there was passed round the College dinner table a sketch by Fraser, who was tutoring that gentleman's ward at the time, of " Dr Candlish on the Down Grade." He was shown on a safety bicycle, in tight knee-breeches and striped stockings, his legs over the handle-bars, speeding downhill over a volume of Hodge's *Systematic Theology.* The sketch at last reached the hands of Professor George Adam Smith, seated at the head of the table, who had a chivalrous reverence for Dr Candlish and could not bear any allusion to him which was in the least degree disparaging. He crumpled it up and flung it under the table. One could

understand and respect his feeling, but there was no harm
in the sketch, and I cannot think it would have hurt Dr
Candlish if he had seen it. I do not suppose he did, but
he got his own back on Fraser not long after. In connection with the same article, an attack, characterised by his
peculiar style of humour, had been made on Dr Candlish
by the Rev. John Robertson of Gorbals, and a report of
this had appeared in various papers. It was Dr Candlish's
practice on Fridays, instead of lecturing, to devote the first
half of the hour to answering questions put by students,
and the second half to a textbook. Great latitude was
allowed in the matter of questions, and, naturally, full
advantage was taken of it. *A propos* of Mr Robertson's
reported sermon Fraser rose one Friday with the question,
" Dr Candlish, do you think a man has a right to make
bad jokes in the pulpit in order to increase his popularity ? "
The Professor hitched in his chair and turned red in the
face, as he had a habit of doing when he was obliged
to make any personal allusion. " Well, Mr Fraser," he
answered, with his peculiar nasal drawl, " that depends on
the larger question whether a man has any right to make
bad jokes at all ! "

In later years his pencil was used to illustrate his letters,
to children especially, and great in consequence was the
disappointment of her little cousins at home when his first
baby arrived from Africa, and turned out to be white like
everybody else. " Uncle Donald " had *always* drawn her
black, and had not their own father, when appealed to
about her colour, said that while he, of course, had never
seen her, and therefore could not say for *certain*, he knew
for a fact that the vast majority of babies born in Africa
were black !

Donald could laugh at his chums, and also enjoy
being laughed at by them. When he came back from a

country church where he had been preaching, he would tell how the elder who drove him in the gig said, " Well, Mr Fraser, that was a mighty fine sermon, but yon ——" (a student who had previously preached there) " *he's* an oarator ! " And then, at his expense, would come a story by Hugh Macluskie, in charge of the Students' Mission in the Broomielaw, of a well-meaning young fellow coming to him and saying he wanted to be a missionary. When asked what had aroused his desire, " Weel," he said, " I aye had a notion that wye, but efter I heard Mr Fraser speak, I felt something stirring in ma inside."

Some letters written before he had finished with the Hall show Fraser watching his friends as they leave College and get settled in charges at home or abroad. He chaffs one, a missionary, about his growing backbone, and asks if the rumour is true that he had locked the door of his church and telegraphed to the Viceroy requesting him to come and see him at once ; he discusses another's chance of being added to the two hundred millions of gods in India. He tells of the sensation caused by the preaching of a famous sermon—apparently well known to his fellow-students—by one who remained in Glasgow, and of the " detestable effeminate clerical dress " adopted by another who with it dons a regrettable professional change of manner, " does not laugh much, says things very precisely and must not be teased." " It was a merciful deliverance for you," he tells R. B. Douglas, " that you had to leave the country, for I was afraid when I saw the black shroud about you that I would be present shortly at the ' coffining ' of your humanity." And, for the writer, the Hall is " wretchedly lonely." He is " like a pelican in the wilderness," for his theological studies are still being intermittently pursued in the intervals that can be snatched from the work he is doing among the British Colleges. But that his influence had first been felt in his own College is the unanimous testimony of his fellow-students. I quote what one of them, Dr James Moffatt, says :

" Donald was a College chum, and we all followed his career with pride, we who had been with him at the start of it. It's a gift of God to have witnessed such a life ! I can't be too thankful for all it meant to myself and, I know, to others of our fellowship. He was so lovable and humorous and natural. And then with it all he showed us such unsuspected resources and capacities ! Unluckily our paths did not often cross, but whenever I saw the name Donald Fraser in some record of new achievement and honour, how my heart glowed to think that he called me his friend ! . . . I'm sure you must have heard, amid the countless tributes to him, the special cry of our ' Celestials.' I've some snapshots of our meetings, taken over forty years ago, in which he appears. It takes one back to far-away days to look at them. But even then, though none of us dreamed of the vocation to which God was going to call him, we all felt that when he entered our group it was like a breath of fresh air, or the tide rising on the beach ; his personality put so much into our lives."

CHAPTER III

Bliss was it in that dawn to be alive,
But to be young was very heaven !

DURING his second year of Theology Fraser was offered
by Professor Henry Drummond a trip to Egypt and
Palestine. Three other College men were going, and
Drummond had apparently been intending to go ; but
he was prevented, so his tickets for the tour were at Fraser's
disposal. Tempted though he was, for he had always
longed to travel, he declined, explaining that he must
help the family purse by tutoring that summer. Drummond consoled him by saying that he had never known
anyone with a passion for travel who did not find the opportunity come to him sooner or later. In this case there
was not long to wait : for the next two years he was to
be traversing the British Isles from Bristol to Aberdeen,
from London to Belfast.

For some little time past religious and missionary awaken-
ings had been taking place in student centres, most notably
in Cambridge, as the result of Moody's visit, and in Edinburgh, where Drummond had held a wonderful series of
meetings. Wilder's visit was the means of causing these
to unite in an effort to increase their influence by extending
it among the universities and colleges of Britain. Within
a year of his coming the Student Volunteer Missionary
Union had been formed, incorporating various isolated
student missionary societies already existing. Its members

22

were those who signed the Pledge, " I am willing and desirous "—afterwards altered to " It is my purpose "— " if God permit, to become a foreign missionary." Polhill Turner, one of the famous " Cambridge Seven " who had created such a sensation by taking the decision to go abroad as missionaries, was appointed Travelling Secretary, and it was arranged to hold a S.V.M.U. Conference at Keswick in the summer of 1893, immediately preceding the Convention.

J. H. Maclean, of Glasgow Free Church College, was one of the three original members of Committee, and was wondering whom they should propose at this Conference as successor to Polhill Turner. In the Settlement one night someone remarked to him, " I'll tell you who is the man you want—Donald Fraser." Maclean had already had him in mind, and, with this encouragement from one not himself a Student Volunteer, he suggested him to his colleagues, Byrde and Williams. Dr Tatlow in his *Story of the Student Christian Movement* tells the sequel : "Byrde hesitated. He might be the man they wanted, but he would like to write to him about his spiritual qualifications for the work. This drew from Maclean the response : ' As to Fraser, you may write him if you please, but I don't know that you will get very much satisfaction. Some of the most spiritual men are, from humility and other causes, the least able to give clear answers when catechised about their spiritual state. On this please yourself. Let me just assure you again that he is a man of great zeal and real spiritual power ; he will do all his work in simple dependence upon the Holy Spirit. As to his English you need have no fear. I trust we shall be guided by God in this matter. But while praying to Him we must use common sense in looking about ; so far as I can see the leadings are in the direction of Fraser.'

c

" The reference to Fraser's ' English ' is amusing.   He
spoke with a distinct Scottish accent, but was always an
accomplished speaker, and one of the few born orators
the Student Movement has had on its staff.   Byrde was
satisfied, and less than a fortnight later Maclean wrote,
' Fraser has accepted the post of Travelling Secretary.'
They had chosen a man of vision, power and great gifts
of leadership."

It was no easy task he had undertaken.   The Movement
was then unknown, and there was great difficulty in getting
a foothold in the colleges, the theological ones proving
quite as hard to enter as the others.   There were some
hospitable doors open to him—such as Sir Alexander
Simpson's in Edinburgh—but in many places he had to
find economical accommodation for himself.   Unhappy
experiences in cheap commercial hotels, where everything
sickened his soul and sent him wandering into the streets
to find some church where he could get silence for thought
and prayer, made him vow that if ever he had to accept a
church at home in sordid surroundings he would make it
a condition that its doors should always stand open.

But the Summer Conference had braced him for what he
had to face.   For him " Keswick 1893 " was summed up
in one meeting on the lake, where the students in their
boats clustered around R. W. Stewart of Fukien as he
spoke to them of what it meant to be a missionary.   That
morning they had had an address on " The Care of the Body
in the Mission Field," and, in relation to other things, it
had perhaps seemed over-emphasised.   Stewart spoke to
them on " agonia "—the word so often on Paul's lips.
What did it mean ?   Did it not just mean the thousand
wearinesses and hungers and thirsts and discomforts and
dangers, and, deeper, the strivings, the desires, the travail-
ings, the bitter disappointments, the " deaths oft " of the

missionary's life ? Well, "agonia is the measure of success.
They who know most of that, know most what it is to bear
fruit ; those who suffer it not, know least."

This talk, in conjunction with the lovable Christlike
personality of the speaker, made an indelible impression on
at least two of his listeners, the more so because, within a
year, Stewart was killed in the Boxer Risings. These two
were Temple Gairdner [1] and his friend, Donald Fraser. In
a little Greek Testament which Gairdner gave his friend on
his departure for Africa was written in Greek, " Agonia is
the measure of success," and Fraser never parted with it
till two years ago when he handed it to his son, going out
to serve the people for whom he himself had known such
travail " that Christ might be born in them."

With this recent memory to brace him Fraser conquered
his shyness, and faced his task of interviewing unsympathetic and unbending Principals, tackling unknown and
startled undergraduates in the corridors of the colleges by
asking them if they knew any Christian students, addressing meetings generally remarkable for the smallness of the
audience, and, perhaps greatest ordeal of all, occasionally
speaking at a Women's College.

These experiences impressed on him the advantage it
would be to have a strong inter-collegiate union uniting the
Christian organisations in the different centres. Such a
movement had been started, but it only comprised a few
of the older universities, and was an alliance rather than
an aggressive influence. But by 1894, when the summer
gathering took place it was a joint Conference of the
Student Volunteer Missionary Union and the Inter-
Collegiate Christian Union (as the Inter-University Christian
Union had re-christened itself), and Donald Fraser had been
appointed, in succession to Frank Anderson, Travelling

[1] The late Canon Gairdner of Cairo.

Secretary for the Christian Union. During the previous
year, in addition to his travels in the British Isles he had
been in America as a delegate to the Students' Conference
at Detroit, where he gave them an account of the beginnings
of the Student Movement in Britain, telling them of the
700 Student Volunteers in their British Union since Wilder
had started it in 1891, confessing that their Movement
had " not been blessed with very remarkable leaders,"
but had been carried on " by commonplace men among
commonplace men " by the efforts of every volunteer. In
suggesting the cautious use of the Pledge, he told of his
own experience when a whole Welsh college was ready
to sign the Declaration, and he had to dissuade them and
advise prayer and consultation. He also pointed out,
what some have failed to realise of the early days of the
Student Movement, how varied were the schools of thought
to which their members belonged ; what united them was
their " heartfelt devotion to Jesus Christ and an enthusiasm
to bring Him to the world."

Impressed by the strength it gave to the American Movement to have such outstanding and experienced men as
J. R. Mott, he had urged that these men should come to
help the British students, with the result that at the 1894
Summer Conference the 143 men and 39 women present
(there had only been 6 the year before) had the great privi-
lege of listening to R. E. Speer giving Bible Readings on
The Man Christ Jesus, and of learning from Mott much
affecting the work, problems and personal life of the
members of the Christian Union and Student Volunteer
Missionary Union in their colleges.

This contact with Mott, both in public and personally,
helped to impress on Fraser the spiritual influence that
might be exercised by a brotherhood of Christian students,
such as Mott visualised in his projected World Federation

of Christian Students. His soul rejoiced in the " bigness " of Mott, and he became his henchman, not only in his student career when he helped to start these Movements on the Continent and in South Africa, but till the latest years of his life, as when in 1930 he had a conference of leading Scottish laymen to meet Dr Mott, and was delighted to see how he impressed them.

Before the week of that Student Conference at Keswick was over, something happened of which he seldom spoke. Here is the story as witnessed by another student, one of a lively, hilarious group under canvas. " One evening there had been impressive talks by Mott and Speer. After the talk we strolled, returned, slept. But next morning it was reported that one of us had not come back to bed after the meeting. We were at breakfast discussing his absence when Don walked in and greeted us, washed, had breakfast : and so the day went on. No one asked him where he had been. Something held us back. But during the day it came out that he had spent the night at the Druid Circle—alone. Who knows what happened that night ? Explain it as we may, after that we all felt the prophetic touch of leadership was upon Donald Fraser. He had had an experience that none of us could follow, and so he led. My own idea is that that night was a great time for the Kingdom—a turning-point of crisis not only for that one soul but for hundreds who followed in Africa, Scotland and the Student Movement. I have often been uplifted in my own soul by the recollection that I was there, among that bunch of men."

A picture of that Druid Circle by moonlight still hangs above his desk.

Yet it would be wrong to give the impression of a young fellow serious beyond his years, or fanatical. The very integration of his life left him extraordinarily free to enjoy all the humour and fun it afforded, and appreciate all the varied interests it offered. There were among his colleagues of the early years some who had little use for anything beyond their Bibles and religious literature. He insisted on the need of a good and varied library ; and he freely used his judgment and spoke out his opinion. At one Conference when, on the last night, there was a meeting for testimony, and one after another, in saying what it had done for him, mentioned with unusual frankness sins and habits that had been spoiling influence and ruining character, he rose and began by referring to his mixed feelings as he listened to their " disgusting candour. . . ." Yet he admitted his conviction that there was depth and sincerity behind it, ending by saying that he too wished to tell of the uplift and inspiration he had received.

The writer of this reminiscence remembers him, " a typical Scot, fresh of countenance, eager and alert, with an unusual flow of language and eloquence which always appealed to me as particularly surprising in one who had not yet emerged from student life. Whenever he spoke he captivated his hearers, and won their admiration and allegiance."

Fraser enjoyed telling the lighter reminiscences of these travelling years. Listening to the stories of the Cambridge men he had longed to be " progged," and when, walking out with an undergraduate who noticed a proctor and his " bulldogs," he was told to " run," he entered into the part with glee. Captured, he admitted being a student and gave his name. " College ? " " Glasgow University," was brought out with keen enjoyment.

Knocking about the country in the way he did, he met with varied and amusing experiences. In Wales, after a long tramp from one town seeking for a college, he lost his way, but presently saw the building, on the top of a hill in the distance, with a mile or two of flooded fields between. There was nothing for it but to tramp through them. At last, wet and tired, he arrived at the gates, and at the porter's lodge inquired, " Where does the Principal of this college live ? " " This college ! " said the man ; " this is not a college ; it is a lunatic asylum ! " When eventually he found the college, he preferred the greater friendliness of his welcome at the asylum.

In Ireland, after a wretched journey redeemed by the kindness of a sailor who at 3 a.m. found him crouching over the cook's galley-fire trying to get a little warmth, and gave him a cup of boiling tea and two enormous slices of bread and butter, he seems to have met with a fine response. The students remembered long afterwards the attraction of the smile that broke out as he met them, and the handshake ; and also a talk he had with Alvarez, a rowing man from Cambridge and a keen Student Volunteer, in which they got on to theology. An Irish student who was to take Alvarez to address a school that afternoon was handed a penny by the Travelling Secretary and told to buy a copy of the Shorter Catechism and present it to Alvarez, while Alvarez was told when he got it to learn the answer to the question, " What is effectual calling ? " It was either in a confectioner's or a tobacconist's that the information was obtained. The one point almost certain is that Fraser could not have quoted the answer himself. His memory for accurate quotation was nil, and he would never trust himself to use another's words, even in poetry, without writing them down.

In Galway he was interested in seeing something of religious intolerance. He left by the same train with half a dozen Protestant clergy who had been preaching in the open air, protected by four or five hundred police, while a raging mob beyond were literally trying to kill them. The

railway for some distance out was lined by double rows of
police.   At the time he blamed the priests, and protested
he was a stronger Unionist than ever ; but in later years
he questioned the real usefulness of such a venture on the
part of the Protestants.   In Belfast the effect of his appeals
for missionary service was so great that the Irish Presbyterian Church, like the Free Church of Scotland, was
unable to accept all the men and women who offered.

Every now and then during these years he would turn
up at the monthly Student Volunteer meetings in Glasgow,
shy and unassuming, and only noticeable for the alert eyes
that looked out under the black brows—eyes which were
really blue-grey in colour, but which everyone who only
saw them blazing when he spoke on a platform was ready
to swear were black.   The meetings somehow always
seemed " different " if he was there ; but still he was so
much one of themselves that it was not till after " Liverpool " that, as A. G. Fraser [1] has said, " we as students
thought of Donald Fraser as above all others the inspiring
first great leader of the Student Movement, and followed,
trying to get done in some measure what he had foreseen
and made possible."

[1] Principal of Achimota College.

CHAPTER IV

"LIVERPOOL 1896" AND AFTER

A NUMBER of Glasgow students saw the New Year of 1896 in as they journeyed in third-class carriages—less comfortable then than now—to a feature quite new in the student world—a big Missionary Conference. They were only one group of many converging from all over the British Isles and beyond. At some unearthly hour in the morning they alighted in the station at Liverpool, cold, tired and dishevelled. There was a gratified "There's Donald Fraser!" as they recognised one of a little group of men waiting to invite them along to the hotel for a hot drink, a tidy-up and a rest, till it was a respectable hour to turn up at their various hosts' houses. Such an action was characteristic of his personal relations with his fellows.

This gathering had been Fraser's conception—a suggestion whose bigness had rather scared the little Executive to whom it had been made until, after prayer, they rose from their knees assured that it was right. For long, preparation had been going on, overcoming difficulties, enrolling helpers, arranging hospitality, securing delegations not only from Britain but from abroad, arranging the programme, and substituting speakers as one after another of those they had hoped for failed them. Fraser had before this retired from the post of Travelling Secretary, and was back in Glasgow giving what time he could spare to his theological studies, but travelling every week to attend to affairs in Liverpool. The Executive—Boyland, Burgess, Butcher, Rutter Williamson, Agnes de

Sélincourt, Ruth Rouse and Emmeline Stuart—were, along with Fraser, living at the Mitre Hotel during the Conference, and making inroads far into the night to overtake the work that faced them.

Yet here was one of them waiting to welcome his fellow-students, and noticing, though none suspected it, that one of the women medicals had her hair a little untidier, and her hat a little more to one side than usual as she stepped from the carriage. Only once again that week did he meet her and walk a little way with her in the street ; but later on, on the day of that chance encounter, she was amused to be approached almost reverentially by an unknown student who in awed tones inquired, " Didn't I see you speaking to Donald Fraser ? Oh ! do you know him ? " For during those Conference days he had attained prominence as Chairman at each of the great meetings in the Philharmonic Hall which so thrilled the largely student audience, doing it so quietly and simply that they only later realised—perhaps because they heard older and more experienced people remark on it—that it had been rather wonderful leadership. This prominent position he had been unwilling to accept till a number of his own College men urged him to do so. He appreciated that, for " it showed," as he said humbly years after, " that they didn't consider me altogether a fraud." All his life, when any praise came his way, he used to say, " I wonder when people will begin to find me out."

A full account of the Conference was published under the title *Make Jesus King*—this title being the wording of a telegram sent from 500 Japanese students to an American Student Congress at Northfield in 1889—and recently Dr Tatlow has given a description of it in his *Story of the Student Christian Movement*, so here one only records some of the impressions made on those attending it.

The sight, as Dr Burroughs said, of 24 nationalities represented by nearly 800 students was one to thrill, to impress, to solemnise ; not one discordant note was heard from beginning to end, and there was evidence of a high spiritual note throughout the proceedings. Part of the thrill came from its being so new, so unprecedented. At the opening meeting of welcome Fraser, in replying on behalf of the students, said, " I am not sure that Europe has ever seen a more representative gathering of students, or that the world has seen a more international one, than that before us." There, distinguished by their coloured badges, were African, American (U.S.A. and South America), Canadian, Chinese, Corsican, Danish, Dutch, French, German, Hungarian, Jamaican, Japanese, Jewish, Moravian, Norwegian, Spanish, Swedish, Swiss and Syrian—57 out of the 77 having travelled to England expressly for this Conference.

The singing thrilled. I wonder how many singing since then " Jesus shall reign," or " Crown Him, brothers, Crown Him," have found their thoughts taking them back to the Philharmonic Hall, with a student [1] presiding at the organ ? And is it an apocryphal tale that years later reached Central Africa, to the effect that that organist, then the Bishop of Peterborough, preaching at a Glasgow University service, startled its learned body of professors by speaking of the pride it gave him to visit the University of Donald Fraser—a man not even on its list of graduates till they bestowed a " D.D." on him in 1922 ?

Day by day impressions deepened till there came that Saturday morning when the Student Volunteer Missionary Union decided to adopt, as the American Movement had already done, the Watchword " The Evangelisation of the World in this Generation." That Watchword came in

[1] Theodore Woods.

for much criticism and discussion in future years, and was
eventually given up by a generation who felt it made no
appeal to them ; but it was a very real inspiration in the
early years.   " A persistent reminder of the world-horizon
of the Christian mission," it had a deep influence on the
thinking, the planning and the giving of a generation of
students from amongst whom emerged many outstanding
men and women.   Who that was present does not still
remember the Report of the World's Student Christian
Federation, followed by the rising of the whole audience to
greet the foreign delegates with ringing cheers ?   At this
enthusiastic meeting a short speech from the Chairman
marked what some have described as one of the outstanding moments of the Conference.   In welcoming them he
described the place prayer had played in bringing the existing Movements into being, told how continual prayer had
been made that it might spread to the Continent, reminded
them of their mighty responsibility, and ended with an
impassioned appeal to them to join hands in making a
world-wide Christian brotherhood to make Jesus Christ
King.   The power of prayer was behind that appeal, and
before that Saturday was over, the European delegates had
planned the foundations for three Student Volunteer Movements on the Continent.

Another revelation was the financial session—no descent
from the heights, but one of the most solemn and inspiring
parts of the Conference, when giving became a very real
expression of devotion.   The sum of £900 asked for was
far exceeded, £1641 being promised, after a silence full of
prayer.   The address that was to follow was not given, Dr
Pierson feeling that any " words would be out of place
after God Himself had drawn so near," and the Doxology
closed the meeting.

And there was that last memorable Sunday night when

those who hoped to be in the Foreign Field within a year were asked to rise, and nineteen stood up including the Chairman, the General Secretary of the Movement, and three members of Committee, and, among others, Donald Fraser gave a closing address on the Fellowship of the Spirit. " Now God is in us, and it is God who is going to rule in our lives," and his audience were led in a united act of dedication.

" We wait for God ; not for men, not for crowds, not for eloquence, not for emotion or sensation, but for God. Our hope is in the Living God, and we wait with hushed spirits to hear what He will say, and in obedience to do it," was the way in which Donald Fraser had expressed the desire of the delegates at its opening meeting, and they left Liverpool with a real sense of God having been among them, revealing Himself and His will.

Few, perhaps, realised how much they owed to the faith and prayer of the little group responsible for the guidance not only of the Conference, but of the future of the Movement it represented.   Night after night they met to discuss the morrow and its plans, and pray about it, intensely in earnest and yet young and wholesome and merry enough to appreciate such an incident as one which occurred " in answer to prayer."   One of the speakers had been exceeding his given time.   They were very anxious he should not disorganise an approaching meeting by doing so again, and yet so young a chairman shrank from the dis- courtesy of interrupting so respected a veteran.   So they prayed he would keep to time, and Fraser urged on him beforehand the necessity for doing this.   So impressed was he that he said all he had prepared well within the time ; so, finding he had still ten minutes he went on to another point.   The half-hour was almost up, the speaker was in full swing, and they felt anxious.   But, in some gesticulation with his Bible, he accidentally touched the chairman's bell. With a startled glance at the innocent chairman he abruptly resumed his seat, having unconsciously rung himself down !

It was at one of these post-midnight sessions, on the dawn of the very day on which they presented their Report, that the Executive came to the decision to adopt the Watchword. On another of the nights they got on to more personal topics, discussing the influences that had led them to missionary service. It became apparent as they gave their personal experiences how God had been at work, for most, if not all, of them had been influenced in childhood, and their lives had begun at a period when in England the urgency of the missionary situation had been drawing into united prayer the leaders of the S.P.G. and C.M.S., and in Scotland, Moody's evangelism had brought about an awakening which was strongly affecting the religious life and missionary attitude of many in the land.

With the close of the Conference, and the opportunity given them by its generous gift of money, the Executive had to consider what steps to take. They had already intimated that any surplus after meeting their own requirements would be used to help other and newer Movements. Some £200 was devoted to sending Mott to Australia to help the beginnings of work there. Donald Fraser, it was decided, should go to Europe to help to build up the missionary interest in the Christian Movements recently started; so, in a short time, he was off again, with nothing but a schoolboy knowledge of French to help him in his travels. He visited Paris, Montauban, Lyons, Geneva, Lausanne, Neuchâtel, Basle, Berne. It was at one of these Swiss towns that he arrived tired and hungry one night, and found no one there to meet him. So he took a cab and indicated that he wished to be driven to an inexpensive hotel. He didn't like the look of it when he alighted in a narrow lane, and was ushered in and found that he had to share an undesirable bedroom with an equally undesirable room-mate. He descended and was asked if he wanted " souper." " Oui, souper et meater et pommes de terre et toutes les autres choses que vous avez ! " Before he had got through his meal, in burst two students who had been frantically searching for him, and the relief was mutual when he found himself traced to and removed from his unprepossessing lair. A Franco-Swiss Student Volunteer Missionary Union was formed at a Conference held in Geneva, and M. Daniel Couve became its first Secretary, and a lifelong friend of Fraser in spite of very infrequent meetings.

In Holland he arrived to find that the " Liverpool Eleven " delegation had caused a great stir on their return, and other previous influences had combined to create a real spiritual work among them. Passing on to Scandinavia he received a warm welcome, and was struck by the interest displayed by the nobility and members of the Court. It was most embarrassing, he confessed in speaking about the class in which he found himself moving, to have to say he did not know So-and-so and So-and-so as they reeled off the names of friends in England moving in much higher circles than the young Scotsman ever dreamed of entering. " I began to be afraid they'd think me a downright impostor. I knew no members of the Royal Family, and only *one* Lord ! " Count Moltke proved a good friend. Copenhagen, Lund, Stockholm, Upsala and Christiania were all visited, and the meetings were apparently very impressive. His interpreters, instead of being the " interrupters " that Egerton Young had spoken about at Liverpool, were so fine that they seemed to add to, rather than detract from, the effect of the addresses. One of his most interesting meetings at Stockholm was a gathering of some hundreds of boys aged from sixteen to twenty. Next he went on to Copenhagen, and at a conference there a Student Volunteer Missionary Union for Scandinavia was organised.

Thence on to " poor dead " Germany, where he felt the contrast from the eager spiritual life manifest in Scandinavia. But there, too, at Halle, where students from six universities gathered to meet him, they spent two days organising a Missionary Union for Germany. A big bundle of faded photographs was the only tangible reminder of that visit to the Continental student centres ; but, more than once as we travelled to and from Africa, or visited some French or Swiss Mission Station there, we would meet some Continental missionary whose face, on hearing Fraser's name, would light up with remembrance—if not of him personally, of his association with the early days of the Movement in his own country.

The student world now had other and abler leaders, Fraser considered, to carry on the work he had pioneered, and he was longing to get to the mission field. Candidates must have been plentiful, for the Foreign Missionary Secretary reminded him of the claims of his own Scottish Highlands ; others pressed him to consider India ; but he himself felt sure that he was better fitted for Africa, and wished to be appointed to the Livingstonia Mission, in British Central Africa, as Nyasaland was then called. The Continental work had once again interrupted his theological studies, and the Free Church did not lightly ordain a man who had not qualified by taking the full course, so he offered to go as a layman. But his professors took up the matter and his ordination was agreed to by the General Assembly. The service took place in Glasgow just before he sailed. A Pan-Presbyterian Council was being held there at the time. So many foreign ministers took part in the " laying on of hands " that it was said to be the most international ordination in the history of Presbyterianism.

Eager though he was to begin his missionary career, there was awaiting him still another bit of service to render to the student world. When, after disembarking at Capetown, he travelled to Stellenbosch to attend the first South African Student Conference, convened because Luther Wishard was visiting there from America, such pressure was put upon the ex-Travelling Secretary to go round the colleges and schools of the Colony that he felt he could not refuse. He *did* refuse the offer of a professorship which came to him in the course of his tour, wondering amusedly what his own old professors would think if they knew such a post had been offered him ! He found the students very impressionable and responsive, and the wonderful work he did then and the permanent effect produced were often alluded to when, almost thirty years later, he was again touring South Africa and meeting many proofs of how he had so won the hearts of the Dutch that not even the Boer War, so soon to follow with its aftermath of bitterness, could affect their attitude to him personally.

D

CHAPTER V

THE YOUNG MISSIONARY

It was the close of 1896 before the long journey up country was over, and he arrived just in time to spend the New Year at Bandawe, the first-reached station of the Mission on Lake Nyasa. A few days later he was completing the last lap of his journey across the hills rising from the Lake to the Nyasa-land plateau on the farther side of the Vipya, as this mountain range is called, there to be met and greeted at Ekwendeni by his future colleagues, Dr Elmslie and Mr Stuart.

It is little wonder that his senior colleague, Dr Elmslie, had been awaiting with some secret misgiving the coming of this young man of twenty-six who had been taking so prominent a place in student affairs for the last few years, wondering how he would settle down and work in with them. He was relieved to find him a modest, rather shy young fellow, interested and thrilled as he sat listening to tales of the experiences Dr and Mrs Elmslie had been through in those early years.

A few months later the Elmslies went home on furlough, and he and Mr Stuart, his educational colleague, were left to carry on. Of that time of partnership Mr Stuart writes :

" Those were great days when we were together, and it is a joy to me to look back on them. We were young and energetic, and there was the lure of the distant horizons, and the unknown beyond, beckoning us on. I have a vivid recollection of the abandon with which Fraser threw himself into the work, and the great faculty he had of

LIVINGSTONIA

The Livingstonia Mission was started by the Free Church of Scotland in 1875, a year after Livingstone's burial in Westminster Abbey, and in response to his historic appeal for the evangelization of Central Africa.

Its sphere comprises a number of stations in Nyasaland and Northern Rhodesia, indicated in the relief map overleaf.

The name Livingstonia was also given to the head station on the hills overlooking Lake Nyasa; but to avoid ambiguity, this station is in the narrative referred to as Kondowi, the native name, by which also it is generally known in the country itself.

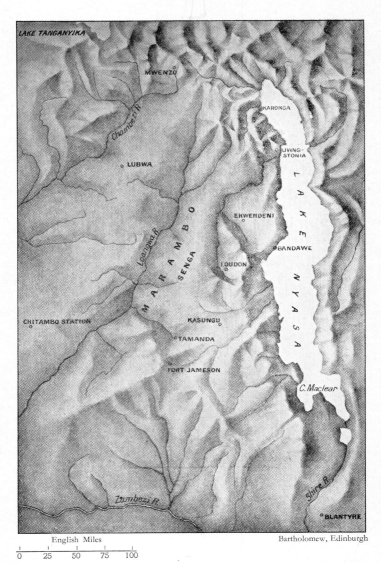

English Miles

| | | | | |
|0|25|50|75|100|

RELIEF MAP SHOWING AREA OF LIVINGSTONIA MISSION

attracting the people. He always managed to make the fullest use of the material he had at hand, and drew the best out of the native teachers. Very soon our little school was all too small and had to be enlarged, and the whole country soon lay open to his evangelising zeal."

There is a great wealth of material dealing with this period, when the waiting-time of the pioneers, with its first faint streaks of light, was to break into a glorious dawn. Of the people and the work Dr Fraser has written in *Winning a Primitive People*. Here it can only be treated from the personal point of view, and perhaps his own letters can best tell the story.

"I am enjoying my work and sphere intensely. Since coming here I think I have broken the record by my capital health—not a touch of fever yet. The people, my parishioners, are a splendid race of warriors, part of whom are now living peaceably. I have come among them just at the most interesting period. After thirteen or fifteen years' pioneering the people now seem ready to receive Christ. Two months ago signs of this began to appear. And during April nearly 500 people interviewed me who wished to be prepared for baptism. This has been a bright introduction to my work. I am up on the hills, nearly 5000 feet above sea-level. The air is bracing, not nearly so enervating as at Bandawe. There is plenty of outdoor life. Apart from the teaching I have to superintend manual labour—and to spend fully half the year tramping round this great parish, of which five-sixths has not yet been even touched.

"My language is Zulu : our people (Angoni) are a Zulu offshoot who made a wonderful raid up to these quarters, and then settled down. In spite of the wretched ' clicks ' I am getting into the thing, and have been taking entire services now, after six months' silence, although to-day I

completely broke down when trying to say quickly
' Kaqoqeke,' the ' q ' being pronounced by smacking the
roof of the mouth with the tongue.

" I have been saying that there is no sacrifice in being
a Livingstonia missionary. I take it all back. There's
a terrible sacrifice. Discomfort, fever, a short life, are
nothing. But when you find that you have to sacrifice
intellectual and spiritual life—the price becomes awful.
The first sacrifice is necessary, perhaps the second need
not be. Somehow this climate, and the fever that is
always lurking in one, absolutely unfit one for concentrated reading or thinking. I know that many of the
missionaries scarcely read one serious book through in
the half year ! And what a fight one has to grow in
Christ ! Here one knows that life must be short. We
are always looking into death's face. Men who laughed
with us last week we bury to-day. Yet we cannot live
with proportionate intensity. I found that one hour's
intense crying to God has physically unfitted me for work
for hours afterwards. But the pity is that it is only by a
severe effort of the will one can get these times for prayer.
Then the fever makes one terribly irritable. It is an
awful, humiliating thing to find that one has been standing
speechless with a spasm of passion because of someone's
slight offence. That is the sacrifice I am daily crying I
may be saved from making.

" This is a very candid letter : forgive me if I have said
too much. I know you sometimes pray for me, as I do
for you. You will know how to pray. I have been
feeling now that I am near that crisis when one's after-
life will be shaped. And without reserve I have given
myself over again to the Perfect Keeper."

To find the solitude in which it would be possible to
seek communion, he built a small hut on a hill at a little

distance from Ekwendeni. There he could be free from the constant interruptions which occurred on the Mission Station.

Later on he wrote :

" I am isolated here with only one white companion in the whole country, and most of my time is spent quite alone in long journeys. But my happiness in it all is unbroken. I am so certain that God is here, and that you and the other fellows are in the same fellowship.

" Just now we are living very near the other world. There has been a terrible death-roll among the white people. No mail comes up to the hills without news of another death. Our Mission has been wonderfully well, but when Dr Prentice passed through here a week or two ago he was asking who of us was to go first ? And with him came the news of the death of Du Toit—one of the Dutch section of the Mission. It is strange to think that one may see Christ's face before yours.

" But this sounds a gloomy strain—especially for me ! For I have quite broken the record of the Mission in my freedom from fever. When Prentice arrived, I had to lead him out of the 'machila' (*i.e.* hammock) into my house. The poor fellow had been travelling along all morning in a bad attack of fever.

" I have just returned from a long and interesting tramp. Recently there was a great gathering of the chiefs and councillors to appoint a new king, or paramount chief. After the appointment was made, some of the old warriors were very keen to have a monster raid like the old raids. There was great discussion, but nothing definite was agreed on. However, we heard that some ' impis ' had gone out. If serious raiding was begun again, it would mean terrible disaster to the nation and war with the British. So I determined to set out at once and visit the chiefs myself.

I had just come off a tramp of 120 miles, so, after resting a few days, Stuart and I started out."

The " freedom from fever," judging from what follows, would seem to have been comparative only. " The start was rather disagreeable, as I was very feverish. Not far from the Station in crossing a river I slipped and fell in. So I had to change at once in the bush. All thro' the walk I was dazed with fever and neuralgia, but at last, in the dark, we arrived at Elangeni where we have a school. I got into bed and managed with the aid of hot water bottles to sweat off the fever without having a bad attack. Next day, however, it was back, and I tramped along in the same condition, over a thinly populated and rough country. In the afternoon we arrived at the village where Mperembe, one of the great chiefs, was staying. Messengers had been sent on the day before to tell him that we were coming, and he had sent back word that it was well. When we arrived we sat down opposite the cattle kraal gate. A number of people were there, and, after a few minutes' pause (which is a sign of welcome), came forward and saluted us. Then we waited for ten minutes longer, when a number of warriors fully armed came along, saluted us and sat down opposite. Another long pause.

" Then we were awakened by shouts of ' Ete, Baba ! ' (the royal salutation, which seems to mean, ' Give us the heads of our enemies, father ! '). On looking up we saw Mperembe himself striding along, with a dignity that would do credit to the Czar of all the Russias. As he passed the people they all shouted, ' Ete, Baba ! ' till he came to us. Then he sat down, saluted us, and remained silent. After several minutes' awkward pause he rose again and went away, all the people again shouting, ' Ete, Baba ! '

" That opened the ball. We told our teacher that we wanted to pitch our tent in the village. He told our messenger, the messenger told the head councillor, the head councillor told the chief. The chief replied to his councillor that we might do so. The councillor passed on the reply to our messenger, our messenger to the teacher, and the teacher to us. And in this roundabout fashion we had to conduct all our business, for it is the etiquette of the Court.

" That afternoon Mperembe sent us a fine bull to show that ' his heart was white ' towards us. Later on we went to see him, to give him a return present of clothes, etc. We found him very drunk, with a great pot of native beer before him ! He took our presents with very bad grace, complaining that we had omitted some things he wanted. Then he began to distribute some of the presents to his favourites. When he gave a little string of beads to his executioner, this gentleman, who was gorgeously attired in a straw hat and little else, knelt down and at the height of his voice shouted off a long story of praises of the unspeakable wonders that Mperembe had done in battle.

" We left this ridiculous scene, and determined not to speak seriously to the king till he was sober. (Indeed, we found afterwards that all business had to be transacted before two o'clock, or we should find him very drunk.)

" We had not long been sitting in our tent when Mperembe himself came tottering in and squatted down on Stuart's bed. Now Stuart is a very particular man, and sensitive to the presence of creatures. You should have seen his alarm when Mperembe sat on his bed ! I'm certain his bed-clothes have been well washed since he came home. Well, there we had to sit and amuse this drunken log of a chief. I tell you it took some patience.

" Next morning was Sunday. Before six o'clock Mperembe was sitting at his kraal gate, and we could hear the people as they passed and repassed shouting, ' Ete, Baba ! ' I went out to him and found him sober and affable. I talked for some time and tried to teach him something about God. Then Stuart joined me and we asked for leave to hold a service. This was granted, tho' somewhat reluctantly.

" At mid-day, when we began the service we had a grand crowd of people who listened very attentively, most of them for the first time, to the elements of our faith. There was a rare lot of young bloods hanging about Court—fine, proud young warriors. It was a great sight to see them striding about, with a step that seemed to spurn the ground. Their clothing was only a little bit of skin, but their very nakedness made them look the statelier, and set off their muscular build to perfection. After service I got a lot of these lads together and gave them an hour's lesson, chiefly on the alphabet. They asked me to teach again in the evening, so I had a big crowd at sunset, and taught on till it was cold and dark. Mperembe came along while we were singing a hymn, very drunk again, and insisted on singing with us.

" That day one of his wives was caught misbehaving. So he killed her and a man straight off. The news of this spread terror among our little houseboys, and they did not chatter and sing round the fire that night. My cook is a very timid boy ; he trembles and cannot speak if he thinks I am going to scold. One morning on a recent journey I rose before dawn and called for my coffee, as we were to make an early start. There was no reply. I looked out and saw all the carriers crouching over the fires. I asked what was wrong, and they called back that there were two lions beside us : and, sure enough, their roars began again.

All night long the men had sat round the fires in terror, and I had been sleeping soundly in my tent unaware of the presence of danger. My guns were lying at my side loaded : but where was my coffee ? I called again, and found that my boy was sitting at one of the fires, fifty yards off. He was, however, too frightened to run across with my coffee, so I just had to wait till dawn came and brought more courage. At Mperembe's he was dreadfully scared, and, I think, expected to be murdered in the night.

"On Monday morning we talked our business. Mperembe agreed to give up raiding, and promised to receive our teachers at his head village. We left at ten o'clock, mightily thankful for the success of our visit. All that day we marched through a thinly peopled country, sometimes coming upon native smelting furnaces, and sometimes upon great crowds of people scraping the dry river-beds to find salt. In the evening about sunset we arrived at Njuyu, where Dr Steele had lived, and where Dr Elmslie went through some of the exciting days of ten years ago. Next morning we were off again. The sun was very warm, and I was tired and feverish, so that the journey seemed interminably long. Again we were passing through new country, as we had struck out over the hills to the west, but this time we could see large villages everywhere. From about eight o'clock we were travelling in entirely unopened territory, and so for the next few days. We made for the head village of the paramount chief, where we were warmly received. When we presented our case to the Council, we had a hearty invitation to open a school and send teachers. The young chief, a handsome but purposeless fellow, professed to be very eager to learn, and, indeed, I spent hours with him for the next day or two, teaching him the alphabet and hymns, etc. There, as at all our stopping-places, I set

up as quack doctor, and soon had crowds of patients.
But the crowning case was found when the head councillor
came to ask for medicine to keep the cattle from breaking
out of the kraal at night !

" Leaving the King (!), we struck out for 'Ngonomo,
the leading war spirit. He was a fierce warrior in past
days, and still sends out his impis ; and now he has
been threatened by the British, but he has defied them. In
the hope that we might yet save him from disaster we
decided to visit him. I confess that at first we were a
little nervous as to our reception. It was a long march
to his place, through country full of villages into which
no preacher has yet gone : I suppose, indeed, no white
man has been there before. The forest became very
thick, and, when we came to some rising ground, we could
see it stretching out in a great plain to the horizon. Towards
sunset we were hopelessly lost, and could not strike the
river near which 'Ngonomo's villages are built ; it seemed
farther away every hour. At last one of our men went
out to reconnoitre, thinking he heard people's voices, and
we sat down utterly wearied and cross. Soon he returned
with directions for finding the river, and we started off
again—back the way we came. Happily it was full moon,
so the sun had no sooner set than a grand moon arose,
making the country wonderfully bright. The moonlight
in Africa is worth seeing.

" At length we arrived in a village planted down in the
thick of the wood, and determined to sleep there. The
village, it turned out, belonged to 'Ngonomo's brother—
by Angoni etiquette the very village we ought to go to.
Messengers were immediately sent off to tell 'Ngonomo
that we had come, and we lay down to welcome sleep.
Next morning, when we were sitting in the tent, someone
told us that 'Ngonomo had arrived ; and when we looked

out we saw him and a great impi following, fully armed,
sitting opposite us. We had not heard a sound of their
arrival : they could very easily have annihilated us if they
had been of that mind.

" 'Ngonomo was at first very suspicious. I asked him
why he had brought his impi with him : he replied that
they had only come to salute us. Then we talked, and
gradually his fears were dispelled and he presented us with
a large bull and a sheep. For some days we remained
there and talked continually to him, but he would promise
little. He wanted to have one big raid, and then have
done : but one big raid will mean war. At last he promised to consult Mperembe, especially about allowing us
to send teachers. We left, pleased on the whole with the
result of our visit, for friendly relations have been established and we mean to cultivate them.

" After this, Stuart went back to Ekwendeni, and I continued the journey, visiting some outlying schools. With
a few more days' hard walking I reached Hora, very tired
and footsore. A letter came from Stuart to say that
Dewar and Prentice were on their way to Ekwendeni. So
I had to start off at once, though nearly a hundred applicants
for the Catechumens' class had come to be examined, and,
leaving them, make a forced march to Ekwendeni. It was
an awful day's walk. We missed the path in trying to
take a short-cut, and I tumbled into Stuart's house, an
hour after dark, lame and blistered ! Next morning, however—though I could not put on my shoes for a day or
two—I was almost right again and ready to welcome my
guests. Altho' this journey extended over a good many
days, we had not gone very far. The paths are so tortuous
and narrow—they are seldom eight inches broad—that
walking is very hard, and a good pace scarcely covers
two and a half miles an hour. Yet I walked about 135

miles in these past few days. You can see how hard it
is to get over my parish.

"I am now fairly into the swing of the work. For the
past three months I have been venturing to address meetings in the native language—Zulu—but I am not sure to
what extent I am understood. I have a very nice house
here and am wonderfully comfortable. My colleague,
C. Stuart, is a splendid fellow. There is a fine lot of men
in our Mission, but we live very far apart. The married
missionaries out here are all tremendously fond of their
wives, and just bore one with their recommendations.
They all say that it saves a great deal to get married, and
that it makes you much healthier, because your wife looks
after the cooking! But I have a fine boy who cooks
well: and I'm not over-particular. Stuart drew my attention to the fact that I had cornflour pudding every day for
three months. I had not noticed it. So I asked the cook
to give me something else, and he made me arrowroot
pudding every day for weeks. That made me observe
that I had had stewed fowl twice a day for three months.
So I asked the boy to boil the fowl *sometimes*, and he boiled
it every day for weeks.

"Fowl is our only 'flesh.' We eat it *ad nauseam*. It is
dangerous to have an experimentative cook. My boy
made a tea-cake because Mrs D. had one. It is very
clammy, and I am eating it carefully. One of the missionaries died because he made a plum-pudding once!
Stuart and I ate a tinned plum-pudding. We walked ten
miles after; nevertheless I was feverish at night!"

If his fare was monotonous when on the Station, it was
still more so when he travelled round the district without
a ulendo (string of carriers), for then, apart from the
kettle he carried, he depended for food on the ministrations
of some old woman in the village he was visiting, who

would be only too proud to cook for the white teacher. But even the best-cooked nsima (maize porridge), the unvarying main constituent of every meal, is not too palatable to the European ; and, though some of the relishes served with it are appetising enough, others tend to take away every vestige of appetite one possesses, as for example when the savoury is a dish of stewed caterpillars. However dubious, from the standpoint of health, was the wisdom of this way of living, yet the fact remains that, when he left the country almost thirty years afterwards, the people cited his having eaten their native food as one of the proofs how thoroughly he had identified himself with them and thought light of hardships that he might win them to Christ.

It is doubtful whether his house was very well looked after during his bachelor days, though he maintained that it compared favourably with those of some other unmarried men—a modest claim, and one that could easily be conceded. At any rate it was not so perfect that he ever forgot the wild consternation that seized him when he heard that two " Donas " (white women) were on their way to be his guests and would turn up that day. Heavy days he had often put in when travelling, but that was the most strenuous and exhausting of all as he and his houseboys turned to and concentrated a spring-cleaning into a few hours.

One of these Donas, now Mrs Moffat, records the interest with which she watched her host at a native service, preaching to the people. Of the language spoken she knew nothing, but the interest displayed made her realise that here was a man with the power to grip.

CHAPTER VI

" GOD'S FOOTFALL IN THE LAND "

ABOUT this time there was awakening a new interest among the people, the Sunday congregations increasing till the little brick church could no longer contain them, and a new building had to be put up. School attendance within the last year had risen from 1300 to 3000, and demands for teachers could not all be met. And the people were not only getting, but giving. In a letter to Dr Laws Fraser wrote :

" The collections are doing well on Sundays. Yesterday's offerings amounted to 64 lb. flour ; also beans, maize, a knife, ivory rings, a goat, a fowl, beads and money, and to-day a large quantity of flour, fowls, etc., has come in.

" There is now no difficulty about getting fees for medicine. People who come a day's journey for medicine bring their fowl, and it has not decreased the number of patients. Last Monday there were seventy in the morning. Nor has this asking for money caused any estrangement. I have begun to get presents from the people. The other week different people sent me as presents, not expecting a return, a leg of a sheep, a large quantity of flour, and a big cock. To-day an old woman appeared with a basket of flour to thank me for having cured her child's ulcer. I am deeply thankful for these signs of liberality. I am sure giving is an essential part of true spirituality.

" Books are going like wildfire. We are giving none free. Stuart is making a splendid job of the Ekwendeni school this term. The building is packed to overflowing,

and there is a great improvement in discipline and
enthusiasm.

" I have been giving a series of sermons to the people
on the Atonement. I found that not one of the teachers
understood why Jesus died, so I have preached every
Sunday on the same subject, trying to explain from different
standpoints and by plentiful illustration. I think that a
fair part of the audience was able to understand me. At
any rate there has sometimes been a great solemnity in the
service, and once or twice what Brainerd would call " a
sense of melting " as one spoke of Christ's sufferings. I
don't know whether it is purely subjective. But these
past weeks have been full of great blessedness."

A great Communion gathering was arranged for at Ekwendeni, the people pouring in from all over the country :
large grass sheds were put up for those who could not be
accommodated in the near villages. Meetings were held
from the Wednesday till the Monday, the numbers swelling
on Sunday to almost 4000. The impression it made on
the people can best be shown by the description given of
it by a young Tonga (a Lake-side tribe) who was present.

He told how he stood at Ekwendeni and saw band after
band coming over the distant ridges, and steadily marching towards the Mission Station, where they were gladly
received by the Christians, and taken away to the villages
to be entertained. The villages were crowded with
guests—men in some, women in others—and there seemed
room for no more. Still, however, other bands appeared
on the horizon, and, as they arrived, the warmth of Christian
feeling made elastic the possibilities of hospitality. " As
I saw this," he said, " I marvelled." Then the services
where, with an elder or other Christian leading, small
companies gathered by themselves for prayer, and many
were melted to tears. " As I saw these, I marvelled greatly.

Then at the Baptismal Service, as I saw those who were to
be baptised coming forward one by one and receiving the
rite, till Mr Fraser's arm grew tired and he sat down and
Mr Henderson continued in his place ; as I saw men with
scars of spears, clubs and bullets on them, and as I saw
Mpangela, the widow of Chipatula, baptised, I marvelled
exceedingly.   I said in my heart, ' Can these be the Ngoni
submitting to God—the Ngoni who used to murder us,
who killed the Henga, the Bisa and other tribes ? '   And
then, at the Lord's Table, to see these people sitting there
in the still quiet of God's presence, my heart was full of
wonder at the great things God had done."

After this gathering, the work greatly increased ; but,
as he wrote :

" One could not grudge any price for the mere sight of
what God is doing daily among us.   Here is a field where
we live by sight, not by faith, for the monthly progress
and the great transformations are very visible.   One cannot
move out on tour round the Stations without meeting
continual surprises of His power.   The Communion season
in May, of which you may have heard, has brought new
life to us all.   Fancy the inspiration of preaching daily for
five days to a congregation of over 2000, which increased
until it reached 4000 !   And the thrill of talking with your
teachers, nearly one hundred of them, while they wept
before God, and sometimes were unable to control themselves !   And that is not only a memory of the past ; it is
part of the present.   Daily as I moved around in my last
tour, the kindly welcomes, the continual little presents of
vegetables and other food, told of lives that had been re-
created, and kindliness that had been awakened by the
presence of God.

" Now I sit in my house every morning to speak with
those who wish to make public profession of their faith in

Christ : and they come to me sometimes in twos and threes, sometimes in tens and twenties. Old scarred grandmothers, and bright, happy little children are among them. And all the weariness and depression of fevers are forgotten before this army of the Lord.

" Liberality, too, has begun in earnest. No less than 150 carriers were required to bring to me the August monthly collection. And the produce, and baskets, and beads, and hoes overflow from my veranda into my rooms. Now, too, we have ceased building schools for the people ; they are erecting their own buildings at their own cost, and some thirteen of them are at present going up."

Most of all, he rejoiced in the " delightful spiritual fellowship " he had with the teachers over the fires at night, as he travelled among the villages. " It is glorious to be allowed to live here," he concludes. " The sense of God, so near, so strong, so triumphant, does not allow one moment's depression. All that one may lose here of health, of home luxuries, of mental development and inspirations, is made up a hundredfold in such a partnership."

His letters reveal much that is characteristic of the man. More than one expresses his longing to get beyond the corner in which they are sitting to the farther bounds of their great parish with a population ten times the size of that which has been touched. " I am afraid to go on and see more people," he writes, " because of the oppression of helplessness before their need." And against that, for his forward vision never blinded him to what lay near at hand, there is an overwhelming sense of personal responsibility for a sad case of moral failure in a teacher—" and I his pastor ! " His medical work seems to have been constant, and the cases of ulcers very numerous, to judge by

E

the incessant demands for iodoform and boracic that he sent to Dr Laws.[1]

Another service he had been rendering consisted in buying cattle for his colleagues in the Mission; but while getting for others the means of securing a clean and regular milk supply, he had not had time to buy any cows for himself. He draws attention to the fact that a very valuable set of stamps are being issued—" three shillings crossed ' one penny ' "—which should be kept to help Mission finances; but he failed to do what would have been so easy, as the King long afterwards pointed out to him on his visit to Balmoral, the making of a private fortune out of these early B.C.A. issues! He notes, too, where good timber is available, and has started in one village a Co-operative Building Society which is putting up a row of brick houses. He seems to have done more than his share in helping to provide articles for *The Aurora*—a quarterly paper published by the Mission—and is projecting a native paper, which came into being at a later period.

Above all he is rejoicing in the evidences of personal friendship that are being shown him. Yet, when the suggestion comes that he should relieve Mr Henderson at the Overtoun Institution, though he discusses his lack of qualification for teaching and the understaffing of Ngoniland, he goes on to say he must not take a selfish view, nor think he is necessary for God's work in Ngoniland. If there is no other solution, " gladly I shall do anything I can for His Kingdom. I shall take "—he hesitates and pauses over this, strokes it out and substitutes—" I suppose I shall take the mind of the Council to be the voice of God." This was not the only time his loyalty conflicted with his misgivings.

[1] Head of the Mission at the Central Station at Kondowi.

CHAPTER VII

THE SENGA : A VISIT AND ITS RESULTS

THE remarkable feature of the gathering at Ekwendeni had been the number of those in the early strength of manhood who in past years had been a troublesome element to the missionaries' efforts to promote peace. Accustomed to hearing of the warlike expeditions of their fathers, they had often been found clamouring for the opportunity of wetting their spears in human blood, that thus they might prove their manhood and so take their place among the leaders of the tribe.

There was surely sound psychology in the way the young missionary tackled the situation that had arisen. No one felt more keenly than he the need of the revelation of God in the individual soul and the necessity for fostering the beginnings of the new spiritual life that had come to them. At the same time he recognised that these new converts were an integral part of their tribe, with an instinctive tendency to take a communal rather than a personal attitude towards life. And so, instead of trying to segregate them in any way—a principle which has sometimes been adopted in African missions—he made no attempt to safeguard their lives by keeping them apart from the evils of paganism that surrounded them. He looked on them rather as the leaven that was to work in the tribe ; so, seizing on that tribal instinct for war, he turned it into a new channel. The fighting was dying out, partly because of a moral uneasiness that had arisen as a result of the new teaching about God, and partly because those who would eagerly have led new hostile

expeditions were realising that they were now surrounded
by European rulers who would not permit such raids.
But inaction was a dangerous policy for such a people ;
so, when Fraser drew their attention to the Senga people,
who had so often in the past been the victims of their war
parties, and suggested a new invasion of their territory that
they might incorporate their hereditary enemies in the new
Kingdom of God, the project was warmly received.   There
was no lack of teacher volunteers for such service, and the
Ngoni Church entered on its foreign mission enterprise in
spite of the great home mission problem presented by its
own tribe.   It was perhaps the most effective way of tackling the latter.   It showed that the new religion was no
affair of mere suppression of the old evils, but gave an
aggressive outlet to the new life.   One of the first volunteers
was Daniel Mtuso Nhlane, an early convert of Dr Elmslie,
who, for some time after he was attracted by the message
the missionaries preached, alternated his time between
teaching in the Mission school and going off to join the
war impis when the time for the annual raids came round.
There can be little doubt that this crusading spirit gripped
his warrior soul, helped to integrate his life in the service
of Christ, and prevented his ardent spirit from hankering
after the excitement of the old days.

Who, then, were these Senga ?   This letter sent home
to the Foreign Mission Secretary gives an account of Fraser's
first visit to them.

"When I reached Chinde's on this tour, I found that I
was within two days' march of the Senga.   As they are
subjects of the Ngoni, and are supposed to be within the
limits of our parish, I decided to push across the fifty miles
of separation, and see them for myself.   An induna gave
us two of his elephant hunters to act as guides, and we set
off.   Crossing the Rukuru, we marched all day alongside

of a great marsh, until in the evening we reached the belt
of low hills which forms the watersheds of the Rukuru and
Loangwa.   Next morning we were up before the sun,
and off.   By mid-day we came within sight of the great
Loangwa Plain.   As far as the eye could reach it stretched
before us, until in the far west it was closed in by a dim
range of hills.   Nothing but trees could be seen, and in
the light blue haze the great featureless plain looked like a
vast lake.

" Then we began the descent ; down dry river-beds,
sinking four inches in the sand with each step, over huge
boulders, through reeds, thorns, and an entanglement of
grass, until our clothes were hanging in rags.   When at
last we reached the plain we pushed on with all speed,
hoping to arrive at the Senga villages before nightfall.   We
passed the spoor of elephants, zebras, buffaloes and other
large game, but nowhere could we find water.   The sun
set, and we were still pushing on.   Happily a bright moon
rose, and allowed us to see our path.

" At last we reached the river towards which we had
been pressing.   But it was dry.   The guides had hoped
to strike the river near where the villages were built.   We
listened, but no village sound could be heard.   Men went
up and down stream straining to hear the voices of the
children.   But there was no sound, save the night voices
of the forest.   So we decided to camp where we were,
if water could be found.   After digging for about four feet
in the bed of the river, to our great joy we came on water.
Fires were quickly lit, sheds thrown up, and we settled down
for the night.

" Meanwhile our guides returned, saying that farther
down the stream they had been met by a hyena, and had
heard the village sounds.   So we sent them off to warn the
villagers not to be afraid when they saw our fires, for we

were not Ngoni raiders. Presently a body of burly Senga were seen striding up the river-bed. They had come to welcome the white man. They remembered Mr John Moir's visit nearly twenty years ago, and welcomed me as they had done him.

" Next morning we camped in the head village of the chief, Tembwe. All the villages are surrounded with a great stockade, and are built in what is, during the rainy season, a huge marsh. They are completely hid from view by a circle of high thorn trees, and, owing to the crowded and aged state of the houses, are in a most filthy and insanitary condition.

" The people gathered round us in hundreds, and brought presents of meal and fowls. They eagerly welcomed the idea of having teachers among them, and begged for white men to protect them from their enemies. On Sabbath we had a congregation of about 800 people, and the teacher who was with me addressed them. In the evening I spoke with Tembwe, the chief, about the insanitary condition of his villages, and pointed out that they are never swept, and that more children are dying from this than from all the past raiding of Ngoni and Bemba. To this he meekly assented. I had been asleep for some hours when suddenly I was startled by a great voice shouting in the village. It was the chief. At first I thought he was mad ; but, as we listened, we soon discovered that he was not mad, but inspired—perhaps by his midnight potations—and was taking his first step up the ladder of civilisation. All through the village he strode, calling like a village bellman, ' Women all take heed ! The white man says we are dying because the village is not swept. Sickness and death are coming. Rise and sweep ! Rise and sweep ! ' And all around we could hear the women in their huts waking out of sleep, and murmuring. But his voice of thunder went roaring through the stillness of the night until all the village had heard.

" Then when he had finished, some foxes outside the stockade began to bark ; and the Natives say that when foxes yelp, death and war are at hand.   When the sun rose some women were sweeping ; but the foxes had been their evangelists.

" Leaving Tembwe we marched south, passing through some large villages, and resting for a night within a large stockade.   Next day we arrived at the head village of the chieftainess, Chikwa, who seems to have many people under her.   She is a plain, unclothed, unimposing woman. Her husband, who seems to snuff and drink excessively, did business for her with as much intelligence as his fuddled state would allow.

" This was our last halting-place among the Senga before turning east on our journey back to Ngoniland.   The first day's march home will not soon be forgotten.   We were tired when we started, for we had daily been making forced marches in a close and enervating country.   Our road was the moist, sandy bed of a river.   On either side was thicket and entangled grass, impenetrable.   We strode along sinking deep with each step, and leaping every minute or two over some cross stream.   ' How long is this to continue ? ' I shouted to the guides.   ' Until we reach the hills,' they replied.   But with every bend of the river the hills seemed more distant than ever.   By mid-day I thought I could go no farther, and threw myself down on a bank of sand. . . . But when I got my boots off, and had changed my dripping clothes, and had a cup of tea and an hour's rest, we all wanted to push on.   Soon we were round the final bend and at the foot of the hills.   Here the guides would have us camp, as water was far off.   But the hills had put new vigour into us, and we would not wait.   So, dismissing our guides, we set off. I warned the men to carry water, as we might not find any on the road. My little cook alone did so, but after marching a mile he poured it all on the ground. He could not be bothered carrying it.

"At four o'clock the men began to wish they had water. At five o'clock they were decidedly thirsty. At six we were marching full speed in dead silence, too thirsty to speak. The sun set. Still no water. The dusk came on. It was getting cold in the ravines. We could not see the hills about us. Still no water. We could only feel the path. It was dark, when the wild beasts come out. A man behind dropped his axe, and could not see it. He was afraid to fall behind to look for it. Another axe fell. Then another. At last we cried, ' It's no good ; we must sleep here.' And we threw down our loads, hungry, thirsty and tired. Sheds were soon built, fires kindled, and we went to sleep. What delicious dreams one had of running brooks, of the clearest and coldest of water ! One spent the night by Scottish burns, except when wakened up to the sad reality.

"Long before sunrise we were off again. But we had not gone three miles when we reached a marsh where cold delicious water was found. What a shouting went up ! I thought I could drink bucketsful of water, and was disappointed to find how little satisfied me. And then we gave thanks—every one of us from the heart—for water in a thirsty land.

"Next day we crossed the Rukuru and were among our own. Our troubles were at an end, for our land flows with milk and honey, and the people with kindness. Sheep were killed for us in the villages, for the people said, ' You have come from a far land.'

"We have seen the Senga, and by elaborate inquiries have gathered some information about them. Formerly they were a great people. But internal strife, and forays from the west and east, by the Bemba and Ngoni, have decimated the people. They now number perhaps 20,000 or 30,000, and live in groups of large stockaded villages. The men show considerable intelligence. They are expert hunters, good weavers, and artists in brass and wood. The women, however, seem to be very degraded. They wear little clothing, and have made themselves as ugly as possible with tattooing, and horrible ornaments in the upper and lower lips. The darkest customs prevail among them. The language spoken is almost the same as our colloquial Tumbuka. Unfortunately the vices also of the Tumbuka seem to find a hot-bed there.

" Here then is a people, living in unspeakable degradation, in continual dread of their enemies, alone, uncared for, yet waiting, now twenty years, to welcome the messengers of peace. When shall they too be claimed in our Lord's name ? "

They were a weak, craven people, with all the faults of those accustomed to oppression ; but in them he recognised the " little brothers of Christ, sons for whom a place was waiting in the family of God, men for whom the eternal sacrifice was made," and all through his life they made a peculiar appeal to his heart. What he said to the Ngoni about them on his return so aroused the feelings of the Christians that they agreed that they must pass on what had come to themselves, and so a month or two afterwards there was a dedication service at which nine teachers were set apart to carry on a new warfare among their old enemies.

CHAPTER VIII

POLITICAL TROUBLE

In the beginning of 1899 Fraser had a new role to play. Ngoniland was seething with rumours and unrest. For long the only contact with other races had been through the missionaries, but latterly other white men had been coming into the land to buy cattle. They offered thirty to fifty yards of calico per head, and, for a while, the Natives had been glad to sell; but cattle meant more to them than calico, and once their needs had been satisfied they were no longer anxious to dispose of their beasts, and the white men who turned up found no such bargains awaiting them as had at first been possible. These whites were not as amicable as the first-comers had been, and some of them were behaving very suspiciously.

One day a messenger arrived at the Mission with a tale about one of these "Bazungu" (white men). He had put up his camp at the paramount chief's, and his "boy" had said he was wishing to build a "Boma"—which to them stood for Government station—this man whom they knew to have come from Mpezeni's, where there had been war, where indunas had been killed, and where the white men had seized cattle and taken away the power of the chief! They had told this stranger that they had no desire to sell more cattle, but he refused to go away. He was wandering about desecrating the graves of the dead by removing the stones which they had heaped up to prevent the hyenas from scraping up the corpses. Mbale-kelwa was alarmed, and he wanted "Framo" to tell him what to do about it.

Fraser set off in person, visited the solitary white man, who was sitting playing with a dirty pack of cards, and then went on to the chief to tell him that his fears were groundless. The white man had stated that, if he could not get cattle, he must make his journey worth while in some other way. He had found traces of gold in the streams, and wished to stay and work in the river during the rains. He had not intentionally interfered with the graves ; to him they had only been heaps of stones, and he had been breaking up the quartz boulders to look for gold. The Boma he proposed building was not a government fort, but a wattle-and-daub dwelling-house for himself. Fraser did his best to create a friendly feeling, but the prospector was as unwilling to move off as the chief was to let him stay. Finally a Christian teacher, Daniel, proposed that the gold-digger should remove to his village not far off and put up his building there.

Scarcely had the missionary returned from settling this difficulty when fresh suspicions were aroused by the arrival of two men at Mperembe's. These two were believed to come from the North Charterland Company's district in which there had been recent abuses, and the chief feared their intentions as they refused to leave. Fraser sent him back a reassuring message, telling him that he was becoming like a child—afraid of a shadow : these men only wanted cattle. But to the men themselves he sent a courteous note apologising for seeming to interfere, but explaining that he thought they should know that their presence was really alarming the chief, the more so as he was a brother of that Mpezeni who had had political trouble, and suggesting that it would make for peace if they would move on to another village.

A few weeks later other and more alarming rumours began to spread. Another white man, named Ziehl, was now in the country with armed followers and native women from Mpezeni. His sales were forcible, cattle being seized and some calico flung to the owners ; men were being chikotied (the " chikoti " is a whip of rhinoceros hide), and women were being raped. If this were true, it meant a case for Government interference, but it had to be confirmed before any message was sent to the Administrator on the Lake Shore. So to one of the most reliable teachers in that district Fraser despatched a note telling him to ascertain the truth about these rumours. Daniel did so by walking into the lion's den, saying he had been sent by the missionary to inquire into the truth of the stories that everyone was telling about his treatment of the people. The white man flew into a passion at his interference, and lashed out at him with his chikoti. Furious at this treatment of one who was not only a teacher, but also a chief's son, one of those who had accompanied Daniel struck out at the white man before they fled, followed by several shots from the Muzungu's revolver.

A letter was hastily sent to the Lake, and now Fraser's task was to keep the people from doing anything rash till Mr Cardew, the Administrator, arrived. Heavy rains kept him from starting for three days, and meantime it became a difficult job to hold in the indignant chiefs, expecially as the white man had taken fright, decamped during the night, and was now heading south. To see their cattle being driven out of the country was more than the people could stand, and some had already pursued him and seized between fifty and sixty head which were lagging behind. The white man's carriers had fled, leaving some of his loads. Everything must be left untouched, Fraser warned them ; the cattle must be put in a kraal, and nobody must remove a beast, even though it was his own. He had sent off a second runner on hearing of the white man's flight, and expected Mr Cardew every hour. But day after day passed, and he did not appear. The only news that was arriving was the latest report of the retreat : the white man had sent back some of his followers to try to regain possession of the cattle ; people had been shot at in their gardens. Urgent messages came from the chiefs to ask what they were expected to do : were they to sit quietly allowing their people to be killed and their cattle stolen, without punishing the culprit, because he was a white ? Their people could not be restrained from following him !

Fraser compromised by asking them to wait till the following Monday : if Cardew had not then come, he would start himself. At four a.m. on the Tuesday, accompanied by Dr Scott, who had come up from Bandawe on hearing news of the trouble in Ngoniland, he set off, seeing *en route* plenty of evidence of the indignation of the people. At one point, for example, an old blind man awaited him by the roadside to tell of armed men entering his village, taking eight cows, stealing his cloth and snuff-box, whipping him and assaulting two of the women.

At the chief's kraal, which they reached that afternoon, they were overwhelmed with evidence of the wrongs that had been inflicted—spear- and gunshot-wounds and marks of chikoti lashes, as well as tales of theft and rape from one after another. It was obvious that the people could no longer be held in from avenging their wrongs. When it came to the turn of the missionary to speak, he said the Mission did not forbid them to punish the evildoer. It was the chief's business to protect his people and bring criminals to justice, but *this* man was not one of his own people, but probably a subject of the Queen, so he must not molest him. However, as they had waited some days and had heard nothing from Mr Cardew, it was right that the chief should take action before the man had left his

territory. If, therefore, Mbalekelwa would send out a
picked body of men next morning to ask the man to return
to hear the charges against him, or, if he refused, to take
possession of the cattle, he himself would accompany them
on the conditions that he should pick his men, that no beer
should be touched on the road, that he should be absolutely
obeyed, and that no one but himself should have any
dealings with the white man.   " You understand," he explained, " that we go as interpreters and to protect the life
of the white man."   The chiefs gladly accepted this offer,
but that night a runner arrived from Ekwendeni to say
that Cardew was on his way.   The chiefs were persuaded
to await his arrival, and the missionaries' part was ended.

The delay thus caused gave the offender time to get
across the border into North Charterland territory, where
he lodged grave charges against the missionary and the
Ngoni, stating that an impi from the Mission had followed
him and seized cows, goats, cases of gin, trusses of calico
and other property.   Another impi from the Mission,
attacking him at Mhlola's, had been repulsed.   Two other
North Charterland men arriving with cattle reported that
'Ngonomo had tried to kill them, and that the missionary
had practically ordered them to leave the country.

The complaint lodged at Fort Alston led to a demand
being sent to Zomba[1] for Fraser's arrest.   By this time,
however, the Government officials there had received Mr
Cardew's report, and considered this step unnecessary !
Ziehl was sent back for trial, which took place at Ekwendeni.
With him he brought as witness the gold-digger, who told
of the ill-usage he also had received at the hands of the
Ngoni and their missionary, and produced a certificate
from a doctor to say that he had returned suffering from
pediculosis.   This statement rather impressed the judge

[1] Government headquarters in Nyasaland.

till he learned the nature of the trouble! The charges against the prisoner included stealing cattle, assaulting Natives, threatening with fire-arms, and carrying on operations of war. On all these and other charges he was found guilty; though on the charge of shooting and wounding Natives he was excused on the ground of provocation. His sentence was six months' imprisonment with hard labour, or a £50 fine. The fine was paid; and, after the few Natives who happened to be in court as witnesses had recognised and claimed their cattle, he went off with the remainder, much the richer for the escapade in spite of the fine. And then the judge, to show his impartiality, censured the missionary for having sent a native teacher to speak to a white man, though a letter telling Daniel to find out if the reports were true scarcely bore on the face of it such an interpretation.

Such censure, though it hurt, had little effect compared with the knowledge of the feeling that had been aroused in the minds of the Natives, that in the Mission they had a true friend and defender of their rights.

CHAPTER IX

AN IMPORTANT FURLOUGH

SCARCELY once during all his years of service in Africa did Donald Fraser go home for the simple reason that furlough was due. Invariably he was ordered home on medical grounds.

By the end of 1899 he was admitting the intolerable strain of the work, for the scores of people who daily waited to be interviewed were proving an overwhelming task quite apart from the ordinary routine. This admission was, not by way of complaint, but that the Church at home might be led to realise how full of crisis the situation now was—far more so than in the dark days that had preceded. All Ngoniland seemed ready to come under the influence of the Gospel if only advantage could be taken of the floodtime. Yet, in spite of all this press of work about the doors, he had deliberately decided to send seventeen native missionaries to the Senga in answer to the appeal of two of their chiefs, because it seemed to him a serious thing to crush the new spirit of missionary zeal which had manifestly been born of God among the Ngoni.

Imagine his dismay when he heard that the Mission Council, which he had been unable to attend, had resolved that he must take furlough at once. He wrote pleading impossibility. Dr Elmslie, as acting head of the Mission, was adamant, and he had to " pack up and go, sick to think of leaving all this work "—a marked contrast to the delight with which a first leave is generally anticipated.

On the journey home he crossed swords with a professional evangelist who found fault with him for presiding at a secular concert, and wanted to know what his Missionary Committee would think of him. Donald spoke out. "Man, I wonder what *your* Master thinks of *you*? Don't you think it would be more likely to commend Him to others if you laid aside your greed, your inconsiderateness and selfishness, instead of 'scunnering' everyone on board the ship with your conduct and your Pharisaism?" It was not often that he spoke out so plainly and hotly to anyone, but when at times he did, it was invariably to someone making very open professions of piety and at the same time showing smug satisfaction with himself in comparison with others. Above almost anything else he disliked to hear scandalous or uncharitable talk about others. Once on board the steamer on Lake Nyasa he was overheard to say emphatically, "It's a lie!" "Hush! people will hear you," said the man to whom he was talking. "I don't care. It *is* a lie, and I don't care who hears me say so!" His companion again asked him to lower his voice. "If you consider it true, and a fact that you as a Christian think it necessary to make public, it is only fair that people should know that I consider it a lie!" He heard no more gossip on that trip.

His time at home gave him more change than rest. Still, probably he himself with his inability to say "No" was alone responsible for his preaching almost before he had renewed acquaintance with his mother tongue. He had to omit the Lord's Prayer in a church one day because he could not remember it except in the Zulu version, and felt that "speaking with tongues" might not be to edification. Not realising what the consequence would be, he threw himself only too successfully into the task of trying to create new interest and support for Livingstonia. There was, however, one project that he was faintly cherishing

F

in the back of his mind about which he showed an unwonted diffidence; it was that of securing a permanent
medical colleague at the expense of another mission field.
He had not been long in Glasgow before he received an
invitation to attend an evening meeting to bid farewell
to two of his old student-day friends who were sailing
that year to the foreign field. One of the two was a
woman medical appointed to Rajputana. He escorted her
home after the meeting, and a few days later called on her.
For more than four years he had been dreaming of the
possibility of having her out to share his home in Africa,
but had never had what he regarded as the presumption
to believe that it might become a reality: yet here he was,
home unexpectedly soon, to find that she was still unmarried
and delayed by student work from sailing the previous year.
Had it not all perhaps been providentially planned? Yet,
though he set out that afternoon with some such thoughts
in his mind, he drank tea and departed without broaching
the subject. When teased about it later, his excuse was
that no man wanted to propose to a girl in a room that
smelled of iodoform.

He met her again at a Students' Conference at Matlock,
where once more he heard her being farewelled along
with the other student volunteers sailing that year. On
this occasion at least one sharp-eyed young woman guessed
at his state of mind, and greatly embarrassed him by counting the cherry-stones on his plate to the rhyme of, " He
loves her, he don't; he'll have her, he won't; he would if
he could, but he can't." He blushed profusely, especially
as the " her " he had in his mind was sitting almost directly
opposite, entirely ignorant of his feelings. And still, like
Brer Rabbit, he " lay low and said nuffin'." It was only
when he had rejoined his brothers and sisters for a month's
holiday that he summoned up his courage to write—this

young man who had always so keenly believed in personal interviews. When the answer came from someone who by this time had her passage taken and her boxes addressed and waiting to be packed, his family did not find him a very cheery holiday companion. He did not want to do anything or go anywhere. They put it down to the effects of malaria, and were very indignant with the Livingstonia Committee when, on receiving a letter, he announced that he was called away and must catch the first train. His letter was not from the Rev. J. Fairley Daly, Secretary of the Committee, however, but from a total stranger who wrote inviting him to visit her and meet a mutual friend who had come to say good-bye to her. She had had a faint suspicion that her guest was half inclined to regret a recent decision she had made, though she only guessed at, and would not guarantee, that fact. Still, if he thought it was worth while risking a second disappointment, she would suggest his coming. He turned up in trepidation, but by supper-time was gratefully accepting his hostess's invitation to stay on for a few days.

Twenty-four hours later two young people decided that they really must write some letters. Dr George Robson of Perth was startled to receive from the young student whom he remembered presiding at the Liverpool Conference an entirely unexpected application to be allowed to become his son-in-law. Dr Laws, also home on furlough, got a note from his young colleague to say that the impossible had happened, and asking for his blessing. The episcopal benediction applied for began, " Tonal, you sinner ! " The Fraser family received an explanatory telegram. The Ladies' Foreign Mission Committee, who were having so many disappointments with their agents that Miss Rainy had to remind them that " after all, marriage was not apostasy," had another—an eleventh-hour—withdrawal, which elicited from their President an unofficial letter of warm personal congratulation—" seeing it was Donald Fraser, she could do nothing but rejoice."

In a very short time the unknown young man, who had discovered to his dismay that his engagement brought him into a very large circle of relations—of which he never quite mastered all the ramifications—found himself one of the family at Garry Lodge, Perth, loved equally as a son and a brother before he was entitled to any relationship. So warmly did they feel towards him that it was no surprise to find one's sister thirsting for the blood of two old ladies who, on the strength of having seen him for ten minutes, had made up their minds that Dr Agnes's young man was not quite good enough for her ! When they left for Africa the young wife, going to face for the first time what really were remote regions in those days, found that among the younger members of the family there was no tender solicitude for *her*, but that the parting injunctions all took the form of " *Do* be kind to darling Donald."

This departure did not take place till the spring of 1901. When this was decided on by the Committee, it was a terrible blow to Donald. As soon as the doctor pronounced him free from malaria, he had begun to plan for his return : the wedding was to be in October, and the sailing, he hoped, early in November. In the beginning of September, in order to get Dr Laws' backing which, he felt, would influence other members of Committee, he wrote an urgent letter to him. After putting forward his arguments he ended on a note of entreaty : " I am remarkably well, and my work and responsibility are not at home, but out there. I cannot endure this delay any longer. I am sure it is wrong for me to be away from my post. Please do not write to delay me any longer. I feel as if it were going to be a curse to our work that I have been allowed to appeal with a little power sometimes." He could not accept the view of others that his speaking was doing so much for the interests of the Mission that it was advisable to put off his return. When they vetoed his plans he was in the depths of depression and distress. He was obsessed with the thought of his neglected people, for Stuart, who had relieved him, had been invalided home after an attack of blackwater fever. If he had known that this delay would happen, he told his future wife, he would *never* have agreed to be sent home ; and when she suggestively inquired whether nothing had happened to make it worth while, his emphatic " nothing ! " seemed scarcely complimentary. The next minute he was saying, " Oh forgive me, but God meant us for one another, and He would have brought that about ; but I can't feel that *this* is the will of God." Yet it was like him to refuse to let the question be settled on the ground of personal considerations when one member in Committee, seeing his distress, suggested that perhaps their proposal was inconvenient through conflicting with such private arrangements as his marriage.

The keen disappointment he felt did not prevent him from promptly setting to work to make as good use as possible of his time. He took on a strenuous programme of work, involving so much travelling and speaking that in premarital letters he got many lectures on overworking and knocking himself up when he should be getting fit for his next term's work. He turned up whenever he could to report to the writer how he was getting on, but it was often in such an overtired condition that she began even then to have a faint inkling that her mission in life was to be the task of patching up a worn-out missionary to make him fit for a further spell of service. The one thing he impressed on her was that she must never try to interfere with his doing his duty, and of that he must be his own judge.

In the intervals when he was not addressing meetings he was learning book-keeping and tile-making. The necessity for the former had been impressed on him in the many weary hours he had spent during his first term trying to balance the Station books. The tile-making rather puzzled one young lady to whom it was mentioned. Her idea was that one didn't wear tile hats in Africa !

Moving about the country Donald was brought in touch with some of his old friends and greatly enjoyed meeting them. One had already attained his doctorate and, after he had pumped his guest dry about Africa, discussed Ritschlian theology with him, unaware that he made his guest feel what a " profound fool " he was. It never seemed to dawn on Donald that anything he had done could ever make another feel a " poor creature " in comparison : yet that was what his friend wrote concerning him. Once he let himself go in indignant criticism of a host, who wrote urging him to come and help to awaken missionary interest, and would take no refusal on the score of overwork. When Fraser arrived, it was to find that the minister was not at home and had never intended to be. " The house was atrociously furnished in bad taste, and the pictures on the walls were a torture to look at." This letter brought an amusing sense of something like relief to the reader. He had always wanted her to be candid to him about his faults, but up to this point they had seemed to be confined to spelling mistakes ! Laziness, which he considered his besetting sin, had been appallingly conspicuous by its absence. Here at last was a reassuring proof of his being very human after all. Even when he was laughed at about it, his excuse was that no one who had not seen the pictures could understand the provocation !

In what leisure moments were left he was making out a Tumbuka Grammar for his future colleague. There were not very many opportunities of *viva voce* lessons, so a good deal of the learning had to be done by correspondence. On one occasion, when a rather bulky letter from him had arrived, some teasing remark about what he could have to say led to an immediate offer to read it aloud. After listening to the way in which one formed the plural in the " li- " class, along with the information that the prefix was often absent in the singular, the family quickly lost interest. A few days later his future father-in-law was overheard telling some visitors that Donald's love-letters appeared to be unique dissertations on classes, concords and prefixes— a hasty conclusion to draw.

Our marriage had, like the return to Africa, been postponed till the beginning of 1901, so that he might carry on the full programme of work as long as possible ; and he did it until within two days of the wedding. The first part of the honeymoon was, usefully if prosaically, spent in London, largely in the Army and Navy Stores. It happened to be the week in which Queen Victoria died, and the bridegroom was rather distressed that his wife's trousseau had to be hastily discarded for some ready-made black clothes, in order to save her from being mobbed. He had a subconscious discrimination about dress and food. He could never describe what anyone wore, any more than he could tell whether he was eating beef or mutton, but he knew when eye or palate was gratified. Yet he had a very keen and accurate observation of the things in which he was really interested, and often wondered at my lack of it. For instance, when building was going on at Loudon, I could not tell him, after merely passing up the road near which they were working, whether the bricklayers had got to the first or the third course above the window-level. But when it came to where he had laid down his pipe, I scored!

One incident occurred during our stay in London which showed up the loyalty of his nature. We had gone to see our first " moving picture." It depicted some imaginary episode in the South African War. Within a brief time three instances of dastardly treachery on the part of the Boers were shown. The war was going on at that time, and feeling running very high, and to my dismay Donald's voice, raised to an audible pitch, remarked emphatically, " They have *no* right to give that impression of the Boers. It's unfair! It's untrue!" Applause of the picture rather drowned the last words, but I heard a snarl beside me, and hastily proposed that we should go out. I rose, and he followed, not realising that my action was not due to my sharing his indignation, but to my fears for his safety. It was only a month or two later, when we were staying in Stellenbosch with Dutch friends who, in spite of their bitterness about the Boer camps, were treating us with great kindness, that I appreciated the loyal spirit that could not let the calumny pass without protest.

London was followed by various parting visits to friends. Among other memories, there stand out two—one of Lady Aberconway (then Mrs Charles M'Laren) crossing the drawing-room floor at Newington House after talking to Donald, to tell me that he was thrown away on Africa and should be using his gifts in Parliament; and the other of his boyish enjoyment of the sport of tobogganing down a long avenue on tea-trays. It may have been the recollection of that that made our friends carry him off on his next furlough to Switzerland for winter sports.

Then home to pack a miscellaneous collection of goods and books—he believed in having plenty of literature— a last week at Bournemouth spent with my parents, to whom by this time he was a very real and dear son; and then came the day he had so long looked forward to, when we should start for his beloved Africa. That last hour before sailing he never forgot, because of the frightful quandary in which he found himself. We had parted on arriving at Southampton, I going off with an aunt to do some last-minute shopping, while he went with my parents to the boat. Time was passing, and there was no sign of our appearing. He began to get worried. The steamer was very crowded, as it was carrying troops to the Cape. While one kept an anxious eye on the gangways, the others searched among the crowds on deck, he all the while facing in his mind the difficult dilemma whether to go ashore or remain on board if the last minute came and his wife had not turned up. Suddenly he came face to face with two ladies who had been distractedly trying to find their party, and heaved a sigh of relief that he had been spared the necessity of choosing.

CHAPTER X

BACK TO AFRICA

In prospect, Donald's voyages were always to be a time of absolute rest : in reality, he always found something to keep him well occupied. His books were often written on board ; and those that were not, were composed during the long trudges in Africa as he passed from village to village, and were scribbled down at night by the light of a camp fire.

On this occasion he found an obvious bit of service awaiting him. Some 700 Yeomen were aboard, for the war was dragging wearily on and the Reserves were being called up. That first Sunday presented a very distressing spectacle : drink had been going freely and the effects were visible. Some men were singing or gambling ; others, many of them mere lads, were looking sick and sorry for themselves. The officers paid little or no attention to the men ; the one man who stood out in the crowd was a non-commissioned officer who, in the midst of some rather undesirable music-hall songs, had the courage to stand up and sing " The Holy City " in a voice fine enough to command silence and attention. The sight stirred Donald as he watched them and realised the hopelessly demoralised condition in which they would land in Capetown. If a Christian nation could send these men to face death—and enteric was rife—and failed to provide a padre to attend to them, he must do something. Obtaining permission, he appeared next evening on their deck with a little party which included two of our Livingstonia missionaries,

Miss Scott, who had a fine voice, and Mr Meldrum, an artisan, who was also a violinist. The Evangelistic Campaign began. The men were in just the mood to be influenced, and daily meetings on the well deck became increasingly attended, everything else being dropped as the time for them arrived. Not a day passed without men holding up their hands to show on Whose side they had enlisted. Before a week was over, little Bible-reading groups were being formed, and the second-class passengers were being asked to part with their Bibles and Testaments to supply the demand for them among the Yeomanry. All this naturally attracted the attention of the other passengers on board. Amongst them one of the most interested was a Jewish Rabbi who used day after day to come and talk with my husband. The morning before we reached Capetown he asked if he might address the meeting that evening, and received a cordial assent. He spoke with great effect, prefacing his talk with the admission that he was of a different persuasion from them, and then going on to say what would be expected of men who had proclaimed themselves followers of Jesus. We never met him again ; but, when the papers published the news that Dr Donald Fraser was to be the next Moderator of the United Free Church, there came a letter from him saying that, if he was addressing the man with whom he had travelled twenty years before, he wanted not so much to congratulate him as the Church which had discovered his worth. As we left the steamer, one of the ship's officers came up and said, " We've you to thank, sir, for not having had a hell of a time on board."

Meetings in South Africa, more meetings in Blantyre, and now we were on the last lap of the journey to Ngoniland. The very day we started off, proof met me of the place he held in the hearts of his people. He had pushed ahead on his bicycle, leaving me to be carried in a machila. For hours we had been monotonously jogging along the road, when suddenly along came a wild, yelling, excited horde of scantily dressed men flourishing spears and clubs. My carriers were unceremoniously pushed aside, the bamboo of my hammock was lifted on to the shoulders of two of the newcomers, and off we went ! I hadn't an idea of what was happening : they had paid no more attention to me than if I had been a truss of calico. At least they were carrying me in the right direction, and I could only " wait and see." I felt a momentary dismay when they suddenly swerved into the bush, but the next minute they had drawn up with a disconcertingly sudden jerk opposite the door of a rest-house at which my husband was standing—one broad beam ! Before he had helped me to alight I was surrounded by the men, their fierce yells exchanged for friendly smiles as they dinned my ears with shouts of " Sikubona Nkosikazi." [1] " It's our Ngoni," explained my husband ; " I found them here on their way to Blantyre for transport work ; and, when I told them that my Dona was coming behind, they set off to give you a convoy." We visited them at their camp-fire that night, and it was easy to see how delighted they were to welcome him back, now no longer a " boy," but with that increased status that marriage brings in African society.

[1] Literally, " We see you, woman chief."

CHAPTER XI

HORA

FRASER had always felt the need for a second centre of work among the Ngoni, and now that there were three married couples on the staff it had become possible, and we were consequently assigned to Hora. This was no new choice of site : it had been occupied for some time, but for the past ten years had stood derelict. It lay within the area of the chief Mzukuzuku, who with his warlike impi had startled the newly-arrived missionary five years before when he had caught sight of them threading their way through the bush, little knowing that their errand was to put in a claim for him to be sent to their district.

We arrived to find the house being repaired and made fit for habitation. It was a simple three-roomed cottage, surrounded by a veranda, portions of which had been walled in to provide a little extra accommodation for visitors, pantry, store, etc. The walls were of rough sun-dried brick, and were unplastered ; the thatched roof had no ceiling, and the floors were beaten mud. Rather nervously had the husband been waiting to see what his wife would think of the home he had brought her to, and he was relieved to find that his frequent warnings had led her to expect something even more primitive than the reality. The roof was still being thatched and the walls washed with local clay, and workers swarmed around all day long. One small veranda-room seemed to offer privacy, but I was surprised by the midnight gloom that appeared suddenly to descend at mid-day while I was putting up my hair, until, turning round, I discovered the window-space blocked by closely-packed faces keenly interested in the operation. Everything Fraser's Dona attempted to do seemed to create this profound interest.

I quickly made the discovery that I need expect no interference in domestic matters! The house and all personal affairs were left to me by a man whose mind was wholly given to his mission work. There was very little time for private life, for the Mission claims superseded all else. When I asked for a rough table to be knocked together for the living-room, he promised me I should have it as soon as all the district schools had been supplied with black-boards. A year later the table which stood there, concealed by a large cloth almost reaching the floor, still consisted of an edifice of soldered flour-tins surmounted by the lid of a wooden box! I had held on firmly to the packing-cases which had brought out our personal possessions, and of these most of our furniture in the early days was composed. Experience taught me that a better plan than asking for a thing was to let him find me attempting to make it myself in a hopelessly crude fashion; then instinctively the superior male element in him made him take it out of my hands and finish it himself. Yet he was keenly appreciative of the changes effected. On one occasion, certainly, he did voice his misgivings as he surveyed the mid-day meal of chicken in jelly and stewed guavas with cream :

" Don't you think this is unnecessarily luxurious ? " he gently inquired ; " a simple lunch of bread and butter with a cup of tea would be quite sufficient." " Yes, but unnecessarily extravagant," I protested. " We can't afford to feed on bread alone with flour costing ten shillings a stone, when I can get a fowl for twopence, pick the guavas off the tree, and pay three or four shillings for the month's milk." After that he enjoyed his cheap luxuries without demur. There was one bit of understanding forethought for which I often felt grateful : he had urged that one large cheque received as a wedding gift should be spent on a suite of folding bedroom furniture, explaining that when one was well it was easy to put up with anything, but that in fever it made a great difference to have things that did not get on one's nerves.

If I found some scope for the creative faculty within the mud walls of the home, how much more he as he looked around? Apart from our dwelling-house the Mission Station consisted of a ramshackle school and an old saw-pit. It was on 1st June, his birthday, that we arrived. The Council which could sanction the putting up of buildings would meet a few weeks before the rains were due in November, when it would be too late to do anything till the next dry season. It was not in Donald to let opportunities be wasted in that fashion. With that contagious enthusiasm and energy of his, he got the people worked up into wishing for a proper Mission Station with church and school, and then called a big " indaba "[1] of the chief and neighbouring headmen, explained his plight, and made them feel this was their job. In a short time there were 1000 people giving a fortnight's free labour.

To one whose impression of a brickfield had been derived from picturing the Israelites working under their Egyptian overseers, what a contrast this merry African scene presented! The mud was being tramped to the accompaniment of singing, and the moulders kept up cheerful shouts of " Dongo, dongo ! " to encourage the children to bring the necessary supplies of clay for their moulds. The Mzungu was here, there and everywhere, seeing that their easy-going unmethodical ways did not lead to unnecessary delay ; he shouted many a " Hurryupi ! "—a phrase learnt

[1] Public discussion.

from the lips of the impatient white man—to the file of women coming leisurely along with their pots of water balanced on their heads—good reason for no unseemly haste. At mid-day baskets of food were brought to refresh the resting labourers.

A three-roomed building went up quickly as office and dispensary. Meanwhile the foundations of school and boarders' houses, and lastly the church, were being laid, and the superstructures rose as fast as bricks were forthcoming. Sun-dried bricks were used for the smaller buildings, but kilns were now burning those required for the church, and so fast were the bricks removed for use when ready that they had no time to cool and were singeing the hair of those who carried them on their heads. The Station was complete with nine buildings, and Fraser was busily devoting himself to the spiritual side of the work before the Council met. There was awaiting them no request to sanction the expenditure of money on Station buildings—a gift from a Baptist friend having covered the cost of what was not provided by the liberality of the Natives themselves. Nevertheless, they felt it incumbent on them to bestow a reproof *in absentia* on their impatient colleague. If he felt it, he tried not to show it, and did his best to allay the indignation of his wife by telling her what a very nice lot of fellows they were personally. He knew he could not put first the best interests of the people without sometimes involving himself in trouble.

The return to Africa had been saddened by the evidences of much laxity and retrogression among the people. Many of the teachers had lost heart, and their lowered spiritual level had affected the tone of their communities. It was the result of the insufficient attention which lack of staff had made inevitable. New influences, too, were among them. Many of the men had been away in distant centres of work and had come back with material wealth, but poisoned in mind by their contact with a society in which cupidity and lust were so evident. Their tales over the evening fires spread the evil contamination.

One watched how he set to work to stem the tide. There were the teachers, starting off with new heart and hope to carry on their work after a few days spent with him on the Station. There were the increasing numbers, and the growing silence with which they listened in the church. By and by there were little groups staying behind after the service for further talk. Outside his office day by day they were sitting waiting to be interviewed as to their fitness for baptism or the reality of their desire to enter the Catechumens' class. There were days when the missionary's wife scarcely saw him. Even at meals there were sometimes continual interruptions, and the last hour or two after dinner, when surely he needed relaxation, were given to what she called " The Translation Committee." The missionary and a native teacher sat at a little camp-table putting the Scriptures into Tumbuka. I can see them still, trying to get the right Tumbuka equivalent for some Hebrew word of which Donald has been explaining the meaning—Hebrew which he studies more interestedly now than in his student days !

So strenuous a programme might well become mechanical, but that is not the impression conveyed to the Africans, so sensitive to the European's mood. Among the 400 catechumens examined, here is the effect made on one. " I have learned many things from you, the crown of these things being God's love to me. Your life and work have greatly helped me to understand though dimly God's grace and love towards the poor sinners. I am a great debtor to you, not in things that can be handled, but in spiritual and intellectual things. . . . On your

G

second arrival from Scotland you found me at Hora, where one of the most remarkable things in my experience happened.   It is this : I came to you as a Church candidate for baptism.   I am sorry words fail me to express how you helped me in your private room, where your words, look and loving face all joined together to make me understand what following Christ means.   I must frankly say that before that time I did not understand what I was doing, but after hearing you speaking to me that following Christ meant casting oneself in Christ's hands, so that He might lead me, soon the light shone in my heart and so I knew myself better than before, and, as you interceded for me, joy which was a new thing to me appeared in my heart. I shall never forget that memorable day when you and my-self were alone in that room : that room was my heaven."

The culmination of these months of work was the Com-munion gathering in November, the close of the working season, for during the rains that follow, the whole popula-tion is hard at work securing its food supply for the coming year.   Little goes on during that time beyond the ordinary Sunday services, and even they may be made very un-punctual, if not impossible, by severe tropical downpours. There was one Sunday when we began a service with a handful of people from a neighbouring village.   Towards the close in came a larger contingent from other villages two or three miles farther off.   The Benediction had just been pronounced when a still larger crowd arrived, who though setting off when the downpour had ceased, had a longer distance to travel.   Once more the service was held and the sermon repeated—in a somewhat condensed form. Those who appreciated it most were the ones who were listening for the third time and feeling that they were getting full value for venturing out !

The need for paying more attention to the women was

one that Fraser realised more than most, I fancy.   At that
time they lagged far behind the men in intelligence, though
there were some with real spiritual life.   In the first services at Hora they used to sit at the back of the church
and seemed to consider themselves onlookers, as at a
village indaba, rather than worshippers, maintaining their
sitting posture throughout.   But this Donald could not
let pass without remonstrance.   In the middle of a hymn
he would stop and address them, " Amama " (you mothers),
" why are you not worshipping too ?   Does not God love
all His children ?   Did not Jesus die for His sisters as
much as for His brothers ?   He wants *your* love and
praise."   Already he was pleading that one of the ladies
from the central station might be spared for Hora, but it
was only later, and then very intermittently, that we had a
woman missionary for work among the people.   The care
of the women members of the Church was a difficult task
for the elders to carry out efficiently, for native customs
made any interest taken in them liable to be misinterpreted.
He therefore appointed, from the best of the Christian
women, a number of deaconesses to undertake the pastoral care of their sisters.   There might be no sanction for
such an office, but the need was enough for him.   In later
years these women were called " bararakazi " (female
elders), and to them, because he hated the effect on the
members of his Session of having to inquire into the un-
savoury details of many a case of discipline, was deputed
the duty of meeting with the women involved.   All the
Session had to do was to accept their judgment without
any publishing of particulars.   At the Communion Services, though they did not go round with the Elements,
they sat on the platform with the men elders.
   One attempt which Fraser made to alter the communal attitude proved a failure.   He spent some Sundays

emphasising the importance of parental responsibility and of the Christian home. This was necessary in view of the claims of other relatives to the children, which often led to baptised children being left to be brought up in the villages and customs of their heathen grandparents. After these talks he suggested that in church they should sit as families, parents and children together. Hitherto the men and women had always tended to sit apart. It was very sheepish-looking family groups that turned up the following Sunday, and one was amused to watch the way a woman would make for the space left in an almost full row, her little girls squeezing in beside her, while with obvious relief her husband began a new row, to be hastily joined by the next man who entered. It was too new an idea to be successful, but at the Communion Services at least the tendency to form into groups according to sex quite died out.

One of the most vivid memories of Hora is the first observance of Christmas among the folk there. Donald had told them that we were going to celebrate it along with other Christians all over the world, and had asked them to bring flowers when they came to the church. On Christmas Eve a group of teachers had been busy helping me to decorate it with the best substitutes I could get for evergreens, and later in the evening they gathered to practise some hymns for the service, though I cannot remember that we had any really Christmas one in the vernacular except " Adeste Fideles." It was dark before we finished, and we started telling them of the waits in the homeland who would be out singing their carols. Then, somehow, the suggestion arose, " Why not here ? " and presently the boys were carrying the little folding organ (to be played by the most unmusical of women) to the chief's village. It was all in darkness : the huts were closed, and the folk seemed asleep. But no sooner did the strains commence than exclamations of wonder were heard, and the light of fires streamed out from huts whose door-coverings had been pushed aside to see what this meant. "Had the angels come back to sing once more?" was the question that had flashed into at least one mind. There was great excitement, and it resulted in a splendid gathering the next day. How it touched Donald to see old men still wearing the warrior's "crown,"[1] relic of former fighting days, bringing their little bunch of flowers as their gift to the Prince of Peace!

And what a memorable Christmas dinner it was, with our unsophisticated black guests being taught how to handle knives and forks and spoons Bazungu-fashion, their beaming host making them feel it was all part of the fun, and suppressing his amusement at the unnecessarily full anatomical details with which they politely refused further supplies! He had a moment of anxiety when he noticed that the plates that had had a plentiful supply of plums were soon after empty, with not a trace of stones; but next morning completely relieved his mind, for the stones were then found under the table, having been got rid of surreptitiously with considerable manual dexterity. Donald loved such occasional meals with Africans as our guests. I can remember one morning some years after, when, in the middle of entertaining the boarders' prefects to breakfast (this honour was to impress on them the responsibility of their position), we heard the sound of boots on our veranda, and mentally faced the problem of what to do with a white man in such circumstances. Fraser rose, met the stranger on the veranda with a genial welcome, and said, "We are entertaining some Native boys to breakfast: I hope you won't mind joining them." The man,

---

[1] Hair worked into a ring and stiffened with wax.

by this time entering the room, looked very astonished at
the scene which met his gaze, but replied politely. He
was seated beside me, and I thought I must do my best to
entertain him, as the conversation had been going on in
the native dialect. But Donald turned it on in English,
and the boys were delighted to air what they knew. Our
guest soon began to give rather abstracted answers to my
remarks—he was getting interested in the company—and
presently he, too, was joining in the conversation. On
leaving he told us that he did not know when he had had
so interesting a breakfast, adding, " I had no idea that
Natives could behave so nicely." This was one of the
very reasons that made Fraser wish to have them become
accustomed to European meals, knowing how unfamiliarity
with customs will make anyone, white or black, seem
boorish. He felt it unfair that Africans, so courteous in
overlooking our blunders, should have no chance of
learning how to acquit themselves when contacts with
other races arose. This introduction to foreign ways was,
as one of our teachers described it, " our BO-class "
(syllable or lowest class) " in the white man's way of life."

Occasional visitors turned up. There was the man who,
after much wandering in the bush, was so impressed by
the " Mayfair drawing-room " into which he was ushered ;
there was the Government man who rather shamefacedly
asked me to reduce a dislocated thumb—the result of an
encounter between his fist and a native carrier's ear which
he had been attempting to box ; there was a Swiss whom,
on returning from a little tour, we found singing hymns
in our house. He had had the misfortune to lose all his
clothes and other possessions in crossing a swollen river,
so he said, and had to be supplied from Donald's wardrobe.
The only thing he professed to regret was the loss of his
Bible. We did not take long to discover that he had

already been re-clad at other mission stations he had passed through, and that when he went for a stroll, still humming hymns, it was to go and pester the chief for the beer that was not available on the Station. Still, it was the rainy season and pouring without intermission, and it was a week before so hospitable a Highlander as his host could send him on his way. He had listened to, and been temporarily sobered by, a very straight talk from Donald. He travelled south, securing a welcome from other missionaries—until they in turn found him out—by representing himself as a friend of Fraser's with whom he had been spending some time! There were two white women visitors in that first year, a welcome variety for a lonely woman who had felt the strain of trying to suppress her desire to dilate on the delinquencies and stupidities of her black staff. The effect on her husband was always to reduce him to silence that had at first seemed unsympathetic, but which, she found out later, resulted from his " wanting to kick himself for having brought out the poor girl to face all this ! "

Silence was always his refuge when he felt deeply about things and could not trust himself to speak. There was a day when, through the carelessness of a cook-boy, his favourite dog, the constant companion of his bachelor days, was poisoned. Three days passed and he had not said anything to Elijah, giving as his reason, " I could not trust myself to speak." But next morning he had his usual greeting for the boy, and Elijah looked as if an intolerable weight had been lifted.

CHAPTER XII

On Dr Elmslie's return to Ngoniland the two men had had a talk in which they mapped out the division of their parishes. The more evangelised part, of course, lay around Ekwendeni, so the greater share of the organised church and school work came within Dr Elmslie's sphere. To Fraser fell the more southern outposts, the Loangwa valley with its Senga population, and an untouched area to the south. This division offered him great scope for extension work. Hora lay to the north-east corner of his district, and various circumstances combined to decide that a more central site should be occupied.

One Sunday morning in the early part of 1902 we were all gathered in the church. While the service was going on, something outside seemed to be diverting the attention of some of the congregation. Looking through the un-glazed window-spaces I could see a distant black cloud which appeared to be moving steadily in our direction. As it came nearer one could hear the continuous and increasing volume of sound. The noise caught my husband's ear just as he was giving out his text. He turned round, for his back had been to the windows, took one glance, and then, telling the people to rise, he gave the Benediction. " Now go and try to save your crops," he said, and almost before the words were out of his mouth the church seemed to be emptied, the nearest window-space being the most popular exit for the men that day. The Sunday peace gave place to a din which was a combination of all the noises it was possible to produce. I reached home to find my husband handing out empty tin cans, a gong, a bell, a tea-tray, *anything* from which sound could be extracted.   For a year or two there had been invasions of locusts, but this was the worst.   We went that evening for a walk to see what had happened to the ripening crops, and met one of our teachers.

"Good evening, Joseph."

"Good evening, Sah."

"Where have you been, Joseph?"

"To see my garden, Sah."

"And how is your garden?"

"It isn't there, Sah."

That was almost everyone's experience, and it brought things to a crisis.   For some time there had been growing a strong desire to move away from the denuded soil and the exhausted maize-plots of that district.   Now, with no harvest to reap, they were keener than ever to open new patches for cultivation in the wooded land that lay to the south.

Hora was the main difficulty.   Naturally we were loth to leave it, and the people were equally unwilling to move away from the missionary for whom they had so long been asking.   They could see our objection to abandoning buildings so recently occupied; but they promised not only that they would give free labour to erect others, but that the Mission should have the first choice of a site in the new territory, so that we might be satisfied that our water supply would be as ample and free from contamination as we fastidious white folk considered necessary. There was in reality no alternative but to accompany them if the work was to be efficiently done.   A few villages might out of loyalty remain in the vicinity if we refused to move, but the vast bulk of our own people would be far to the south.   We knew, too, the danger of the insidious temptations that would assail them when they settled down in a district already inhabited by a pagan people of a lower moral type. The only effective way of meeting this danger was to bring Christian influences to bear on these hitherto untouched villages.

We were very reluctant to say good-bye to our first little home. Behind it, separated only by the green Kasitu valley, lay the hills of the Vipya over which we watched the sun rise. Near by towered the bare granite kopje of Hora, from which our Station derived its name. This mountain was a page in tribal history, for on it had perished many of the BaTumbuka who had risen against the domination of the Ngoni. In front stretched the far western horizon which held for Donald the irresistible lure of lands and people unknown. The new station would be built in flat and featureless country.

" Must we go ? " I asked, " it's all so beautiful here."

" My dear," was the reply, " we didn't come to Africa to evangelise the scenery."

But, although the people came first, there was hardly anything connected with the beauty or prosperity of the land itself that, in Fraser's view, lay outside the scope of mission work. To him all creation was waiting to share in the redemption of the sons of God, and he found it of thrilling interest to evolve out of the spot we finally selected a literal as well as a spiritual " garden of the Lord."

Putting a place on the map is a responsibility : an unsuitable site is a bad handicap to health and effective work in future years. Fraser did not want to have successors regret his choice, so we took some time to fix on it. Our first camp was at Lwasozi—" the river of tears "—but it proved unsuitable, and we were relieved when a better place was found beside the Kakoma—" the pretty little stream." Before we got that length we had travelled a good deal about the country, and could not help noticing the contrast between our new neighbours and those we had had at Hora. Here the people were very scared, and it was often more than two days before we could get a glimpse of a woman or child in the villages beside which we camped ; they were all hidden away till they had made up their minds about us. These local people were the first to start working for us, for the folk from Hora were moving into the district by slow degrees only.

A site had to be cleared in the dense wood, the cut trees serving to feed the fires of the brick-kilns. Ant-hills had to be hacked down and converted into bricks ; trees for timber selected, felled and marked for the sawyers ; saw-pits dug and grass collected for thatching.

It took some time for those employed to lose their fears. Even the approach of the white man tended to alarm the women workers, and if it was hastily made they would sometimes break into flight. One thing helped to make them lose their fear. It was the great friendship a little native child of three or four struck up with him. The mother was our water-carrier, and the child was left to hang about while she did her work. In no time he was the inseparable companion of his adopted " Dada." He sat and played in our little grass shelter content with occasional notice, but as soon as the Mzungu rose to go he had slipped his hand into his to accompany him, chattering gaily all the while. His great delight was to wear the Mzungu's big sun-helmet, beneath which the small brown body was almost hidden. While lunching we were entertained to a dance performed by a very miniature but deadly-in-earnest warrior, brandishing a toy spear, who chuckled delightedly when he finished, and sat down to suck the meaty bone of a fowl. No one could be really afraid of a white man whose biggest chum was a small black piccanin.

The end of November came, and the house we had

hoped to erect before the wet season was not ready, but neither had the expected rains broken. The building was hurried on and hastily roofed, and on Christmas Eve, half an hour after we had moved our beds out of " Exeter Hall," as the magistrate later dubbed our marquee tent, down came the heavens in an almost solid sheet. One of the workers standing sheltering on the veranda turned to Donald, clapping his hands and thanking him. " For what ? " Donald asked. " For hurrying on with your house so that God could let us have rain," he replied, and we found the willingness to work well those last few weeks had arisen from the conviction that God's messenger must be safely housed before their thirsty gardens could be attended to !

After the rains were over, the building began in earnest, thousands of people coming in to give three weeks' free labour, the more willingly because they knew that after that they would continue as paid workers. A temporary log church was put up, and not only on Sundays, but daily at sunrise, Donald had all the greater opportunity of giving his message because of the activities that brought such crowds about. Before the larger buildings had been tackled (for the builders had to be trained by their work on the less important) a colleague, Mr J. Riddell Henderson, arrived to share the responsibility. It was an immense relief, for it was a big undertaking for amateurs to build a church capable of holding 3000 people with only a sketch of the design and no building plans. Many a consultation they had and many a sleepless night they spent when it came to some ticklish point in the construction. Fruitless efforts used to be made by their wives to get them to return from their all-absorbing task to a mid-day meal and rest. After vainly ringing bells and sending summonses by houseboys, they often ended by going in person to effect their capture. Then one of the husbands would say to the other, " Here come the Donas ! Let's get up on the roof," and on that unattainable height they were free from anything more serious than vocal interruption.

There were some narrow escapes for the builders. Once a row of pillars collapsed from having the foundations undermined by white ants, but fortunately no one was inside the building at the time. Still more serious might have been the consequences on another occasion when a ladder reaching up to the tower of the church was struck by lightning and ripped and blackened from top to bottom. Ten minutes before, it had been crowded with children, one on each rung, handing up bricks from hand to hand to the builders on the summit. Fraser had come along just in time to summon them to another job which he wanted completed immediately. It was with a very thankful heart that he gathered them inside the church to give thanks for their safety.

The new Station was planned on a much bigger scale than Hora. Thought, meaning and purpose were put into everything. The permanent European houses were a little removed from the big square of the Station. Symbolically situated in the centre of its life rose the great cruciform church, simple in design, a pattern on a larger scale of what might be done still more simply in any village. Thatching and wooden shingles were both used for the roofing, for Fraser was always unwilling to introduce imported material until he had exhausted the possibilities of any local product to serve the purpose. The interior walls were plastered, and, on the wall behind the pulpit, against a grey background, was a plain cross in the red clay from which Ngoniland gets its name of " The Red Land."

The square on which the church stood was bordered by

roads, on the farther side of which stood all the other Station buildings, facing towards the church. Besides hospital, school, office, carpenter's shop, book and food stores, there were a number of dwelling-houses in a variety of designs. Several of these, circular in shape, were intended to show how the native huts, if built even partly of brick, could be modified to offer greater comfort and convenience, by the addition of a fireplace and chimney to eliminate the smoky atmosphere caused by having a fire in the centre of the hut.

The school was a quadrangle, the buildings composing two sides of it being open to the centre, so that in the hot weather there was plenty of light and air, while fires could be lit, when necessary, in the two which formed the remaining sides of the square.

The hospital might have been a fairly ambitious building, as £1000 was offered for its erection. But one of Fraser's strongest principles was that gifts should not influence policy, but that policy should guide giving. So he wrote to his friend and supporter, Mrs Loudon, to suggest that, instead of having a memorial hospital, she should contribute this sum towards the building of the Station, which might be called after her husband, Dr Loudon, a friend of David Livingstone. One of his reasons, he confessed, was that he would like to retain some claim on his wife, and too large a hospital might absorb all her time and energies. So the " house of medicine " that went up was more of a hospice than a modern hospital, although it provided sufficient facilities for the necessary treatment of the cases.

The Mission was not the only place where building was going on. All over the district the Ngoni were putting up their new villages with all the elaborate observances that custom enjoined. The chief Mzukuzuku had allowed

Frasara's Dona to watch the ceremony of building his head village, though no native woman dared make her appearance at such a time. So we let them see *our* native customs when Mrs Riddell Henderson laid the foundation *brick* of the church, above a hollow that contained papers and current coin of the realm, while the lady who represented the future medical and nursing staff, superintendent and board of directors, laid that of the hospital.

As the country became more populated, and the trees were felled to make garden sites, it was a great joy to find that the view opened out. To the south a ridge of hills became visible, and to the west, over the successive rises that marked the division between the streams, we got that distant horizon which Donald said was *almost* essential to keep one's missionary passion alive. Long vision and vast stretches satisfied his soul.

From time to time through the years something else was undertaken to make the Station more complete. He never felt quite happy about anything that would only increase our comfort, though he recognised that health was such an asset that anything tending to promote greater fitness and leisure for our work was worth while. But something we could *share* was what he really enjoyed undertaking. That dam, for instance, which Mr Livingstone christened " The Wonder Lake." Dr Prentice first suggested it, and a generous friend—Mr J. C. Hunter of Glentyan—sent money to cover the cost. Donald pored over the *Encyclopædia Britannica* till he had mastered the science of dam-construction, and then set to work. It was built almost entirely by children, eager to earn something at a time when their fathers were so many of them away doing transport work in the East African Campaign. One was drawn irresistibly two or three times a day to the " dambo " (little valley) to watch that merry scene, active as an ant-hill, but by no means so silent. Farther down the valley some of the villagers were grumbling that the Mission was going to keep all the water and their supply would be cut off. At last the great bank was complete and the basin began to fill up, and incredulous wonder gave place to excited interest as the water steadily rose, until at last the surplus was making its way once more into the stream-bed below, and the grumblers realised that they were better off than before, with the stream still flowing and a great reservoir to draw on when the season advanced and it ran dry. There was no sight that Donald loved better than that lake, with the little brown heads of the school children bobbing all over it like apples in a Hallowe'en tub, as they swam about shouting merrily to one another in the heat of the day, while crashing through the wood and down the banks came thirsty cattle, making for the welcome water in which they could stand and drink their fill.

Here was the beginning of a redemption in which the brute creation shared. Dr Laws used to say that the very dogs in the villages ought to be the better for the coming of Christianity. Donald often quoted that, and did his best to lessen the thoughtless cruelty meted out to dumb animals. He would allow no killing of birds within our Mission grounds, and they seemed soon to realise that it was a sanctuary : especially down near the garden, below the dam, they became so plentiful that the gardener remonstrated, saying that not only did they destroy the fruit, but, still less pleasant a result, attracted numerous snakes to the spot ! Donald had a theory, based on the silence of the woods through which he travelled, that the vicinity of a village with all its varied noises stimulated the birds to vocal rivalry. Certainly we always thought that the birds sang more on the Mission Station than anywhere else.

It took time to instil into the utilitarian minds of the people a sense of pity and an appreciation of mere beauty. Passing through a village one day he noticed hanging from the eaves of a hut a dozen beautiful little dead song-birds. When he expressed his aversion to such a sight, our carriers offered the excuse that they were good to eat. "One fowl," said their white teacher, "would give more food than all these put together."

"Don't you remember," he pleaded with the men, "how, when we were camping up on the Vipya, we were wakened each morning by the beautiful songs of these birds?"

"Yes," they agreed unenthusiastically, "but here in the villages we don't *need* them to waken us. We have the cocks."

CHAPTER XIII

OF the uncontrolled, turbulent condition of the people we had come among there was plenty of proof, even without going beyond the boundary of our new Station. A local girl, who was engaged in carrying our water from the well which we had sunk, mysteriously disappeared one mid-day. A few months after, her remains were found in a thicket quite near the well and within a quarter of a mile of our house. Apparently the murder was one of revenge, for it came out that her mother had some time before burned her own husband alive by setting fire to the hut in which he lay sleeping. Within one week three people who had drunk "muavi" (the poison ordeal) were brought in for treatment. On ulendo one morning I had to stop to see if there was still life in a body by the side of the path—that of an old woman dead from a spear-wound. A mile or two farther on we came on men lined up with shields and spears, who had heard and taken us for the marauding party. In two of their villages they showed us newly-made graves and brought a number of scalp wounds for treatment. It was not easy for the missionary to confine his interference in such circumstances to trying to stimulate the chiefs to exert control, for to the people he seemed the right man to do what was necessary.

Things were more difficult when white men were involved. One night there turned up a headman with a prisoner—a man from the north—whom he accused of assaulting a European camping in his village. " Not that

I object," he added magnanimously, " to his killing his master, but I don't want it done near my village where it might get me into trouble." Having had a passing visit that afternoon from the very unpleasing European, we scarcely wondered at the mildness of his view of the crime, and less so when the prisoner displayed a wound right through his foot caused by transfixing it with an iron-pointed stick. It was this injury that had made him attack his employer. After having the wound dressed he was put into a hut for the night. Next morning he had escaped—to his gaoler's relief, for what could he do with a prisoner ? The missionary was always having to avoid any assumption of civil power, lest by putting himself in a wrong position with Government he might lose his power to help the weaker side if trouble arose.

Such trouble was not long in coming. On one of our tours we arrived at a village to find the men all fully armed and looking grim. They explained that they were waiting to defend their village from a band of native police who were in the vicinity collecting taxes and burning villages. This was well within the watershed of the Rukuru, and quite beyond the administered district of the Tonga on the Lake Shore side. Trouble seemed brewing, and Donald wanted to prevent it if possible, so he sent a message to the village where the police were reported to be, asking them to await him there. We arrived to find them looking somewhat scared : they were beginning to realise the growing hostility of the people among whom they were. Their story was that they had been sent out to collect taxes, knew nothing about boundaries, and had had no instructions as to where they were to go. The people who had paid taxes displayed their papers : one man had received four 3s. receipts in exchange for £1, 1s. ; another, who paid 10s. and a 5s. blanket, had been given three 3s. receipts,

and so on. Donald rebuked their dishonesty in carrying out
their job, and said that they must now return to the Boma
(Government Station) for instructions, and that he would
give them a letter for their master. He wrote in a friendly
way, telling how he had found them far beyond the boundary—indeed they had actually penetrated into Rhodesian
territory—said he had told the people who had been
molested that these police had exceeded instructions and the
white man would put it all right, and ended by remarking
that he thought that, if compensation was given for burned
huts, etc., the whole matter might be quietly finished and
go no further. " There is no use his getting into trouble,"
he said to me. " He is young, and new to the work."

The suggestion so kindly meant was not taken. The
young official resented Donald's action and spoke to others
about it, and an inquiry was ordered. This took place at
the Lake Shore, and, when Donald went down to attend it,
he found that instead of investigating his charges against
the police it took the form of investigating *their* charges
against *him*. The inquiry was not without its humorous
side. In the first place a Tonga Mission teacher had been
much impressed because the Government men had a
policeman out trying to secure a Bible for them, not knowing that it was only for the purpose of swearing in witnesses.
The official conducting the inquiry was not feeling very
well, and cups of Bovril, thermometers and quinine were
much in evidence in the court, which was partly at least
held in the Resident's bedroom. For a couple of days it
had been postponed owing to his malaria, and he was
looked after by the virtual prisoner at the bar, who insisted
on the third day that proceedings must be resumed or he
would go away back to his interrupted work. Mr Mac-
Minn, a Mission colleague, was there to support him. The
police made wild charges of Mr Fraser having incited the

people to murder them, defying Zomba (Government Headquarters) and trying to rouse the Ngoni to rebel. One policeman told a story of what Mzukuzuku had said to him about Mr Fraser, quite unaware that a large and enraged-looking man sitting in court was the chief he purported to be quoting, until the latter rose to his feet shouting, " He's a liar ! Let me get at him ! "

The whole affair was Gilbertian. The leading Native accused by Donald acted as interpreter. After two police-men had been heard the magistrate remarked, " My judg-ment on the question is so and so, and I shall write so to Zomba," whereupon the accused interposed, " I protest against your forming a judgment when you've only heard one side : not one of my witnesses has yet given evidence." At another stage he said to the Government official, " If I thought there was the least likelihood of these statements being considered serious accusations, I should object to being tried in such a court as this." " I quite agree with you," was the reply.

The day the inquiry was closed Fraser, passing through the Boma, was accosted by a prisoner. " Hullo ! Samuel, what are you doing here ? " he asked. " I was imprisoned till my people paid their taxes," the chief explained (he had moved into taxed territory), " but they have paid up long ago. I don't know why I am being kept." Fraser said he would ascertain. So, turning back, he entered the house and said, " By the by, I see you have Samuel Jere in custody here. What is he in for ? " " Oh ! is he still there ? " was the answer : " I meant to have him released long ago. Take him with you ! " Fraser did so, and received a most cordial welcome from his people when he turned up as the rescuer of their chief.

Donald had left so impressed with the incapacity of those in charge to master the facts of the case, that he wrote to

Dr Laws expressing grave doubt as to the type of report that would be forwarded to Zomba. Certainly his only reward for trying to uphold the justice of British rule was a letter sent to Dr Laws as head of the Mission casting doubt on Mr Fraser's loyalty. Ten years later we travelled home with the Intelligence Officer for Nyasaland, who one day remarked, " Fraser, you are a very different man from the person I had conceived : I thought you must be a regular firebrand." He went on to explain how part of his job had been to ferret into the archives of the Administration. " What was the truth of that affair ? " he asked. When he had heard Donald's story he said, " Now I know you, that is a much more believable version."

A few months after the trouble the Governor suggested that it would save complications if Ngoniland came under British rule. We had been in the west, and, in passing through the paramount chief's village, found him very much disturbed over a summons for all the chiefs to assemble and meet the Governor. This had come in our absence, and letters forwarded to the Marambo had failed to reach us. At Loudon, however, Donald found an invitation from the Governor to meet him at Ekwendeni. A still very resentful wife asked, " Why should you go ? How does he think you can help if Zomba considers you disloyal ? They should withdraw that letter before they ask you to exert your influence to get this put through. Why don't you demand an apology first ? " He smiled and shook his head. " Remember we are here for the people's sake, not for our own vindication. If Sir Alfred thinks Zomba hasn't been quite fair to me he'll be all the more inclined to make up for it. Demanding the withdrawal of charges won't make for a friendly discussion, and what Stuart and I want now is to get as good terms of annexation as possible." He was met most cordially by the Governor, and came back well pleased with all the friendly concessions to the chiefs that made the actual taking over of the country the amicable function of a few hours.

In the London *Times* appeared, over Donald's signature, a letter describing how this annexation had been accomplished, and giving warm praise to Sir Alfred Sharpe for the way in which this new corner had been added to the Empire without expense or bloodshed. Sir Alfred wrote a cordial note of thanks, acknowledging that, without the very fine work the missionaries had done in the country, it could never have been accomplished, and this expression of indebtedness to the Mission he renewed recently on hearing of Dr Fraser's death. When the first magistrate came to administer the district he occupied our old Hora house till his own Boma was built, and he told us that at Zomba he had been advised to consult Fraser about any problem or difficulty that might arise.

CHAPTER XIV

HIS MEDICAL CONTRIBUTION

PEOPLE frequently used to ask if Dr Fraser was a medical. The proper reply always seemed to me to be, " Yes, but without a medical degree." In his first term he developed quite a big practice, and had been able to impose fees without diminishing the number of his patients. When he had a wife to take over that work, he was still often in demand as an assistant and interpreter till a medical vocabulary had been acquired. On tour he helped, taking the dental department into his own stronger wrists. The day he started to nurse his wife through her first fever he had pulled nineteen teeth before breakfast—a fact always remembered because these teeth intruded themselves into the patient's delirium ! Not until almost the close of the Great War was there any trained nurse in the Loudon Hospital, and the native assistants only knew what they were picking up while at work, so he was always required to help at an operation, and there was something marvellously helpful and steadying in his very presence. The simple prayer in which he always referred to the patient by name gave confidence to patient and operator alike. Somehow it always brought God into the affair, and no heathen would have felt he was getting the same chance as others had it been omitted, even if to him it *was* only a magical formula to ensure success. Two European ladies writing of medical treatment in our house both make reference to these prayers of his, one saying she would never forget the thanks he offered after her baby was born, the other

saying how vividly the day stands out in her memory
when after a hard fight to save her child Dr Fraser prayed
in gratitude and intercession for the life restored.   A chief
lying seriously ill on the Station used to comfort himself
by murmuring, "Frasara is praying for me," his hope
resting on that.

One never felt that he grudged the time he had to spare
from his own overwhelming task.   Even when a night
case called me away, it was useless to urge him to have his
night's sleep and not bother about what was another's
job.   I knew that upon my return there would be waiting
a tray set for tea, hot water for a bath, and a man anxious
to know how things had gone.   If, as often happened
during the war period, it was some sudden call to a European patient which involved my being away for a week
or a fortnight—who knew how long it would take before
the patient could be safely left for good?—how rapidly
he made arrangements for my journey, never thinking of
anything but the relief it would be at the other end to
have the doctor turn up.   He felt glad and proud that it
was his wife who could help them.   Or if it was our
house that was turned into a nursing home his hospitable
soul was delighted.   The burden often fell largely on his
shoulders.   One case was brought in by native police who
were terrified lest their "Bwana" should die on their
hands.   They had at last got him to consent to be carried
to the nearest hospital for whites, 100 miles away ; but no
sooner had they got him in the machila than they turned
in the direction of Loudon, which was nearer and thus
brought their anxiety to a speedier end.   The man had
lived so isolated a life that the thought of a white woman
terrified him, and so the unqualified assistant had to do
all the nursing, being told by his wife outside the door
what to note and what to do, while the doctor herself

only took as casual-looking a glance as possible when she went in with the patient's food.

But the sick man to whom he meant most was a poor Boer gold prospector, carried in after weeks of illness in the bush. "It was heaven," his chum said, "to see that room with its comfortable bed and clean sheets and the dainty food, after roughing it in camp." But what brought comfort to the invalid's soul after a life of extraordinary ups and downs was to be tended during his last illness by Donald. "I have never met a man like Dad before," he said shortly before his death (his miner's phthisis having gone too far for cure). "Dad," as he always called Donald, seemed to lead him into his own faith about God without any talking beyond the "Good Word" time the Boer looked forward to when, before settling down to take the first half of the night-watching beside him, Donald used to read a few verses and pray a simple prayer. Before he knew that he was not to recover, the old man had asked that we should make out a manuscript Prayer Book for him before he left, saying that he had never learned to pray and he wanted to know how to say things to God. Often as he lay looking out at the window he would turn and say wistfully, "Dad's long in coming," and his face would light up as he heard him coming up the veranda steps. "You've no idea how I love that man. I *believe* in him," he would say in explanation. We buried him who had entered the Kingdom like a little child beside a tiny grave that Donald had dug one Sunday morning to lay in it the body of his first-born son.

For there had been a day when his wife herself had had to depend on him, and had found how reliable he was. One night he had had to call the watchman and send him hastily to the chief's village to find a messenger who would go with a summons to the nearest white woman—

70 miles away—and a note to the nearest doctor at twice that distance, and then he had gone back to learn from the patient what he must do. All the day that followed he never stirred out of that room. His reassuring, confident voice never gave the least hint of strain. Once a native woman's voice rose in protest, and he quietly replied, " This was how the Dona told me." Only when all was over and his wife urged him to go and get the food he had so long been without, did she suddenly realise what that day had meant for him. For he staggered across the floor like a drunken man, and the next day she noticed that his hair seemed whiter, and for weeks afterwards he had broken sleeps from which he woke to say, " Thank God you are still alive."

The one thing that he had not been told about was the after-care of the patient, and there he struck out on a line of his own, for from the waiting crowd he invited two or three of his best friends among the evangelists to come in that very evening to see his wife and the twin daughter who had survived. Their own wives they would not have visited for a week, but the thrill of seeing a white child overcame any misgivings latent in their minds. When he ushered in the little group he looked so happy that his wife felt she could not tell him that it was not customary to have visitors so soon. He discovered this for himself later on and was most remorseful, at the same time begging her not to tell her mother what he had done ! But indeed it was typical of him—that desire to share our joys and interests with our people. Next morning the crowds who had gathered for service were so keen on a peep at their little white sister (the first white baby many of them had ever seen) that they could only be induced to enter the church when he stated firmly, after half an hour's exhibition, that not another person was to be allowed to see her till the following day. Early that morning, before the crowds arrived, he had buried the baby boy who had failed to live, and it was only when one saw the care with which he covered the little coffin with white linen and laid some flowers upon it, that one realised that, in spite of the child spared to us, his heart was yearning over the son he had been unable to save.

When Donald had first come into the country he had been impressed with the strength of the ties that seemed to bind the missionaries and their wives. Now he understood, for such times of anxiety and danger had come to many another in those early days. They were worth while, were it only for letting the Africans see what the marriage relationship could mean to the men and women who wanted to share with them the possibilities of the Christian way of life.

The health of the people was of real concern to their missionary, and one of Fraser's great contributions to the welfare of the natives lay in his realisation of the possibility of improving health by means that lay within their own power. Physical salvation at least must be largely a question of works, and he would not have them lay on God the responsibility for the results of their own ignorance and carelessness. Everything that was possible in the way of improving water supplies, increasing the amount and variety of the food available, and bettering housing and sanitary arrangements, he did his best to promote. He was always willing to give help and advice about the digging of wells for the villages around; he let people bring in their oxen to be trained for transport work, and had the Station carpenters try their hand at producing an effective type of sledge since wheels were so difficult a problem. His own ox carts were lent out at harvest time to save the labour of the women in bringing in their crops. Those who got the loan of them were expected to pay the ox driver's wages, but there were certain days reserved for the free use of them for the widows in the neighbourhood. The Mission garden was an experimental station for trying what would grow in the district, and the more the people demanded in the way of plants, cuttings, etc., the more pleased he was. His own Station had its roads lined with trees, mostly fruit-bearing, and it was a common sight to see him going along picking supplies of mangoes or loquats for people who had turned up on some errand. He knew the value of letting them first acquire a taste for such things before he began to urge them to plant them in their own villages. But sometimes one felt (he always said I had a more suspicious nature than himself!) that the people who came in the mango season to ask for seeds to plant and got loaded up with fruit, did not always carry the seeds farther than the point by the roadside at which they had finished sucking off the pulp. Happiest of all was he when he moved from tree to tree during times of famine, accompanied by a growing crowd of kiddies eagerly holding out their hands for the fruit he plucked for them. He knew that it was in such ways as these that the literal " open sores " of Africa, and other ailments, were dealt with far more effectually than by antiseptic dressings and medicines.

All his organising capacity was devoted to the task of dealing with serious epidemics when they arose. When plague broke out to the west, not many could so effectively have managed the problem of setting an easy-going, naturally fatalistic people by their own efforts to prevent the spread of plague into their district, at the same time making it an unusually successful money-raising stunt. The magistrate's first idea was to get Government Headquarters to send up people to grapple with the danger. Fraser undertook to get it satisfactorily done by the people themselves if a price were given for the rats killed. Then began a most successful campaign against these plague propagators. Not that the people were worrying about a danger that had not yet made its appearance among them, but the white man had said that the only school fees he would accept from the children would be rats' tails—and their children must be taught. Then the deacons who went round to receive the monthly offerings of the people were asking that these might take this unusual form, and there had been announced a " rat-tail Sunday," when everybody was expected to bring a bunch of tails. After all, it saved them cash, and it was an exciting form of sport, and they did not *like* rats, though they had learned to tolerate them, so they set to work with a good will. The rats' bodies were burned and the tails tied into bunches of ten, and so many of these were sent along to the Boma that the price was soon lowered, and finally it was decided that there was no real menace of plague and no more tails would be bought : it had, however, lasted long enough to make the Mission finances a success that year. Rumour had it later that a new paying industry which had just started among the Ngoni had been nipped in the bud—the manufacture of tails from rat-skins ! Audiences at home were always interested to hear about the rat-tail collections, but it remained for an American girl to pronounce that missionary " real cute " who had invented a " Rat-tail Sundae," and to want particulars about the ingredients.

After the close of the war the bad epidemic of influenza that began in Europe spread to Africa, and gained terrible virulence as it advanced into the interior, laying its grip on many tribes for the first time. Efforts were made to arrest its spread, as might have been feasible in com-

paratively thinly-populated areas, by trying to prevent the
people from moving about and carrying the infection from
place to place. The Government ordered that schools
should be closed and the gathering for services forbidden :
measures which Fraser pointed out to the magistrate would
be quite insufficient in themselves if at the same time
public beer-drinkings, witch doctors' dances, and other
customs that drew crowds were not similarly suppressed.
But such prophylactic steps were not enough.   If influenza
appeared, what was to be done to diminish the dreadful toll
of victims ?   What obviously added to the mortality was
the helplessness of a household attacked, owing to domestic
arrangements.   Each day the woman pounds her flour
and fetches in her water and firewood.   When a household
was stricken they might so easily be left without fire and
food and drink.   And helplessness and fear were responsible
for many of the deaths.   Nor did it help that ugly rumours
had spread among the tribes.   Had not the white nations
been killing one another for years ?   Now they were few,
and they feared the numerical strength of the black races
and had sent this new form of death among them to weaken
them, too.   The very warnings that had been issued respecting the danger confirmed this suspicion.   How was
it that the white people knew it was coming ?

Our schools were shut, but the teachers were not dismissed : they were instead called in for instruction about
this new menace. Personal work and house-to-house
worship were to go on, and in each village besides collecting the children for lessons, now that inter-village schools
were closed, they were to organise a little band of those
who would make themselves responsible for seeing that, if
influenza came, each hut should be visited to ensure that
none were left uncared for or without the necessaries of
life.   Meantime the women were to be encouraged to pound

busily and have supplies of flour available, as well as lay in a good stock of firewood. The teachers were also entrusted with supplies of medicine.

This systematised help was very effective in lessening the risks incurred by those who were ill, and the presence and activity of the Christian teachers among them prevented the feeling of being abandoned by the Mission at such a time. Bad enough though it was, the mortality among the tribe would undoubtedly have been much greater had it not been for the measures adopted, together with the unwearied efforts of the Europeans in the district, Boma and Mission alike, to bring relief to the many victims.

CHAPTER XV

IN THE VILLAGES

ALONG the narrow beaten track running through an African glade a crowd comes rushing, shouting, laughing, whistling, hullabalooing. A few are wearing what might by courtesy be termed " clothes " ; some have little bits of cloth about their loins, some nothing but a string of beads, or some grass bracelets ; but all are as merry and excited as can be. You might easily imagine they were following some Pied Piper, so eagerly do they rush along. Among the children may quite possibly be some perspiring matrons, or even an old white-haired granny, as excited as any. Sometimes a child stumbles, but he quickly picks himself up, joining in the shout of laughter his fall has occasioned. What *is* the attraction ? It is the annual visit of " Chisekeseke " (the one who smiles) and his Dona. There they come, she whirled along in a funny carriage consisting of a seat perched above a single wheel with bamboo shafts in which a couple of men run, one in front, one behind, balancing and drawing the " gareta " ; he on his push-bike. The accompanying crowd have had their school examined and are now convoying " Frasara " to his next group of villages. Suddenly from those in front there is a yell, " Njoka ! " and they dart right and left of the path. The cry spreads, and in a moment numerous clubs are being thrown by all the boys at a big snake which has been sunning itself on the road and is now trying to wriggle away through the long grass. Its back is soon broken by the blows rained upon it, and then the head is crushed. It is then lifted on a long stick to be

I

inspected, and finally hung upon the branch of a tree.   The
interrupted journey is resumed, and the incident passes
from the minds of all but the white woman, for to the
others snakes are a commonplace occurrence compared with
a visit from the white man.   Later there is another halt
where two tracks diverge : a dispute arises between the
carriers and the children as to which is the right one to take.
The road which the children assert to be much the shortest
is selected in the end, but it proves to lead through a
regular quagmire.   The bicycle becomes an impossible
method of conveyance.   It is easy for bare brown legs to
plunge halfway to the knee in rich squelchy black mud
which leads to reeds through which a stream flows, but
the white man has shoes and stockings, so he gets carried
across on a big man's back.

When at last the village they are making for appears in
sight, the bulk of their numerous convoy, with many a shout
of " Good-bye, Dada," " Good-bye, Mama ; travel safely,"
bid them farewell and turn home again, having acquired in
the morning's doings food enough for conversation to
last for many a day.   The path which the missionaries
follow suddenly emerges on to a broad hoed road—sure
sign that a school is near.   There it stands in a clearing
in the wood—a long mud-plastered building with thatched
roof, outside which two rows of children are most ostenta-
tiously drilling for their inspector's benefit.   It is now three
o'clock in the afternoon, and they have been hanging about
since seven in the morning waiting for his arrival.   The
teacher and monitor hasten up to salute.   The children are
then marched, " Left, light, left, light ! " into the school,
and seated on logs laid lengthwise on the floor.   The
windows are just a row of spaces left in the wall on one
side, and the coolness and comparative darkness are refresh-
ing after the glare.   The walls of red mud are decorated

with drawings of animals and conventional designs in grey, yellow and black mud. Among these specimens of primitive art you can pick out leopards, lions and zebras, varied by pictures of men on bicycles. A little raised platform of mud with a roughly made table and a box containing the simple school materials—slates, chalk, pencils, roll-book, wall-sheets, etc.—complete the furnishings. In his writings Fraser has sketched the running of such a type of school.

How wholeheartedly he used to throw himself into the task of inspecting it! Class after class was taken; faults in teaching were noticed, and there and then he would start to show how the lesson should be taught. He would inspect the roll-book, inquire the reason for any unusual variations in attendance, go into the question of the payment of fees, the adequate purchase of school books by the pupils, the hospitality of the village to the teacher, see that there were sufficient supplies of the simple school materials and that these were being carefully kept from the ravages of white ants and other destructive influences, note the condition of the school building, its surroundings, the roads in the vicinity, the community garden, and everything else with which the school was in any way concerned.

But he did more than that. He somehow made the people feel how keenly he was interested in them and in all that went on in their neighbourhood. The window spaces of the school would often be darkened by the heads of interested adults watching the inspection within, and to them he would speak later on about supporting all that the school stood for. Then he would turn the children on to some new and more exciting kind of drill, such as making them form a huge ring and introducing them to the game of leap-frog. Of course he had often to be stern, and, because he was eager about the development of teacher and pupil

alike, he would not overlook slackness, or anything savour-
ing of dishonesty.   Many a pupil he turned out of a higher
into a lower class about whom the teacher made the excuse
that they had refused to come to school at all unless they
were allowed to " climb."   When he was overtired and
feverish there was plenty to make him pessimistic and
irritable in the dullness of scholars and the incapacity of
teachers ; and there were times when the latter would
stand by waiting in nervous apprehension for the interview
that would follow by and by !   But, if fault had to be
found, he never liked to leave the school subdued and rather
scared, so he invariably closed it with singing, which he
encouraged till eyes and teeth were gleaming in the little
dark faces, hands were clapping, feet stamping, and lithe
bodies swaying rhythmically to the growing volume of
song.

If it was the last school to be inspected that day, then
later on there would be time for a little contact with the
teachers, to stimulate their enthusiasm in the sense of
importance of their work.   Stupidity, though trying, he
tolerated more easily than the slackness of a brighter lad.
Best of all, after the evening meal, there would be one of
those gatherings he so loved, when the children would
bring firewood, kindle a cheerful blaze under the starry
sky, and gather round eagerly and expectantly for the talk
and stories, songs and games and dancing that the Mzungu
loved to foster.   " He will be an unforgettable memory to
hundreds," writes one of his missionary colleagues, " for
he was the first white man many of them had ever seen as
children when he visited their villages, and he has left an
indelible impression."

From these tours he used always to return with one item in
his stores quite finished.   No matter what quantity of sugar
one supplied him with, it never sufficed.   When he enter-

tained " company " he enjoyed doling out little supplies of
sweetness into little brown palms, and then watching how
the pleasure was drawn out by little appreciative tongues,
picking up a few grains at a time. Often it meant that he
himself went without for the last day or two of his journey,
till his cook grew cunning and used to secrete a reserve
store for his master's meals. Then he could truthfully
expostulate that the tin was empty when asked to produce
it. Salt, a very satisfactory substitute to the African's
palate, had then to take its place.

Fraser often regretted that there was not time to visit
the people personally in their huts. One year, before the
districts had been thoroughly organised so that the work
was overtaken by native pastors or evangelists, he had
greatly enjoyed entering the individual homes, and had discovered its value. I can see him, sitting on a native carved
stool or on a " tuli " (wooden pounding mortar) turned
on its side, or perhaps squatting, native fashion, while he
chatted away, revealing such interest in all the little affairs
that concerned the family. The prayer and blessing of
the home that followed always seemed so natural an outcome of the talk, for the reverence in his tone was combined with an intimate concern for those with and for
whom he was praying. There was invariably a parting
ceremony on these occasions. If our visit there had been
expected we were conscious of an occasional scuffling noise
inside the hut. If unexpected, the owner would at some
stage disappear outside the house for a moment. Thereafter there was heard the sound of wild cackling and
children's shouts as a hen was ruthlessly pursued round
the village. It was tactful to prolong the visit till the
noise subsided. Then, as we rose to go, the fowl, whether
previously secured under the upturned pot in the hut or
waiting in the hands of a small boy outside, was presented

to us.   A day's pastoral visitation made us look ere long
as if we were returning from a successful raid on hen-
roosts !   He always felt it right to fall in with this kindly,
courteous habit of the people, recognising in a way that is
not brought home to those under more civilised conditions, the need for hospitality to strangers being maintained
as a Christian grace, when it is dying out as a primitive
virtue.   Even when an old widow brought and presented,
in lieu of the customary fowl, two coppers, he had too
much tact to refuse them, knowing that to the African
mind there was no distinction between the fowl and its
equivalent in cash.   So he thanked her courteously, saying
that, as we had received plenty to eat, this should be a gift
to God and go into the local church fund.   That was not
the only occasion on which he rather ruefully received
little personal gifts of money which he was too understanding to refuse.

There were other times in his travels when he eagerly
pursued anthropological investigations.   Everything relating to the people interested him, and, besides getting
one or two of the more intelligent Christians to write all
they could find out regarding the past, he made widespread
personal inquiries.   These brought him into contact with
the old men untouched by the new ideas spreading among
the people.   But they did not feel " out of it " when they
sat round the fire with " Framo " listening to their stories
of the old days, asking for full details of the customs
and traditions of the past, and following with interest the
genealogy of their ancestors as far as they could trace them.
He never mocked, or even smiled at, their beliefs as he
questioned them about them, not even when they themselves
got confused and contradictory in trying to explain them.

Sometimes he used to wonder if, as a missionary, he
ought to be spending his time over this hobby ; but he

never neglected other work for it, only giving up to it the hours of evening when he should be resting after a day's work and travelling. It helped him to win the friendship and confidence of those who kept their old pagan outlook, and to understand better the minds of some who had accepted Christianity, and yet were haunted by the ghosts of their old faith, which had power to alarm and weaken them when nerves were overwrought by outward calamity or the poison of disease. It helped in another way, too. Respecting as he ever did the Africans and all that was best in their culture and the constitution of their society, he regretted the apparently unavoidable result of education and progress in taking the leadership out of the hands of the older men, and recognised how this tended to the disintegration of the tribe. Move they must, but he longed that the older men might not be left behind. He made special efforts to win them. At Loudon he called them in for an *indaba*, reminded them that they were the natural leaders of their people as headmen of villages, and yet they were falling behind. " Could you not travel along with us ? " he asked. Thus began an old men's class, which he held on Sunday mornings, when, helped by that knowledge he had acquired of their mental attitude in matters of belief, he began very simply to unfold the truths of the Christian message. It was done slowly, patiently, informally, allowing them to talk it over till they knew how they felt about each new truth put forward, and had got the length of accepting it. Then, " We have travelled this length together : can you sleep here ? " he would ask, and they would agree. From this mental camping-ground they moved a little farther each week. He led them on till there were some who, to his great joy, were baptised. Others went a certain length ; but there were ethical demands which some could not face, or there were real scruples in the minds of others about such a question as polygamy. These their guide could appreciate and respect, and for their encouragement he explained that, while the Church believed in monogamy as the ideal for married life, and therefore did not feel that it could lower the African by tolerating in him what it would consider wrong for other races, still he could well understand that they might not think it right to part with those who had been their wives for so long. They must remember that the Church was not the same thing as the Kingdom of Heaven, and that they could be members of the Kingdom of Heaven without entering the visible Church. No matter of conscience need keep them from entering the Kingdom and throwing themselves in with all who were seeking to bring in the Reign of God.

CHAPTER XVI

TILL he was invalided home at the end of 1905 Fraser spent strenuous days divided between Loudon and its ever-increasing outposts. The things that have to be done on a Mission Station are extraordinarily varied, and the ordained man, when he has no educational or artisan colleague, has to develop considerable versatility. All the years the Station was in process of building there were brick- and tile-moulders and their crowd of workers to supervise on the brickfield, as well as sawyers, carpenters who needed help with the making of roof-couples and frames for doors and windows, builders who went off the plumb and off the level if not watched, thatchers, women beating the mud floors smooth and level, road gangs, etc.

All these had to be paid weekly. On Saturdays Fraser was to be seen surrounded by an unruly mob answering sometimes to names that might be theirs, but were not the ones they had happened to give when they were being engaged—a habit that led to much confusion. What times those early pay-days were! The wage of each man, woman and child had to be calculated according to the days of work they had put in, and then they had to make up their minds whether they wanted red, blue or grey calico, or which of several varieties of beads. They wished first to see how much they would get of one or the other. The calico was measured off and not quickly could they decide the momentous question of whether to choose it or something else. After all, why should they? It was

127

perhaps the first chance of " shopping " some of them had ever had. If " Donald Fraser could suffer fools gladly and meet them with a smile that was almost a benediction," perhaps he had learned his patience through much tribulation. It was those experiences that led to the starting of a store. When a man looked at a shilling and asked what use this was for clothing him, he learned that it too could speak like a book and tell how much calico he was entitled to receive ; but it took longer before he could understand that two sixpences or a dozen of coppers were equally capable of giving the same message. Men who had worked the same time and received different coinage had to come and argue that some mistake had been made. It was not easy to send them all away without a grievance, yet how much one's Saturday behaviour affected the influence of one's Sunday preaching.

Mondays were no respite. At the sunrise service the abnormally large attendance would have been gratifying had he not known only too well what it signified. Almost before he was out of the building he was surrounded by a crowd clamouring for work. There was no lack of local labourers in those days : it was the necessary work that was not forthcoming. For a job that required six men he would have three hundred simultaneous applications.

The Station store had to be visited and the books gone over with a storeman whose arithmetic was a weak point, though his honesty was undoubted. Stores had to be kept replenished, for in the early days there was no other place where the workers had a chance to spend their wages ; and at times, when the cash in hand was not nearly enough to meet the payments, there had to be pauses while the first-paid batch went and made their purchases and the cash, handed over the counter, was promptly brought back to the office door to allow payments to be resumed. Men had frequently to be engaged—or, as we said there, "ulendos were written"—to fetch from the Lake shore, or Blantyre, or Kondowi, the necessary calico, beads, salt, Bibles, school books, soap and other articles, and on their return their loads had to be checked and themselves paid. Other files of people came in with school fees and church collections in the form of squawking fowls, maize, beans and other produce. These had to be received and credited to the respective departments.

There was seldom a day when there was not some ulendo coming or going. It might be a number of people in from some district sent by their catechist for examination for the Catechumenate or for baptism. Nervous-looking people they were as they sat outside the vestry waiting for their turn to come. Cheerier, noisier crowds poured in on certain days when marriages took place, but for them, too, patience and good temper were just as necessary. Otherwise in his hurry there was risk of the minister marrying the brides to the wrong bridegrooms, for they did not like to interrupt and explain that they had not taken their places properly. The bride, too, with what she considered becoming modesty, often refused to utter her assent, and there was a temptation to take it for granted instead of waiting patiently while her girl friends prodded her, and the other guests, noting the growing impatience of the white man, urged her in audible whispers to "agree." Yet there was real danger in hurrying on, for once, when a girl kept resolutely silent and Fraser said he would refuse to go on unless she spoke, he saw something like a gleam of satisfaction in the girl's eye, and discovered in time that she was being forced into the marriage unwillingly, and had made silence her last stand against it.

Then there was mail day—very exciting when it occurred only once a month. Its infrequency made it all the harder to leave the letters resolutely alone till the duties of the day were attended to. In hospital there was kindly consideration shown, or perhaps a desire to get less divided attention, for more than once out-patients, on seeing the mail man pass the doorway, obligingly offered to " return to-morrow " instead.

There was always someone willing to open the mailbag and sort out the incoming mail. The outgoing one was not so simple. Natives came with letters to be sent; the addresses were often entirely undecipherable, or, if legible, quite insufficient; and as one knew the value of a letter when sent so seldom, a great deal of time and trouble had to be taken to see that it was posted in such a condition that there was some probability of its reaching its destination. The expert letter-writers needed only a stamp and an envelope, for which they brought a fowl in payment.

Visitors, too, were liable to turn up at any moment. It might be a chief or headman with his little following. Possibly they had something about which they wished to speak. For instance, it might be the desire to have a teacher in their village; but more often it was only because they wished to kill time and had no idea how the white man, sitting trying to talk pleasantly with them, was grudging the waste of what was very precious to him. He grew wise in the art of shortening these visits without discourtesy: if he started to talk to them about religion, they began to realise that there were other and less disconcerting ways of using up their infinite leisure, and would bid him farewell.

The Station schools, junior and senior, were also going on for a good part of the year, and he had to pop in frequently to see how these were progressing. The little boarder boys, for whom, as for all boys, Donald had so warm a place in his heart, had to be encouraged in work and play, their quarters and themselves had to be inspected, and soap doled out on Saturdays so that on Sundays at least, their garments might be clean. Two or three times a year, before the opening of school term (cash on hand determining the frequency !) the teachers turned up to get their schools assigned to them and to receive the necessary school materials, wall-sheets, blackboards, and other items. However carefully their allocations were planned, there was invariably some appeal for alteration of the scheme drawn up, and each got a hearing if there seemed to be any reason behind the desire. If it were the first term after the long vacation of the rainy season, their possible need for cash was taken into consideration, and a month's wage paid in advance. Each of these little extras meant encroachments on valuable time. Monthly pays had to be sent out during term, and at the close all the teachers were in again with their total sheets, attendance sheets, school material and what not. Of course, too, there had to be the annual teachers' school, with examinations to follow, that they might have a chance of attaining a higher standard, with its desirable increase of pay.

Wherever the missionary went from one corner of the Station to the other, there was the chance of his being intercepted by someone " with words " to whom he must listen either at once or later, or it might be have thrust at him a split reed with a " karata "—generally a dirty little piece of paper with some message or request scribbled on it. Anything in writing, they seemed to think, must command instant attention.

Outside the office people might be seen hanging about with sheep, fowls, mats, hoes, honey, etc., for sale. Of course some of these should have gone to the store boy, and others to the dwelling-house ; but what did those people from distant villages know about that ? They were slow to learn the methodical ways of the white man and the importance to him of time. Even if he did send the vendor of sheep to the Station employee responsible for buying, the two would come back to him about the price. " But I've told you what price I would give for a sheep." " Yes, Sir, but this man is wanting an extra shilling." " Well ; don't buy if he won't accept the price ! " " Yes, Sir, but he said you sent him to me that I might buy the sheep for you." This is a brief summary of the conversation that would go on as long as he was willing to listen. It was wonderful how patient he could be, and how he could manage to cut it short with a smile that kept the official buyer for the Mission from feeling hurt that his explanation was not heard out to the full length of which he was capable of drawing it. Of course Fraser did lose his patience sometimes, but there was one thing he could do that a European seldom cares to do—he was willing to apologise if he felt he had lost his temper unjustly.

Evening when it came was welcome. At sunset there were the quiet Evening Prayers for those resident on the Station—an evangelist, or later a pastor, one or two teachers and hospital workers, some of the domestic staff from the missionary's house, and those hospital patients who were able to come. In term time there was the crowd of little boarder boys, and, when we were fortunate enough to have a lady worker on the Station, boarder girls as well. Dispersing outside the church with cheerful good-nights to one another, there was a good chance of peace and rest for us all till morning came.

Along with all this, time had to be found for study, occasional translation work (he had begun to put *The Pilgrim's Progress* into Tumbuka), book-keeping, church rolls and other statistics, and a fairly heavy correspondence. But always on his desk lay his big interleaved Bible, and time was found for that; while occasionally, when the press of work was heavy, he would have the little tent put up in some quiet place in the woods and go there for a day's retreat, to find the strength to carry on. All this burden would have been intolerable, had it not been for his organising powers and a willingness to trust others that made it possible to put the principle of devolution into practice. As the years went past, the training of native clerks, school inspectors, elders, voluntary preachers, women deacons (really taking the visiting and ruling function of the elder), evangelists, and, finally, ordained pastors, made the position of the missionary more episcopal. This he had so strongly advocated at the first Missionary Conference at Blantyre as the right rôle for the missionary that Dr Hetherwick, an inveterate tease, professed surprise at the lack of the episcopal gaiters and apron, and used to address all his letters to him to " The Bishop, The Palace, Loudon."

As years went on and this scheme of devolution materialised, there was less necessity for continual control of all departments of work. But always he was needed to help and guide, and smooth away difficulties and rectify mistakes. Colleagues lightened the burden at times, but never as permanent additions to the staff, for they came and went as contingencies in staffing arose elsewhere. Yet no amount of organisation in Africa can relieve the missionary in charge from a varied assortment of duties. The most constant feature of his work is the frequency and unexpectedness of the interruptions which break into what might otherwise be called the " Station routine."

CHAPTER XVII

ALARUMS AND EXCURSIONS

THAT first term's work in Ngoniland was interrupted by a trip in 1904 to Blantyre for the first of a series of United Missionary Conferences. The journey down seems to have made the deepest impression on one's mind, for we started the Lake journey in the midst of a storm which swamped the barge bringing out our luggage to the steamer. The boxes were retrieved, but the immersion had not only soaked all the clothes so carefully laundered for the occasion—it even meant starched collars !—but had dyed all Donald's white suits blue and red and various other shades, owing to an incurable propensity he had for stuffing as many books as he could get in, between the layers of clothing one had packed for him. We lay on our bunks feeling excusably sick when we knew the skipper also was prostrate, and saw our soaked clothing knotted tightly to the steamer rails and waving in what was doubt-less a " good drying breeze," but one with which we could have dispensed.

The overland journey which succeeded was scarcely less trying. We found no tea, and the filters empty, in the rest-houses where we stayed, and were glad to reach Blantyre and comfort. The younger men of the party had had to walk most of the way, and had turned up at our last stopping-place so thirsty that they were ashamed to mark in the book kept for that purpose the number of bottles of aerated water they fortunately found there. I can remember Donald and the Rev. James Henderson striking an average and crediting Dr and Mrs Laws, who had had one between them, with four apiece to diminish their own total!

The Conference brought us into touch with some members of the South Africa General Mission, and on learning how the lack of trustworthy Native agents hampered their work on the lower Shiré River, he offered them the loan of some of our Ngoni teachers. For many years this arrangement held good and gave our Ngoniland Church another missionary outlet. After the delegates to the Conference had departed, we remained behind that my husband might have some meetings for the Europeans of the district, as he had on a previous visit. Then home again, after having noted all the spoils we wanted from the Blantyre Mission garden, and arranged for them to be sent as soon as we despatched carriers to fetch them.

The following year was one of alarums and excursions. It began with the unexpectedly early arrival of our first baby. Two months later she was getting her first experience of the vicissitudes of life in Central Africa. After three days' travelling with her mother down to Kasungu, where a Government lady was awaiting attendance in the mission house, there was a hurried journey back to Loudon, occasioned by the receipt of the following letter:

" MY DEAREST WIFE.—Excuse Hanania's writing. As I am in my Bed with fever. I got a sharp tuch at Mzimba and again today after preaching. I have gone to bed. I hope I shall be better tomorrow. But I fear I shall not be able for the work for this week. Northern (*i.e.* nor the) journey to Kasungu next week. I am only tired but that makes me wrong (long) to have you here. Also Mr W. Henderson The Boxer and Mr Adimson may be here. If Mrs Henderson will be so kind as to excuse you and if Mrs Rubens can spare you please come back this week. I have sent for your machilla boys just now. But please

K

be not so in hurry. At the councel meeting we were asked to go home. As soon as Dr Elmslie returns. As it depend on you and the baby I did not promise anything. Dr Elmslie was asked to come and stay at Loudon. Dr Boxer was apointed to marambo to open as sufordenets (subordinate) station in under control at Loudon. Tell Mr Henderson that he and Mr Macalpine we are asked to go all Chitambo in August to prospect for a new station and to place Tonga teachers as Pioneers. Please make my excuses to the Dutch missionarys. At last I am having a profuse weat and life seems blighter. Please do not tire yoursel all (or) Violet coming home too fast. I hope to be well tomorrow but I am sorry to ask you to make this journey alone. I shall be very happy when I see you both again."

That letter, which would have been pages longer had not the native amanuensis been so slow in taking down the dictation, showed that Fraser had a considerable temperature, for it was always when over 103 that he used to pour out the news to me. Knowing that things were worse than he would have me suspect, we did hurry, and were relieved to find the District Resident with him and the worst over.

In June the Boxers arrived, and after a few weeks on the Station went on to start building the Senga Station for which Donald had so long been pleading : little did we know then that in a few months it would be abandoned owing to Mrs Boxer's death. In July I was off on another medical trip, and this time was met on the return journey by a letter to apologise for my returning to an empty house : my husband was having *his* turn at making a hurried journey on the Kasungu road, for Mr Henderson was ill. Dr Elmslie, arriving soon afterwards, hurried down after him, and, in August, they turned up along with their convalescent patient and his wife, and somewhat crowded the accommodation of our three-roomed house !

After a Sacramental gathering in September, a hurried packing and closing up of Station books, we were off on furlough at last, hearing on the morning of our start that Dr Boxer was bringing his wife in to Dr Elmslie.

What a journey we had ! The steamer was supposed to be due at Bandawe in three days, and it would take us all that time to get across the intervening hills. The very first day out Donald was running a temperature, and we had to shorten this first stage and camp early. The second day dysentery developed, the baby was cross, and her mother had low fever, and yet we had to push on across the Vipya to reach the Bandawe hill-house on the Lake side. By that time my patient was really very ill, and a messenger had to be despatched to ask that the steamer should be kept waiting for us if we could not push on next morning. Reassuring news came back from the agent to say that it had only recently gone north, and we might wait on without misgivings till he sent us word. That gave us a brief respite ; but if we could stay without misgivings, we could not remain indefinitely without food, and our three days' provisions having quite given out, we moved on to the MacAlpines' empty house at Bandawe. The trouble was that their store-room was as empty as their house, as their last grocery order had not yet arrived. The agent at the African Lakes Corporation's store explained that there was a dearth of flour in the district, and he had none to supply ; but there were a few boxes of mouldy biscuits left in the store. It took a lot of toasting in the oven to make them palatable food for an invalid. However, he was convalescent when the steamer arrived a fortnight late !

When we reached Fort Johnston, at the south end of the Lake, we found the boarding-house full of German Fathers and nuns—refugees from German territory, where there had been a rising, during which a bishop and one of their priests had been killed. We arrived by boat at night, with mosquitoes swarming round. The next rest-house was worse, and we left it at 2 a.m. to get on while it was cool, seeing there was no chance of sleeping. Passing through Blantyre we heard of Mrs Boxer's death. Beyond that point there were far too many travellers going south for comfort. There was a day in a Cholo rest-house, where fourteen people competed for the occupation of the two small bedrooms which constituted all the sleeping accommodation.

The journey across the Elephant Marsh to Chiromo was also done at night. Then off again for Port Herald, which we reached at dark in pouring rain—eighteen travellers, half of them speaking no English, landed on one agent who had had no notice of the numbers to be expected, and who had to provide us all with house-boats, men and food with which to do the next stage of the journey down the River Shiré that night! A Government agent took the English-speaking ones off his hands as far as providing dinner for them was concerned. He himself had only just arrived, and his boys were in the act of opening up the house when they were told to find dinner for twelve. Feverish activity ensued: while some chased and killed the fowls that were to provide the soup and the subsequent courses of the meal, others were rushing to the river with pails to get water. The filtering of this Donald watched in the backyard of the Boma. His host had gone off on some errand after giving him particulars of a bad row he had got into a few years before, when the Postmaster-General in London had been on his track because of some mails that had accumulated in his house for five months without ever being sent up country to some wretched missionaries who had started to make a fuss!

Donald asked, " But why did you keep them all that time ? " " Oh, well ! I used to be out shooting a good deal and just overlooked them, and then there were so many I hadn't bags to put them in." His visitor was more interested in the story than he guessed. *Now* we knew who was responsible for the arrival at Hora of three mailbags stuffed to the brim with magazines and papers, after we had had five months of waiting ! But Donald said nothing beyond sympathising with him, thinking to himself that it was as well his companion had forgotten the names of the " wretched missionaries." !

But, as he watched the drinking-water being prepared, he began to think we might have further cause to remember the casual ways of this man's household. One boy lifted the pail of water, a second boy held out his not immaculate loin-cloth, and the water was poured through it into a second pail, and then the jugs for the table were filled up with what they could truthfully assert to be " filtered water." No wonder he urged me to accept the invitation to dine at the house of a lady who turned up providentially at that moment, in spite of my reluctance to lift a sleeping baby from under the cover of a mosquito curtain and take her out once more into the rain !

At midnight we were all away in our little fleet of houseboats. Our provisions seemed to consist of tins of sausages, but the only cooking utensil provided was a kettle, so we formed a joint-stock company with two ladies and a baby travelling in another boat, and used to have meals together on the bank, when *they* could lend their frying-pan and *we* could boil the water for their tea. We had seen nothing of our baggage since leaving Blantyre, and so our picnic life included a good deal of washing. Ours was known as the " flagboat," from the array of floating garments that adorned it.

One morning, thinking it was about time for breakfast, I suggested that if our sister vessel was in sight, Donald should hail them and inquire if they felt ready for a meal. A moment later he came in to the thatched enclosure that occupied the centre of the boat, and said, " I've done something to offend Mrs G." He was greatly upset, but, in spite of all the suggestions I put forward, maintained that he had shouted to her, and she had turned round, seen him, and re-entered her cabin without a word. We waited some time, and finally went ashore and had our breakfast. Later on they passed us. Donald was inside the shelter while I shouted to ask if they did not want the kettle. They did, and as the boat came alongside to fetch it Mrs G. said, " *Did* your husband see me ? " Those were " Victorian " times, and she had been caught unawares hanging up her one and only blouse to dry, and was much relieved to hear that he had had no idea why she had not stayed to talk with him. But Mrs Grundy would have been more shocked if, when we reached the steamer on the Zambezi, she had heard the attempts made to allot us cabin companions by a skipper who had been waiting two days for us with a whisky bottle for sole companion. We " sorted " ourselves, and managed to give the nuns no male companions.

Our troubles were not over when we reached the coast. Plague had broken out at Chinde ; no steamers would lie off to take us on board, and we were confined to very narrow bounds. While we were there, one of the two white victims died, and Donald took the funeral service, fifty white men appearing at it. After four days it was arranged that the *Kadett*, whose usual trip was across the bar to meet the ocean steamers, should take us down the coast to Beira. The ordinary six hours' trip took us thirty-six hours, in a rough sea that made it of little consequence that the food ran short. The only two people on board

who had a bunk were the two ladies with babies.   But at
Beira, after having our luggage disinfected, we went on
board the *Burgermeister*; and, with the exception of a snow
blizzard in the Bay of Naples and missing a train at Mar-
seilles—whereby we escaped the worst of a bad storm in the
Channel—we travelled in a comfort that was enhanced by
contrast.   Often in later years when we went out with newcomers, Donald used to tell them of the interest and thrills
of travel in the earlier days that they had missed.   When
one reminded him how he had felt at the time, he admitted
the facts almost incredulously, for, when he spoke of
African life as if it had been lived in one blaze of sunshine,
he was giving the real impression of gladness that it left
on his own mind.   When he tried to bring in the other
side of the story it was with a conscious effort to be impartial.
And he was not very successful, for, he used to admit with
a smile, he was like the man who told Dr Samuel Johnson
that he too had tried in his time to be a philosopher, but,
he didn't know how, cheerfulness was always breaking in.

CHAPTER XVIII

FURLOUGHS seldom meant rest to Fraser. In spite of a journey home begun with dysentery and lasting eleven weeks, with a sudden and trying change from the greatest heat of Africa to a snow blizzard in the Mediterranean, he was half-way across the Atlantic six weeks later, travelling in company with his father-in-law to speak at a Student Conference at Nashville. They made friends on board with Sir Bache Cunard, who used to invite them and Sir Stafford Northcote to private suppers, at which the two missionary enthusiasts taught the other two more about missions in a few days than they had ever known before !

" It was great," confessed Donald, " to meet so many old friends among the leaders of the Movement." To judge by the description of him in a Nashville paper as " the veteran missionary from Central Africa," they must have seen a physical change in him from the lad who had been across twelve years before. Though he was only thirty-four, his hair was turning white. After the Conference he travelled around visiting various student centres, and was specially interested to see all he could of work among the negro and coloured students in the Southern States, and to pick up practical suggestions about what might help the work in Africa. His letters were full of interest and fun, and showed how his buoyancy was returning. One friend has suggested that he seemed almost afraid of his own humour. There was plenty of it in his intimate letters, but he never knew what might happen when he let it loose on

142

the humourless. He had once been asked how he had managed to speak at a big meeting in the St Andrew's Halls, Glasgow, after coming out of the dentist's hands. "Oh, when I got up, I just said, 'Excuse me, my Lord Provost,' and dropped my teeth into the speaker's tumbler till I had finished"; and one of his hearers told the tale as an instance of his composure!

A son was born during the Assembly of 1906, and his wife had to be content with reports on his speaking from others. Her latest sister-in-law wrote that goodness just seemed to radiate from him, so that one always felt the better for being in his company, and she wanted to know whether being constantly with him made one get used to that sort of thing, or whether one was always kept bursting with pride. He had had no idea how splendid he was at the annual Livingstonia meeting at Free St George's, but that was part of his charm—he never *did* know what he was like!

Though his shyness kept him from ever looking up the Student Movement Headquarters when he arrived home, he was pleased when they invited him to their Summer Conference at Conishead. If only he had not had to speak, he decided on arrival, he could have enjoyed it thoroughly, for here were Harry Miller, Douglas Thornton, Miller of Hausaland, O'Neill from Manchuria, and others. He spent a whole day, when all the others had gone off on excursions, preparing for that missionary appeal, and he knew that there was a great backing of prayer. An old Student Volunteer friend wrote to tell his wife about it—how he had left no argument unanswered, and yet was so liberal-minded in his appeal: his magnificent voice, too, was easily heard in the big tent which speakers often found so difficult. "It was as of old I remember him, the man hidden behind his Lord and Master. I told you at Matlock that he seemed to me to live that verse with which he opened a meeting at the Liverpool Conference one day—'Not unto us, O Lord, not unto us, but unto Thy name give glory.' I am glad he has not changed. You are surely a happy woman."

He had been given twenty minutes for his address, but when he tried to sit down the men shouted to him to go on. That he made a profound impression is evident from the fact that men have written saying they remember that address after twenty-five years. In one tent six men decided for the Foreign Field; in another almost as many. When he went into the Edinburgh tent for prayers, two of the most brilliant men stood up and said they had made the same decision. From that night on to the end of the Conference he was spending his whole time—apart from an interval of uproarious fun on Sports Day—having interviews with men up to midnight. It seemed as if many were going through a spiritual crisis. A High Churchman accosted him with the remark, " I want to make a confession to you. When you stood up to speak I said to myself, ' Now has that man anything in common with me ? Is there a single point of contact between us ? ' and when you had finished, I said, ' Is there a single point of difference between us ? ' " " I don't know what to say," said Donald in reporting it; " I just wanted to go away and cry with humiliation and wonder. And of course I have felt throughout the ministry of intercession."

On this furlough, as on the previous one, he was asked to remain a second winter at home, doing deputation work up and down the country. This he did with one break, when some friends carried him off for winter sports at Christmas time.

From Switzerland he returned safe and sound, in spite of an attempt he made to find his way back from the top of some height they had climbed by starting off on skis in a direction that would have led him to a precipitous descent!

In the early summer of 1907 we were sailing again for Africa accompanied by some ladies for the Mission, one of whom we hoped to retain for our own Station. Before we reached Madeira he had a language class going.

CHAPTER XIX

ANOTHER FIVE YEARS

OUR first welcome on our return was from two excited, perspiring matrons whom we met running along the road "lululuing" (by a rapid motion of the tongue from side to side of the mouth) a vocal welcome. As we appeared in sight they stopped and danced, and in another minute we had alighted on the ground beside them and were shaking hands and laughing, almost as excited as they were. It was good to be back. Many a time, wherever Donald was, he could scarcely enjoy the present for his impatience to get on to the next place—but he never felt like that when back in Africa. It was *home*.

There was plenty to do and see. The permanent dwelling-house, a two-storied building with six rooms and comfortable verandas running round two sides, had clean plank flooring instead of beaten mud or brick, and made a delightful home. This, for the children's sake, we greatly appreciated, though it had only been rather reluctantly that Donald had agreed to this type of building. The upper story—once a six-roomed house had been decided on—had been his suggestion, to save roofing and reduce the amount of lead required to make its walls ant-proof.

Miss Irvine, a teacher, was with us, and cheerfully did the head of the Station look forward to the day when she would relieve him of the bulk of the school work, though the visiting of out-schools would necessarily remain largely his job because of the time and travelling involved. He had done his best to qualify for this side of his work by seeing as much as possible of educational methods and diligently studying the subject. Two volumes of biography were on one occasion sent back to the Station with a note to say I should not have forwarded them; they were *far* too interesting, and only by returning them at once could he hope to master the educational volume he had carried with him. That he had mastered his subject, and was regarded as something of an authority on education, is evidenced by the fact that Dr Edgar H. Brookes, in his book on *Education for South Africa*, devotes some time to discussing the views on the education-for-life theory of " one of its most recent exponents, that brilliant and devoted missionary leader Dr Donald Fraser," and the volume on *Education in East Africa* quotes from an article of his in *The International Review of Missions*, January 1921.

The colleagueship with Miss Irvine was all too brief. He could not refrain from expressing his appreciation of another's work, and she was promoted to a post on the teaching staff of the Overtoun Institution. Meantime she was sharing our house, and our family meals took pedagogic turns, with wild discussions about meanings of words and pronunciations. The table-boy could not follow, but he got into the habit of bringing in a large dictionary from the study and laying it before his master whenever we seemed to be arguing.

Visitors were frequent—missionaries passing or on holiday, trade or Government agents, travellers and patients. It is astonishing how many guests a house can hold in Africa, especially when there is a top veranda on which beds can be put. Tents, too, can be erected if necessary, and the bicycle house can hold a camp-bed if its miscellaneous contents are shoved aside. Donald's hospitable Highland soul loved to have visitors about—if they did not interfere with work ! When we took a flat in Glasgow

which had no spare room, he wanted to know what we
would do with visitors. " Do without," I suggested,
adding : " After all, we have been hospitable for twenty-
five years ; I shall be quite glad to have a rest." He shook
his head with a reproving smile : " What about not being
weary in well-doing ? " But indeed at times the " well-
doing " tended to be overdone, as even he admitted when
different parties arrived simultaneously, and his letters
were illustrated with pictures of his wife fainting at the
sight of a motor-bike with two riders, a donkey, a couple
of bush-cars and a machila, all converging from different
points upon her front door.

There were many young families in the Mission in those
days, and from time to time the children had some white
playmates arriving from other Stations ; but in their
absence there were plenty of black ones, and their Daddy
took care that their lives were full of interest. There were
donkeys to ride, and villages to visit where they got the
warmest of welcomes. " Daddy " would sometimes take
one or other off with him on tour, and then there were
streams to bathe in, all sorts of animals to watch breath-
lessly, and sensations to be produced in villages by the
mere sight of white children who could jabber like natives.
Many a time their father broke the Tenth Commandment
as he listened to their linguistic powers ! The loadmen
were not altogether keen on taking a little tender-hearted
girl with them when they went to a district where there
was game, for after watching the unsuspecting buck she
would beg her Daddy not to shoot them, and he was only
too glad to promise ; he disliked taking life, and only
did it because it was necessary for food or for a treat for
the men.

There were generally pets on hand. Besides the donkey
mare and her offspring, Peter—politely re-christened *Miss*

Peter when she in turn foaled—there were at various times dogs, a cat, a monkey, bush-buck, cranes, a family of mongooses, besides other unauthorised pets, such as the bongororos (millipedes) found crawling over the bedroom floor after having been smuggled in in bulging pockets. Their father was always doing something to give the children pleasure. He built a little house for them to play in. When they got tired of it, it was converted into a garage in which was a weird collection of bits of broken-down bicycles, for which he was always ready to pay a shilling or two, and scraps of all sorts. No one passing and in difficulties would fail to find any ordinary part that might be required, and many a Native who thought his bike was useless could get it put together again there by means of the collection at his disposal.

Christmas became more exciting than ever, for Santa Claus, who held a popular if vague place in the minds of the people, suddenly took bodily form in a beard that would have greatly impressed them if it had not looked so uncommonly like hospital dressings. Children's parties there were, too, and no party was more successful than the birthday one when, owing to an epidemic of whooping-cough that made it necessary to keep all native children at a distance, a company of old grannies were invited in their stead. They were far more appreciative than the children, who were accustomed to get an occasional meal from their white playmates, and left the house hugging their parting presents of packets of salt and singing the praises of their small host, " Jorodji."

Anxieties were not absent. From one ulendo both father and daughter returned very ill and very thankful to be home again. There was a day when the father darted anxiously off in pursuit of a small and apparently hatless boy, visible in the distance in the dangerously blazing sun-

shine, and was greatly relieved on approaching him to see
his head well covered by a yellow tea-cosy ; and another
occasion when he was just in time to prevent a small couple
from lifting a snake they were pursuing under the impression that it was a giant millipede. Going his rounds of
the Station on his motor-cycle, he was often accompanied by
one child seated fore and another aft—not necessarily one
of his own children.

This term might be called the " era of wheels." He
delighted in the vehicles which would save men from being
turned into beasts of burden. In the past there had been
a push-bike, a wagon presented by the South African
students, and a rickshaw. This last, its body having been
smashed against a tree by a runaway donkey, was now
converted into a tinker's cart which was most useful in
various ways, and on one occasion served to take our
children to Livingstonia. Protected from the sun by an
awning, they sat with toys and books around them, and did
not find the week's journey thither a moment too long. The
cart was well surrounded on that occasion by a bodyguard
of carriers, for the district was being ravaged by a man-
eating lion, and no one dared to straggle. There were
the Scotch carts and two wheelbarrows ; and finally, there,
was the bush-car that he invented, from a description of the
Millford bush-car which we could not afford to buy. It
was the most convenient form of travelling yet hit upon,
and, once tried by anyone, was so much in demand that he
built several for friends. Consisting of a seat placed above
a single motor-bike wheel with shafts for a man fore and aft,
it enabled one to move along a narrow track raised sufficiently high to see about one, yet free from that apologetic
sense of one's weight which troubled one when being
carried. When they had once acquired the art of balancing
this bush-car, four men could easily do a good day's work

with very little fatigue, keeping up between five and six miles an hour. I remember the amusement when, trying to make up a team for me, Donald refused one man on the score that he had not learned the job, and got the answer, "Bwana, if I can run with the donkeys, I can run with the Dona."

Cycles he had always made use of in travelling, more than once to the extent of seriously straining himself and bringing on illness. Later, through the kindness of friends, he tried motor-bicycles. The first of these was an old, second-hand and not very powerful machine. He had learned very little about it when he started off to ride to Loudon on it, and he prayed that he might find no obstacle on the road. By the time he arrived he had found out how to stop it, and a day or two later he started off on an adventurous journey to Council which had a perhaps undeservedly happy ending, for a good deal of it was done after dark in the attempt to reach the camp of the men who had set out five days before. By swerving into the bush he avoided killing any of the babies whom the mothers forgot to remove, when his sudden appearance interrupted the picnics they were having in the middle of the road ; and, by the speed with which he dashed past, he avoided being killed by two terrified Ngoni standing at the bottom of a drift with spears uplifted to strike at the unknown monster bearing down on them through the darkness. He had departed looking like the White Knight, with all sorts of things tied about him, but these were strewn along the road as he went. Articles that mattered were lost for good ; but, a week after his start, I had to pay a man two shillings for bringing me in a parcel which he had picked up seventy miles away—sandwiches and bananas no longer appetising !

The following term he took out a "Triumph," and,

L

later, a side-car in which his wife spent some anxious moments as it was slowly driven across the very rickety and narrow little bridges over the gullies. Such bridges were made by laying branches transversely on two logs that spanned the ravines, and plastering them over with mud that too often only hid the ravages of the white ants beneath. Running his wheels as close as possible to *his* side, he would ask, " Can I take another inch or two on your side ? " Anxiously watching my narrow margin I would reply, " Not more than one." Safely across, he would say to me with a smile, " It's good you didn't see the wheel right over ! " Natives he often picked up for a ride, and the older ones sometimes wore a relieved expression when they once more set foot on mother earth. But when he went out, perhaps to bring some old blind patient into hospital for operation, he took great care not to scare his passenger, who accepted this mode of travelling as one of the wonders that were so easy to the white man.

Yet, while appreciating the saving of time which mechanical transport effected, especially for long journeys —in one year he calculated it had saved ninety days—Fraser was aware of the risk that such a method might prevent that close contact of the missionary with the people which is obtained by the journeys on foot, when one shares the life and interests and hardships of the way, and learns to know the folk more intimately than is possible on the Mission Station. He got fun as well as fellowship out of his wanderings with his men, and his good-humour kept them cheery. One of them was a big-chested man, named Majamara, with an extraordinarily booming voice—bad at night-time if one wanted to sleep. One of the duties the tired men used to avoid was the filling up at night of a pail with water, for a wash and the early cup of tea before setting off : without it there was delay in getting an early start. We would hear the cook pleading with man after man ; but, seated by the blaze of the camp-fire after a satisfying supper, they were loath to move. Then the Bwana's cheerful voice would be heard shouting, " Maja-mara, maji ghamara "—a play on the name, for " maji ghamara " means " the water is finished." The joke never failed to amuse, and the man, with a happy grin and a bellow of assent, would go off on his errand. All of them knew his thoughtfulness for them, and that, although he told them it was their own fault when at mid-day they were panting for the water which, in spite of his warnings, they had been too careless to carry, he would share with them the last drop in his bottle, and, however tired he was by evening, would do his best to cater for their larder with his rifle. They in turn looked after him with rare, if rough, concern when he was ill, sitting up all night in his tent as he lay unconscious with fever, or making forced marches to bring him home.

The houseboys were all devoted to him in their various ways. Solomon, a big married chap known as " the poor orphan " from a " sob-stuff " way he had of appealing for help from the children whom he wanted to bring in a supply of firewood or to clean his pots for him, would think nothing of picking out a tin from the food-basket and darting off across country to milk some cows he had descried in the distance, if it seemed the only chance of obtaining milk for a pudding or coffee that evening in camp. Any row made by the owners was met with a pathetic tale of the white man's need. Of course, these house-boys grew lazy and careless, but they had just to be reminded that their way of serving the Kingdom was to keep their master fit for his work, and there would be a promise to " buck up "—a phrase which made its way into the local dialect. Alone once at Loudon and far from well, he asked the table-boy

to remove the breakfast he had laid on the table, as he had
a sensitive dislike to the smell of food when not hungry.
" Then what shall I bring you instead ? "   " Nothing."
The lad continued to make suggestions.   " Peter, leave
me in peace to drink my tea : I've told you that I don't
want to see any food."   Silence ensued, and he began to
have an uncomfortable suspicion that something was
wrong.   Turning round, he saw a tear trickling down
the boy's face.   " What *is* the matter, Peter ? " he said, a
little testily, probably, for he hated having a fuss made
about himself.   " The Dona said I was to see that you ate
properly when she was away, or you would be ill, and now
you are getting ill."   So for the unhappy lad's sake he
despatched him to bring a poached egg, which the dog
ate while Peter was sent on some other superfluous errand.

His reports on domestic matters to the absent mistress
were generally that the boys seemed to be doing all right,
though to keep them up to the scratch he was giving them
an occasional row in turns.   She knew these would not
be serious—he was more concerned about averting the
trouble there might be on her return.   When he was
coming home after an ulendo without her, he used to make
the cook stop at some stream near the Station and give
the pots and pans a better scour than they had been getting
on the trip, so that she might be satisfied that they had
been attended to properly ; but the signs of damp and of
sand still adhering told her what had happened, and the
cook would guilelessly reveal the whole story.

In Africa, years are dated by their happenings.   In 1907
we arrived during a series of earthquakes which (according
to our carriers) was explained by the death which had just
occurred of Ng'onomo, the old chief, who had been so
good a friend ever since that first visit of the young missionary, and who always cherished the belief that " Framo "

was the re-incarnation of Koyi, the Christian Kaffir, who had come with Dr Elmslie to open up Ngoniland. 1908 was the year when Mzukuzuku, our own local chief, died. The following year was remembered by the people as that in which one of our oldest and most esteemed evangelists was heartlessly murdered by the roadside where he was sleeping, for the sake of his clothes and the bundle he was carrying. There was overwhelming circumstantial evidence as to who had done the deed, but, as reported to Government headquarters, it was deemed insufficient at Zomba, and the accused were acquitted. The inoffensiveness of the victim and the heartlessness of the crime had roused much feeling among the Christians, and it was largely on that account that Fraser had refused a suggestion made to him by the magistrate that he should be public prosecutor in the case. He feared that it might seem to the people that he was out to avenge Andrew rather than help in the administration of justice. But he had not for a moment imagined that, through slackness in summoning witnesses, the verdict would be such that it would seem to the people, not the technical flaw that he tried to explain to them, but foolish weakness in bringing criminals to justice, carrying in its train a feeling that the hold of the law was not the thing they had imagined, and, thus, a renewed sense of freedom to act as they pleased.

At the death of our chief in 1908, Fraser had an anxious and responsible time, knowing that on such an occasion there is a recognised sort of interregnum when violence can be resorted to with impunity. Mzukuzuku died on the Mission Station after an attack of pneumonia, from which it seemed he was recovering; and he might have done so had it not been for the strain of receiving strings of visitors who could not altogether be excluded once the crisis was past. Their one inquiry was, " Whom do you

blame for this ? " and earlier in the year there had been a
tragic misfortune in connection with one of his daughters
which left no doubt in his superstition-ridden mind as to
whom to blame for his present misfortune.   It was while
he was angrily discussing this very subject that he collapsed
and died.   Immediately there was a wild uproar on the
Station, and, as the death-wail spread the news, in came his
sons and a neighbouring chief, accompanied by a following
of their people, and working themselves into a state of
frenzied wrath and grief.   Some had to be held and the
weapons forcibly wrenched out of their hands.   In the
midst of this confusion Fraser arranged that the ceremony
of removing the body to the first of its resting-places in
the long series of burial observances to be gone through,
should take place as soon as possible.   But he dared not
let them start off without his restraining influence, and he
followed them, first there, and, later on, to the chief's own
kraal.   He had considerable influence over both the sons,
and fortunately there were many Christians in the head
village.   When he got hold of one of his elders who
resided there, and asked him to see that the Christians did
not get carried away by the excitement round them, he
was assured that they were all quiet, and had been helping
to disarm the most excited.   Presently Fraser caught sight
of an angry commotion in one corner, and found it was
one of the chief's widows—the mother of the dead girl
whose case was blamed for this.   She was surrounded by
a group of Christians trying to shelter her from the blows
aimed at her by the angry mob.   He sent her off to the
shelter of our house under the escort of some of the Church
members.   The head induna of the chief was giving way
to exaggerated demonstrations of grief : by quietly laying
his hand on him Fraser got him to stop and listen, and
warned him that he would be held responsible for any

bloodshed. One of the sons was more difficult to manage, but at last Fraser managed to get together a little group of the sons with the head induna, and had a serious talk with them, telling them that, if they had any charges to make against anyone, these must be reserved for a full inquiry after the funeral. Influenced by the quietened behaviour of the leaders, the tumult subsided into weeping; but, going among them, Fraser could see in some, traces of the terror which underlay their wild demonstrations of grief. He demanded silence, prayed with them, and then, feeling their passion of grief had exhausted them, felt it safe to go home. But he knew the danger would break out again with the arrival of distant chiefs from various quarters, and he sent a message to the magistrate, warning him and suggesting that he should come across. He was up at daybreak, calling together his elders and proposing a meeting with the Christians, to remind them of their function as peace-makers and to warn them to take no part in bringing charges against anyone; but the elders assured him that it was unnecessary—none of them had taken any part by word or action. It was the *old* men of the village who required to be restrained. So into the kraal he passed to talk to these of Mzukuzuku's death and what had caused it, and to speak of the danger of making wild accusations. How blandly they agreed and protested their innocence of making charges against anyone! Why then had certain men been forced to flee? What but their guilty consciences had driven them away? replied they. But he knew they would now be careful, and let it go at that, though on the Station we were still guarding carefully not only the widow who had been attacked and had several wounds from club blows, but also a good deal of property which had been brought in till the risk of pillage that so often accompanied the incoming of funeral parties, should be over. When, finally, the funeral took place, with all the elaborate ceremonial of the past—save for the absence of other victims to accompany their dead chief into the hereafter—Fraser obtained a hearing, read some passages of the Bible and prayed, while, for a time at least, there was silence throughout the great crowd of mourners.

CHAPTER XX

" WHAT *is* your husband, Mrs Fraser ? " asked a Johannes-burg business man one day on the steamer, as he watched him pacing the deck. " He's a missionary." " A mission-ary ? Good heavens ! Do you mean to tell me that a man like him could not get a better job than that ? " " If he could, you may be sure that he would have jumped at it." " But surely," he began ; stopped, looked at me, realised what I meant, and then, with an " I'm blowed ! " he got up and strolled off to consider this strange phenomenon.

People were so often entrapped into liking Donald before they discovered that he was a man they should by rights have avoided as one of a type they could not tolerate at any cost. It interested me to watch the growth of interest from casual contacts, and to see how often real friendships resulted with an astonishing variety of people. He was always himself—never professional—and padre though they sooner or later discovered him to be, they never veered off when they made the discovery. Only once did I hear a disparaging criticism of him on board, when an irate female in whom class-feeling ran high, remarked, " That man call himself a missionary indeed ! He's a second-class passenger himself, and yet he goes and gives a decision in favour of a first-class passenger ! " He had been acting as a judge in the sports, as so often he seemed to be asked to do. These class distinctions on board ship, with the feeling they sometimes engendered, he heartily disliked, and he never was so happy as when we were travelling on a

one-class boat.   After seeing how a Johannesburg parson
had captured the third-class by travelling with them, he
always regretted that his wife's inability to enjoy sea travel
prevented him from suggesting a voyage in the nearer
neighbourhood of the screw.

The friends he made were a cosmopolitan crowd.
Missionaries, of course, of all denominations.   He attracted
High Anglicans and Roman Catholics as much as he did
Salvation Army friends ; but he seemed equally at home
with some of the music-hall artists who were often our
travelling companions.   How we teased him once when
the Capetown press coupled him with two music-hall
performers as the " stars " who had arrived by a certain
steamer !   He discovered " such a nice wholesome affectionate couple " in an Australian step-dancer and his wife, who
was a professional singer.   How pleased, though nervous,
she was to sing " Abide with me " as a solo at the Sunday
evening service, at his request !   Her husband would
wander round, pipe in mouth, looking out for the parson
that he might have a " jaw " with him.   I listened to them
one day as the missionary and the step-dancer discussed at
length the effect which their audiences had on them !

On our first journey home we travelled down country
and up the East Coast with a party of German Roman
Catholic missionaries.   They were very pleasant companions, the nuns being greatly delighted to help in looking
after our baby.   At the head of the party was an abbot
who had been out on a tour of inspection.   He knew very
little English, and my husband practically no German, but
they managed to become great friends nevertheless, and
carried on their conversations and discussions with the aid
of a German-Zulu dictionary.   The abbot turned up the
German, and the other recognised the Zulu, which is
practically the same as the Ngoni tongue.   We arrived at

Dar-es-Salaam on a Sunday morning, and there our German friends were landing. They invited Donald to go ashore with them, and he did not return till late, having spent a very happy Sunday worshipping with them through all the services of the day. We were on a German boat, and there was some political incident at the time which was making feeling on board rather tense between the two nationalities, but it did not affect Donald's relationship with anyone. "After all," as he said, "we have far more in common with these people, who are so devotedly bringing the news of Jesus Christ to the Africans, than we have with those Englishmen who have no interest in either the message or the people." When we arrived at Mombasa, some Brothers of another Order came on board to visit the Presbyterian missionary, having heard news of him from Dar-es-Salaam.

In spite of, or perhaps because of, the subject of Missions not being popular on board ship, he often deliberately chose it to speak about when taking a service, and managed to make it attractive. One of the crew, coming out from a Sunday evening service, remarked to me, quite unaware of my relationship, "That old codger could have gone on a darned sight longer with his yarns. I never knew these niggers were so interesting before."

Before the start of the South African Campaign, the following paragraph, à propos of its leader, appeared in *The Star*:

"Shipboard is hardly the place to look for a new sensation. The best efforts of the energetic passengers often fail to relieve the monotony of many an hour during the voyage. But even on shipboard occasional happenings do occur to jog the even tenor of life out of its accustomed rut and arouse interest.

"One of these incidents occurred on a steamer *en route* to South Africa some little time ago. The curiosity of passengers was aroused by a little notice, which was posted on the notice-board one morning. It read : ' All those who oppose missionary work among the African Natives are invited to meet in the dining-room this evening.' Every passenger was present. They found that the meeting had been called by a keen-eyed, business-like, grey-haired man, who was returning to his Mission Station in Nyasaland after a visit to his home in Scotland. His name was Fraser—Dr Donald Fraser.

" That evening will be remembered by many of those present as the time when their eyes were opened for the first time to the deeper problems of inter-racial relationships. The speaker quietly, but eloquently, gave them an honest, straightforward explanation of the why and wherefore of missionary activity, causing them to see how necessary and valuable was the contribution which the missionary was making to the right development of Africa. The question must have occurred to many at that meeting, Why isn't this done oftener ? Why don't we read and hear more of the work of the people who are handling these vital issues ? "

He seldom argued, believing that argument makes a man entrench himself behind his present position, while friendliness makes him come to meet you. An old farmer in the train in South Africa once cursed missions roundly to Donald as ruining the country and the Natives. Donald asked if he had employed Nyasaland boys, and what he thought of them. He said they were superior to all the South African Natives he knew—a fine, unspoiled set. Nyasaland must be a fine land to live in. " But," he added, " you wait till the missionaries get into Nyasaland, and you'll see how they'll ruin the place and spoil the niggers there ! " Then Donald intimated he had come from there, gave a sketch of how the country had been opened up by missions, and got the old man quite interested—even to the length of admitting that there were missionaries *and* missionaries !

Donald had more than one tale of the sudden conversion of people, through deeds, not arguments, on the question of missions. At Ekwendeni he had as his guest an Italian gold-digger who wept tears of gratitude over the goodness of Mrs Laws in giving him some tins of jam—an act which had turned him " from a swearing opponent to a cursing supporter of missions." One of our Loudon guests once remarked as he left us, " If anyone ever says a word against missions to *me* again, I'll *fell* him with this fist," a strong-looking one which he brandished as he spoke. It is most often those who are in no need of help or hospitality, but expect and accept the latter, whose after-criticisms are lacking in the courtesy due from guests.

If passing friendships often left their mark, still more did long-continued relationships knit him in close ties with others. One of his colleagues has written asking that, in his biography, his affectionate relationships with his fellow-members of the Livingstonia Mission (artisans as well as, or more so than, ordained members) should be emphasised. It is difficult for a wife to insist on this, as she naturally knows only one side of the story, but the lack of seriousness of the only quarrel she ever heard—" overheard " might be a more accurate word to use—may suggest its truth ; for it was while she was sitting on the top veranda that the following conversation floated up from below :

" I say, Prentice, I wish you wouldn't try to enthuse my wife about keeping pigs."

" Why not, Fraser ? "

" Because I don't want her to."

" What's wrong with pigs ? "

" They are nasty, insanitary beasts."

" Not half so insanitary as the geraniums on this veranda ! "

On hearing a chuckle from above they dropped the

argument. It was not Dr Prentice who was finally responsible for the addition of a pig to the farmyard of ducks, turkeys and fowls that he had at different times led me to rear. A Government Resident going home on furlough had accepted one in lieu of hut-tax money, and had grown too fond of it to be able to eat the pork he had at first contemplated. "Little Willie" was fed on our superfluous peaches, and the objector to pigs had no objection to cured bacon.

For his work's sake, if for nothing else, Donald would have done a great deal to keep on happy terms with others. It upset him physically if there was any unfriendliness or trouble between people, and even if he was in no way concerned, he would do all he could to restore friendly feeling. He was so sensitive that, if he had unconsciously caused any unhappiness to others, he was wretched. Once I got quite a disturbed letter from him because, when he visited the Stuarts, one of the children had cried when he came near. "What a brute I must have become, to make a child cry at the sight of me! She was quite friendly with Dr Elmslie when he came in," he wrote, not realising that a white baby in a lonely Station very seldom sees a new face. Dr Elmslie, living on the Station, was probably a daily visitor.

Missionaries in malarial districts are capable of occasionally writing "spiky" letters, but Donald took much trouble to avoid that danger. If he received such a letter, he would never send a reply without first bringing it to his wife to ask if there was any trace in it of sharpness or resentment. Even when his censor was impressed by the lack of such qualities in it, he would often tear it up and see if he could not increase the friendliness of its tone. If a long day's cycling could enable him to have a talk instead, he never grudged the extra trouble. People were always so easy to get on with when you met them! One of the men who arrived on the field shortly after Donald tells what a comfort and delight, as well as a stimulus and inspiration, it was to receive a letter from him.

Yet, this longing to have happy relations with others did not keep him from frank expression of his views when he differed from others on matters of policy, though he always tried to distinguish between matters of principle and personal opinion. On the former he would hold out as long as possible, though he felt keenly resisting the wishes of those whom he respected and admired. If he failed to carry his point, he could accept this with a good grace. Only once in all those years did he so feel the righteousness of the view for which he was fighting in Council as to say that, if the opposite opinion was accepted, he might find it necessary to resign, though he would not take such a step till he had first returned to his Station to consult his wife. It concerned some decision which he considered meant breaking faith with the Natives. Seeing how strongly he felt about the matter the proposal he objected to was dropped. He came home a little unhappy that it was perhaps deference to his personal attitude which had led to that satisfactory conclusion.

One of his best remembered and most successful efforts at restoring perfect harmony was entirely unintentional. It occurred at a Council at Bandawe. All day long they had been in session, and resumed after the evening meal. The evening went on, and Mrs Elmslie and I, sitting on the veranda of one house, could hear the voices of the Council members deep in argument on the other. We looked at each other and shook our heads, knowing that at so late an hour there was little likelihood of their arriving at reasoned and dispassionate conclusions. Suddenly there was a roar of laughter, followed by the shuffling of chairs and the sound of voices pitched in quite a different key.

The break-up was as unexpected as was the change of mood. Fraser had caused it quite unconsciously by saying to Dr Laws, " But don't you see, Dearie . . ." The sentence was never finished.

With the colleagues on his own Station he always had the most pleasant and cordial relations. We had various people at different times, but never managed to keep them as he would have liked. He appreciated them all, valuing in each some qualities he felt he lacked in himself. And he knew the advantage of having the opinion of a second man to counterbalance his judgment of those employed by the Mission, for each man has his favourites, and Donald was always afraid of doing less than justice to those against whom he had some prejudice. He had a surprising habit of being extraordinarily grateful for any tale one could tell that shed a better light on those he himself did not take to, or mistrusted.

His colleagues must have found him an easy head to get on with. He was solicitous for their comfort, especially if there were women or children to be considered, and he trusted them to carry on whatever part of the work had been assigned to them without interference from him. One of them, after leaving our Station, replied to me in answer to a letter telling of a new-comer who was settling down happily, " There's no one in the world like Mr Fraser for getting the best out of people, and making them try to do their best. No one could work with him and not want to. He just sometimes gives in too much to the opinions of people who haven't half as much sense or as much goodness as he. It was a pleasure to work for a man who showed so much confidence in you as to allow you to experiment along your own line, and if you failed didn't throw it in your face afterwards "—not that she did fail!

CHAPTER XXI

THE ECCLESIA : AIMS AND METHODS

" WHEN we think of Christ the King, and the realm over which we would make Him King, we cannot isolate the souls of Africa from the soil of Africa nor from its social structures." It was the attitude which Donald Fraser expressed in these words that so completely integrated all his service for that continent. Nothing helpful lay outside its scope, but the greatest contribution to its future that he knew was to bring it the power that was capable of producing good men and women, and thus transforming society. The last thing he desired was any isolation of the Christian community from the life that lay around it. His ideal of the Church was no aggregation of converts from animism, but a fellowship of those to whom had come such life and light that they would be the leaven which would leaven the entire community. " I fear," he said at the Le Zoute Conference, " the Evangel which denationalises."

When the three Presbyteries of the Livingstonia, Blantyre and Dutch Reformed Missions joined to form " The Church of Christ (Presbyterian) in Central Africa," Fraser was only partially satisfied. He would fain have omitted " Presbyterian " ; but, as Dr Hetherwick has said of him, " If Fraser did not carry his point in discussion there was generally some trace of his influence in the decision arrived at." In this case the brackets at least were the result of his pleading. Some day he hoped to see them, and what they enclosed, drop out. The effects of denominationalism elsewhere made him anxious to avoid hampering the future

M

development of a Church indigenous to the soil and spirit of Africa. He used to quote the description one old African had given of himself in the census, with unconscious candour, as a "Presbyterian heathen." That, he felt, was the danger of denominational loyalty, to those whose religious past was bound up in customs, rites, tabus.

On his arrival in Africa, Fraser found the people in that early and perhaps inevitable stage in Christian evangelism at which, having given up some of those practices that entangled them and prevented them from taking the first step into Christian liberty, they were largely occupied in denouncing what they had abandoned. He lamented this negative attitude, fostered by eloquent sermons from the preachers on such evils as polygamy, drinking and Sabbath-breaking. The people were apt to think of the new teaching as the acceptance of a revised set of tabus. Such a conversation as the following, between him and a woman applicant for baptism, was only too typical. "Why do you want to follow Jesus, Mama?" "Because He died for our sins." "Have you sins?" "No." "Do you mean that you never sin, never do wrong?" "No, not now." "You must be a very wonderful woman! There are none of us who are as good as that. I think you cannot know much about Jesus Christ if you are so contented with your own life. Mama, there are still many things in your life that you have to be saved from." "Is that so? I thought that when I stopped pounding flour on Sunday I had stopped sinning."

It puzzled some of these simple people when they found that no set of rules could cover the demands of Christ: that what He brought them was a liberty controlled by love and loyalty. As in their travels they were kept in the right road by someone going ahead and "shutting" all but that path by casting some plucked leaves upon the byeways, so they wanted obvious and unmistakable directions for this new Way. They had to be taught that the Guide was the Way, and it was His footsteps that they had to follow. Fraser set himself to preach Jesus Christ, and it was after a series of sermons on the Cross and the proof of His atoning love, that the great awakening came at Ekwendeni. He followed this up by trying to give the teachers, especially, some idea of the life of fellowship and prayer open to them. This was not only true of the early days : always throughout the years this was what he sought to impress.

He saw, as all workers in Africa must do, the value of music as an evangelising agency, but saw, too, that it must be of a type familiar to the people if it was to capture the simple and untaught. The pupils in the Station schools were, it is true, learning the sol-fa scale and hymns translated and sung to English tunes ; but it was all foreign to the African ear, and the farther a tune spread from the Mission Station the less recognisable it became. Yet every African is a singer, and can pick up native music with the greatest ease ; and there is little difficulty about the words, for a leader sings the beginning of each verse and then the other voices blend in. It was mingled with such a type of song that their old folk-lore came to them ; the new Message might be most naturally spread in this way too. He therefore encouraged the production of native music, either newly composed, or rescued from the oblivion into which some of the old war- and other songs tended to fall. Words from the New Testament and the Psalms were suggested ; and, when the large church at Loudon was opened with a series of meetings, the first day was devoted to hearing such hymns. The best of these were used throughout the remaining days, and the people, thoroughly familiarised with them, spread them throughout the country on their return to their homes.

Throughout the land, when people sang for the sake of singing, the words were always Christian, the secular songs being retained as the rhythmic accompaniment of other activities. The European had the best opportunity of hearing these when travelling by machila or bush-car, for this, like all other work done by the African, must be made a play of, if they are to be happy in the performance. It was very difficult to make any meaning out of the words, but that was due to the concentration or studied ambiguity of the expression. A common chorus struck up as Fraser was approaching a village was, "Wafika kaluwongwe ho! wafika kaluwongwe; chenjera!" It did not seem to make much sense translated as, "He has come, little ' springing green leaves'; he has come; look out!" But it was really an intimation to the village that it was Fraser who was approaching. The fresh vegetation that springs up all over the land as the rainy season draws near and the heat becomes intense, gave rise to the name, for he had a habit of hanging a bunch of leaves from the back of his hat to protect his neck from the sun. The "be careful!" no doubt helped the teacher to be found in the diligent discharge of his duty when the Mzungu arrived.

For several years, till a large number of hymns composed by the people themselves had been collected, musical festivals were an annual event at Loudon, prizes being given for the best words and music, and the best village choir. Thus, out of a good deal of rubbish produced, those that attracted the people (and it was what appealed to them that decided the judgment) were added to the growing volume of Church music. These hymns were undoubtedly of great value in impressing on those who used them some of the truths of which they sang.

He tried to use to the full the opportunities afforded by Church services. Preaching was almost the only way in which religious education could be given to a people with no literature. But he never talked to them on any aspect of their faith without trying to give its application to the devotional life. Various methods were employed to get their attention and foster the habit of listening, which sometimes seemed so unnecessary, when an African was holding forth, and they all knew what he was going to say and repeat *ad infinitum*. Often he asked questions in church, or got them to repeat the points he was trying to emphasise, so that they carried away with them a synopsis of his talk. Yet, realising that the pulpit had to fulfil a manifold function in the life of the community, as the most reliable way of disseminating instruction and warning, he felt he was no less bringing to the people the will of God when he occasionally spoke about some hygienic precaution, such as the boiling of drinking water or the sanitation of a village when some epidemic threatened. In the absence of a specialised theological vocabulary, a sermon on salvation might turn out to refer to the destruction of vermin. It helped to bring home to his listeners the sense that God's interest in them extended to everything connected with their life, and that their new religion, like their old beliefs, must affect every detail of their daily existence. There was a homeliness about the services that did not in the least detract from reverence. If a baby cried in the middle of the sermon, and the mother showed no intention of taking it out, Fraser might stop his address and say, " Mama, you know you can't listen with your baby crying like that ; nor can others hear when there is a noise. But, if you took the baby outside, the others would be able to listen." In no way abashed or self-conscious, the matron would rise in the silence that ensued, fasten her baby securely to her back, lift any little belongings that were beside her, such as the little gourd containing baby's gruel, and saunter out with the utmost composure. Then the sermon was resumed. The presence of children, even if not devotionally inclined, perturbed nobody, and there were occasions when, with a mother perhaps ill in bed, a small boy played happily at his father's feet in the pulpit, unseen by the congregation though they knew he was there. And nobody but the white people smiled when, seeing two small white children gazing wistfully at one item of the collection which had been placed on the steps of the platform, an old woman in the front row rose during the sermon, filled her hands with the pea-nuts, ascended the steps, and, kneeling down in front of the boys, presented them with what they had been coveting. She did not know that two white women were firmly holding on to the children's belts to prevent them from doing anything so scandalous as appropriating Church funds in kind. Another time a little naked black mite recognised his white friend in the preacher on the platform, and, making his way up beside him, slipped his hand into his, and remained there till he had finished speaking.

That prayer might be an act of the people and no mere ceremony performed by the minister, Fraser often made them repeat it clause by clause after him, or used a form of liturgy to which he taught them the proper responses. Some of the best-known prayers of the Church he translated into the vernacular, and used till the people were familiar with the words, and in confession and adoration were one with their brethren throughout the world. Then suddenly he would drop this liturgical form for a period in order that it might not become stereotyped and mechanical. He wanted to keep their minds alert.

Everyone was expected to contribute to the upkeep of the Church. He was very doubtful, at home as well as in

Africa, of any devotion that did not find expression in giving ; so, besides what the people brought on Sundays, the deacons went round monthly to collect offerings, which were largely given in kind.   Where folk were poverty-stricken they had opportunity of helping, by carrying in the district collections to the Station, cleaning and repairing the buildings in which they worshipped, and assisting one another.   The Christians in a village were made to feel they should repair the hut of a widow, or help the old and feeble to hoe their gardens, or carry some sick person to the hospital.   Yet when the elders suggested some form of compulsory Church dues, because, as always happens, some Christians did not take their share, he opposed it, feeling that any giving that did not arise from the spontaneous liberality of the people was no means of grace.   It was not Church funds as such that mattered to him ; always he was waiting to see the evidence of the fruits of the Spirit.

What consternation he created one night in a village when the people, after long hanging-about, came at last to ask when he was going to have the usual evening service ! We had entered the village an hour or two before, with a very weary, hungry set of carriers.   No presents of food had been given, and when our men had received their week's " poso " (food money) and began to try to buy food, the folk wished to drive so hard a bargain that the travellers said they would rather go hungry than spend on one night's supper what should keep them fed for three days.   When this little group suggested worship, their missionary turned on them to say there was to be none with them that night. " God does not want your hymn-singing," he told them ; " He wants the hungry fed.   You would only mock Him with your prayers.   You are doing what any heathen would feel ashamed to have done."

The news and the dismay spread, and, when he refused gifts hastily produced, because they were no tokens of kindness but were only meant to placate him, other villages in the vicinity began to come in late, with little offerings to make up for their inhospitable neighbours.

In ecclesiastical matters Fraser was, perhaps, something of a suspect in the eyes of some of his brethren. He had an open mind, and looked at everything from the African point of view, and would use any method that he thought might help them. Why it was necessary to maintain among these people the extremes of bareness and lack of symbolism which had characterised the Presbyterian Church in Scotland since the Reformation, he failed to see. Often as he travelled about the country and caught sight of some prominence on the landscape, he expressed a desire to plant on its summit a Cross that, catching the eye, might bring to the memory of those who looked at it their new faith. In the old days—it is true even yet—one saw everywhere proof of animistic beliefs, in the stones thrust into the fork of a tree, the heap of scattered pea-nut shells at the cross-roads, and many another custom. He himself said he found help from a little Cross in his office; it reminded him in the midst of irritating duties of what lay behind them all. And indeed it must sometimes have been difficult not to lose sight of " the wood for the trees," when day after day he sat there for hours examining applicants for the class, often so overwhelmed by the numbers that he was shocked to find himself asking anxiously if there were many more, and breathing a sigh of relief if there were not. There might be as many as 600 before one of the Annual Conventions, and for four months he might be seeing some daily. To him it was no light thing—this admitting of candidates to the Church. Each was seen not only by him, but also by some native leader, and then the names of those they had accepted were sent to the district to which they belonged for scrutiny by the local Church members who knew more about their lives.   It was a responsibility either to accept or reject, and the difficulty of knowing their motives was very great.   Some, through nervousness, might be almost unable to speak ; others to whom it meant nothing might be glib.   Once an old woman seemed to know nothing at all, and yet refused to leave when dismissed.   He tried again.   " Tell me yourself what you *do* know, Granny ? "   There was an indistinct murmur about John the Baptist.   " Yes, what about him ? " he asked encouragingly.   " He lived at Jordan."   " Yes, and what was he doing ? "   " Work." " What work was he doing ? "   A long pause, and then, " Perhaps it was carrying boxes for white men."   Yet when he shook his head and said kindly, " You don't know what you are wanting to do, Granny ; you must go back to your teacher and learn," the old woman went into her hut, and stayed there and wept for twenty-four hours, refusing food a kindly neighbour took in to her.   It took so much patience to try to find out what was really in their hearts, and it was so hard to refuse the old ones.   They were the only ones who were baptised without having learnt to read, and they had generally made at least a pathetic attempt.

The Loudon church building was capable of seating (squatted on the floor) more than 3000, for it had been planned with a view to the gatherings for the whole district, not the local Sunday congregations.   Of the former Fraser made rather a special feature.   They gave an opportunity for teaching those who in their village services got little systematic instruction from the local teacher or elder who officiated.   It kindled in the heart of Christians from remote villages a sense of fellowship, and sent them back with a feeling of enthusiasm and inspiration.   Not only did these " unganos " take the place of the old tribal gatherings for war, but they brought their old enemies into their company to sit down together—as one woman put it—" to eat out of the same Chief's basket."

Before the numerous visitors were due to arrive, there was much preparation for their reception on the Station. Many would crowd into their friends' houses in near-by villages ; but great shelters built of logs covered with green branches were erected to house the main crowds. In the villages all over the land the coming guests were equally busy, preparing their food supplies for the days during which they would be away. When they started—for some of the Senga it had to be a week before the date of the gathering—it was in groups, not as stragglers, that they came, carrying with them sleeping-mats, cooking-pots and provisions. As they approached the Mission Station they formed themselves into orderly processions, and, singing their " Songs of Degrees " with which they had beguiled the long journey, came up the avenue to the Mission House to salute and be saluted by their missionary. The sight of the approaching groups always thrilled Donald, and, however busy one might be, his sense of courtesy made him feel we must both be there to greet each ulendo as it came in. There was a great sense of festival about it all. If there was any time in the year when they flaunted clothes that were new and gay and clean it was then. It was impossible to see them without thinking of the Jewish " Feast of Booths," and, in Ngoniland too, there was " joy when they said, ' Let us go up to the House of the Lord ! ' " For some curious reason which we never fathomed, though the church was " Loudon," the school quadrangle was known as " Jerusalem," and many of them *did* gather within its walls, for it provided better shelter for women and children.

Then followed a period of mixed gladness and solemnity, when the speakers addressed great audiences thrice daily. Sunday was the great day of the Feast. The morning service was often so large that it had to be held in the open air, for the local people, heathen as well as Christian, came pouring in for the occasion from all the surrounding villages, and formed a congregation that varied from 5000 to as many as 7000. Standing in the angle formed by two of the church walls, Fraser's voice could reach and be heard distinctly on the outskirts of the crowd. Baptisms often required a special service, they were so numerous : at the first opening of the church there were 311 adults and 118 children. There was no sermon at that service—enough voices had been raised without Fraser's being added !

In the afternoon, the great crowds having dispersed, the Christians gathered very quietly at the Table of the Lord. They were seated so as to leave room for the elders to pass between the rows, and the limited space that was left was reserved for the catechumens. Nine hundred members were present at that first Communion in the newly-opened church, but as the years passed their numbers increased.

But it was not the increasing numbers that moved Fraser, but the growing realisation in the minds of the people of what it all signified. The hush of awe and reverence which came over the congregation as they gathered gave the impression that it meant something very real to those who participated. Not lightly would they come. It might be that someone who had been prominent throughout the week absented himself. Then, though the last thing he wanted was to rouse suspicion, immediately the fear that all was not right with him came to disturb the minds of those who had oversight of the flock. Not that it was necessarily anything serious—it might only be that he had had a quarrel with his wife the day before. But the man who knew of treason in his heart always kept away from the Table.

It took some time for the bare-footed elders to move around among the communicants with the Elements. After a short period someone would very softly begin to sing some hymn about the death of Christ, the others joining in till the murmur of sound had spread throughout the building. Then, when all had been served, there might be a parting message, or just a prayer and the Benediction, and then they would burst out into the Doxology that Donald was always glad to remember had been composed by one of the early women converts in Ngoniland. He had just to say the opening word, "Tiyabonga," for the whole congregation standing to burst out into a great volume of praise, "We thank Thee, Father, because Thou didst send Jesus Christ to be our Saviour." Sometimes it was not enough to sing it once : it burst out again, and, as they dispersed, there were some still singing it as they wended their way home.

It somehow came about—it may have been Fraser's unconscious influence, but it was not of his ordering, he was always glad to think—that the elders who came up to the house to carry down the Communion vessels formed themselves into a reverent procession as they moved slowly down the road, singing as they went. Again, when they entered the church to place them on the Communion table, the congregation rose to their feet. Fraser never sat among his elders at such a time without overwhelming thankfulness, as he looked around and beheld among the worshippers one after another whose presence there thrilled him. Not that he was blind to their faults : he knew and loved them too well for that ; but he remembered their past, and believed in the Power that could shape their future.

Not all Communions were of this type. For a third of the year he would be itinerating, and each week-end he would be holding Communion Services in some centre, with meetings on Saturday and Sunday, all the time between being passed in interviewing candidates. So much had to be attended to personally—the selection of some quiet site for the meetings, the arranging in orderly fashion of the people for the Lord's Supper, the preparing of the Elements, all to be done in such a way as to help them to have that sense of reverence for the Sacrament to which they had been called. That he in some measure succeeded can be gathered from the fact that once, when he thought one corner of the assembled group were a little inattentive, he found that above their heads, on the branch of a tree under which they were sheltering from the sun, was coiled a large snake ; without wishing to disturb the service they had to keep an anxious eye on it in case it suddenly dropped among them. When there were babies as well as adults to be baptised, it was as well if they became a little familiar with him beforehand, otherwise the unexpected sight of a white man towards whom they were being brought created some noisy alarm among the infants concerned.

Perhaps one of the most memorable to him of Eucharistic gatherings took place during the visit to Marambo, when he took his wife to see the Senga people to whom he had been the first to speak of the name of Jesus. Travelling conditions were appalling, but there was no doubt about the welcome in some of the villages where the Christian teachers had been at work. The thrilling climax for him was the week-end at Tembwe's, where a congregation had gathered from a radius of thirty miles around. The school was packed, and those who could not enter crowded about the window spaces, excluding all light. The service was carried through in deep darkness; but as he remembered the unutterable spiritual darkness of four years before, this troubled him not at all. "At the early morning service," he wrote, "with emotion I could scarcely control, I baptised the first-born of this land, receiving into the visible Church nineteen Senga men and women and thirteen of their little ones; and then a few hours afterwards I spread there the Table of the Lord for the first time. We and some of our Ngoni carriers ate and drank in memory of our dear Lord along with these new brothers and sisters, and thus, by the unceasing feast, linked them on to the family of God over all the world and throughout all the ages past."

One could not travel with him without being conscious of how "with a rush the intolerable craving" came upon him to bring these people into the life about which he knew. Of the last Sunday during that ulendo he wrote, "There were 2000 round the Communion table, so still. When it was all over, and I had spoken three times, and the audience was still there quiet and ready, and the heathen men and women looked on like little children, I got up on a chair for one last appeal to them to come into the Kingdom. But I was too tired to get far in my vehemence, and I had to let them separate with a strange melancholy that they would not understand and taste and see. . . . It is all very well to say, 'Take it easy,' but if there is an audience of 1500 waiting in great quiet to hear you . . . you cannot preach listlessly, but have to wear yourself out a bit."

Eagerly, in the early days, he longed for the time when there would be an African pastorate. In preparation for this he had selected the men of outstanding Christian character and appointed them as evangelists, to do what was really the pastoral work, apart from the Sacraments, in the parishes into which he had divided the Loudon district.   This was fitting them for further service, and every year he gave them a month's theological training, until his scheme of evangelists had been adopted elsewhere in the Mission, and an annual Evangelists' Course was started at the Institution at Livingstonia.   It was from their ranks that the pastors were selected.

CHAPTER XXII

WHAT an asset lions are in missionary work! They so seldom capture a missionary, yet so frequently help him to capture the imagination of an audience. And not only a youthful one—for very few people of mature age seem disinclined to listen to a wild beast thrill. In South Africa there was a head master who, according to Donald, " messed up " his meeting in a boys' school by saying, " Now, boys, this is a very solemn occasion and there must be no applause." The speaker charged ahead with native fables, lion stories, etc., till he had the boys thrilled; but " there was no applause from the meek lambs till the rector led it vociferously at the end." He remained chatting on with Fraser till long after the classes were resumed, and began by saying, " Why, I had no idea that a missionary meeting was like this ! It is perfectly unique."

The first time I heard him speak to children was when he addressed the Sunday school of my father's church in Perth, and the following week I saw a report of it in a letter written by one of the small boys who had listened to him. " Sir Donald Fraser Miss Robersons intended told us about his beasts and small natives and lions in Africa. I have a great noshun to be a mishonary myself." Probably he was not the only one with that " noshun." After a great meeting of young people in their various uniforms in the Caird Hall, a Dundee paper expressed the conviction that hundreds of boys must have left that gathering sure that their future sphere of life lay in Central Africa doing missionary work. That was, I think, the occasion when the young Oliver Twists encored the speaker till he had to rise and give them a second supply of the fare he had been dealing out to them. Of course, he did not confine himself, in speaking, to his own experiences, for his fellow missionaries had had more exciting adventures than he. Mr MacMinn, on his lion-infested walk, became known to many an audience, and once the climax came when at the end they were told that he was present, and would rise and " look at them from over his specs."

Fraser had, however, plenty of experiences of his own with wild beasts. It is the man who trudges quietly along the path, not the one who goes surrounded by a noisy gang of carriers, who has the unexpected encounters, and he had only been out in Africa a short time when, travelling alone and unarmed, he suddenly came face to face with a leopard on the narrow path. They stopped dead, and each surveyed the other. Their alarm was apparently mutual, for, after what seemed an unconscionable time, the leopard turned aside and disappeared into the bush. Fraser never again believed in the power of the human eye : that beast was scared, he said, because it was as big a coward as himself ! We had another encounter with a leopard in Marambo. It was just in front of our tent as we were turning in for the night. Before I could hand out the gun from the back of the tent it had disappeared from sight behind the long grass ; but it was not gone, for we could see the waving tops of the grass where it padded to and fro. It was not safe to shoot at such an uncertain mark, for a wounded leopard is very dangerous. On the other hand, it seemed to have no intention of going away, so we shouted to our men, who had put up a stockade at a little distance, and they finally heard us, armed themselves with burning logs from their camp-fires, and then

N

charged for our tent, yelling their war-cry. Before this onslaught the leopard retreated, and the men, scolding their Bwana for the folly of camping apart in a place where wild beasts abounded, moved our tent close to their stockade, with its blazing fires. Later on, on that same journey, the loud roaring of lions apparently very close at hand wakened us one night, and we waited to see what was going to happen next. After some time the roars became more distant, and finally died away. In the morning we discovered that they had been very close, but on the opposite bank of the Luangwa from that on which our tent was pitched. The river was narrow at that part, but fortunately the banks were steep.

There was another night when lions came into the village where Fraser had camped, and walked round his tent so close that he could hear the twigs crunching beneath their feet. He sat on his bed ready to shoot if one tried to enter ; except in that extremity he dared not shoot, with wattle-and-daub huts all around.

Once he deprived a lion of its supper. He was out stalking a waterbuck—so often at the close of a long and fatiguing day he had to hunt to get food for his carriers— and he could not understand the uneasy snorting of the beast, feeling sure it could not have got his wind. At last he fired. As the buck fell, something else between him and it bounded up in the growing dusk and made off. A lion had been stalking the same game as himself !

Snakes, too, he often met. His narrowest shave was once when one got entangled about his leg as he stepped over a fallen trunk. It glided into the bush, however, and the men accompanying him refused to follow, for they said it was the kind they most dreaded—and the kind he most wanted to see !

But there were other dangers, deliberately faced, of

which he never spoke. There were years when he had to use all his influence to obtain permission to go travelling in the Luangwa Valley, at a time when it was closed to all Europeans and Natives from outside districts on account of sleeping sickness. Only on the plea that his work lay within that area did he get a permit to enter, with the concession that he might take one personal attendant with him, a cook who was so devoted to him that his one great worry was lest his master might die and he be left behind. He had once dreamed that they had entered heaven together, and he wished to be at hand when there was any chance of facing risks. Through these tsetse-infested districts Fraser travelled yearly, that he might shepherd the weakest and neediest portion of his flock—those Senga to whom he had first brought the Message. It was not comfortable, travelling with a feeble lot of carriers who knew nothing about putting up a tent or any other ulendo duties, and at such times he was cut off from all communication with Loudon, unless a letter, handed to the police guarding the boundary and delivered by them to the Government official, might eventually be forwarded if his whereabouts were known. He never stood heat well, and invariably returned from these journeys ill—once so ill that for some weeks one wondered anxiously if sleeping sickness was developing.

One of the evangelists who was more thoughtful for him than any other, came to me to see if I would not interfere to prevent his running such risks. We had recently returned from furlough, and while we had been away the Senga had remained unvisited. " I hear, Mama, that our teacher is going to Marambo." I assented. " Mama, it is madness ; even we black people want to travel in Marambo in the cold weather only. Now it is scorchingly hot and waterless. He must not go."

" Daniel," I said, " the schools have had no visit from a white man, and the Christians there have had no Communion Service since he visited them last. He says he *must* go to them before the rainy season." And then, suddenly, Daniel's face glowed with loving admiration. " Ha ! " he exclaimed, throwing back his head with the brave pride of an Ngoni warrior—he had been an outstanding one—" Our master, he has no fear in him " ; and, watching him, one realised that Donald would not have won the same place in their hearts had there been a more cautious saving of his strength.

Only once did he depart with real misgiving. A short time before, he had had to be summoned home hastily on account of our boy's dangerous illness. He was away, we did not know where, except that he was among the Ngoni villages on the Rukuru, and the messenger could only be told to make inquiries as he went along and find him as quickly as possible. He found him sixty miles away. The moment they heard the news his carriers told him to get into his hammock, and they carried him thirty miles without stopping. He left them exhausted by their effort, and, himself fairly fresh, started off to walk the remaining thirty miles, accompanied by the faithful cook, Solomon, who had done the whole journey on foot. How thankful one was, on hearing them creep softly into the house in the middle of the night, to be able to slip downstairs and assure them that there was some improvement. Their arrival was soon followed by that of Dr Berkeley Robertson, who had also done a non-stop journey over the Vipya on getting my message, and who stayed with us till the child's recovery was assured.

It was soon after this incident that he was due to visit the Senga people. Carriers of that tribe were to be awaiting him on the border on a certain day, and Communion gatherings had been arranged. Again illness came to one of the children. He felt anxious and did not like leaving his wife alone, but his arrangements had been made with difficulty, and could not be altered. So on the Thursday he left—with some anxiety, as letters could not be sent to him. By the Sunday the child was much better, but there was no way of letting him know, much as one longed to do so. Some days later he wrote from across the border, telling how on the Sunday evening, while sitting in his tent and wondering how things were going at Loudon, he suddenly saw his wife in the tent. "I just saw you long enough to know that there was nothing to worry about any longer, for you were smiling reassuringly." Several times there seemed to be suggestions of telepathic communication between us, but this was the most striking.

Frequently there must have been accidents that might have been serious when he was rushing about the country on those various bicycles of his—first a push-bike, then a second-hand F.N., and finally his "Triumph," to which was attached a side-car; but of such happenings he did not speak to his wife. Sometimes they were recounted to her by the houseboy who accompanied him, and sometimes they came out accidentally, as when I heard him being vigorously scolded by one of our employees, an elderly man who had worked for Mr M'Callum, one of the early missionaries, and who felt that his age and official position as foreman gave him liberty to take the missionary to task if occasion demanded. M'Callum, he was assuring him, had never done such a thing—and in Africa what your first white master has done always sets the correct standard for successors. "What has he been doing?" I inquired. "*Doing!* Has he not been trying to kill himself?" he protested. "You haven't heard that last week he tried to swim across the river Mzimba when it was swollen, and

was carried away down by the current ? He would have
been drowned if his men had not raced down to the bend
of the river, and holding together made a chain out into
the stream, and caught hold of him and helped him to
shore." " Nonsense, Kambaso," he laughed, " you Africans
exaggerate terribly." But knowing how he refused to be
delayed by obstacles when " making a breenge " for home,
one felt that there might be more in the incident than he
wanted me to guess.

They did their best to look after him, these folks among
whom he lived. If they were thoughtless, clamorous and
unreasonable in the thousand and one demands they made
on his time and energy, it was because they did not realise
the strain they were putting on him. When they came to
understand it, they could be unselfish and considerate.
Our friend Daniel was one who saw it more than most,
and more than once interposed to lessen the burden. In
the office one day, when Donald had been having a conference with his evangelists, each of whom had charge of
a district, he came to the question of his own visits. Immediately everyone was thrusting forward the manifold
needs of his own parish where, perhaps, attendances were
going down, or fees not being paid, or drinking had
revived, or some school was needing repairs which the
villagers were unwilling to do. Suddenly Daniel spoke up :
" Brothers, when a man has a good axe, he does not ruin
its edge by using it up, hacking at everything that comes in
his road. Any old axe will do for that. The good one
he keeps for the building of his house. If our teacher can
come to our districts for the local Communion Services, let
us try to attend to the other things ourselves." Looking
rather ashamed, they agreed.

At another time I felt most profoundly grateful for his
intervention. My husband had just informed me that he

would not be able to accompany the family and me when we went to our little hill-house for a fortnight's holiday, when the heat on the Station became very trying before the rains broke. His reason was that it proved to be the only feasible time for the evangelists' annual Bible School, to which they looked forward greatly. Knowing how much he needed the change, I asked if it could not be dropped for once, but he refused to disappoint them. After all, it was the only opportunity they had in the year of acquiring new knowledge.

Next morning Daniel stopped me on the road to tell me that he did not think Mr Fraser was looking at all well. " He isn't," I agreed, " and he'll be worse before long, for you know how the heat tries him, and yet he is going to carry on without any holiday because of your Evangelists' School, Daniel." " I see," said Daniel thoughtfully, and walked away. A day or two later Donald remarked, " I'll be able to come with you to Champira, after all." " How are you managing it ? " " Well, when I arranged that school with the evangelists, they seemed quite eager about it, but now several of them have found out that it is not a very convenient time, and so many want to drop out that it is not worth while, the others say, to go on with it." He was evidently just a little disappointed about the lack of keenness displayed. I immediately conjured up in my mind the picture of Daniel going round browbeating those men to give up that on which they were so set, and making them do it in such a way that, instead of showing how unselfish they were, they fell under the suspicion of being slack. But it was only at the end of his holiday that I dared divulge the true interpretation of the incident.

CHAPTER XXIII

Soon after his arrival in the country Fraser was out with a band of teachers superintending the manual labour that was part of their day's work. They were hoeing a road and approaching the grave of Dr Steele—one of the earliest missionaries to the Ngoni. Dr Elmslie and Mr Stuart had been telling their newly-arrived colleague of the superstitious horror with which the Ngoni regarded a grave; so, taking a hoe, Fraser went forward and began to clean the ground himself. By and by the teachers approached, very silent. Presently they began to converse in whispers. Fraser continued his work, occasionally making a remark about Dr Steele, who had won a great place in the hearts of the people in the short time he had lived among them. At last a teacher approached and inquired, " Do you want to do this alone ? " " No, if you like you may clean up too ; Steele would be glad to know that the teachers love him still." In a few minutes as many as could were down on their knees silently removing the weeds, and cleaning down the encircling bricks. When they had finished he suggested that they should pray together, and beside the little mound they knelt, two of them asking God to teach them, too, to live and die for others. Then quietly, without noise or laughing, they finished their work and went away.

It was in this way, not by argument or scorn, but by silently encouraging them to overcome their fears, that he began the long campaign against superstition. He hated its hold, for he saw in all its stark reality the suffering and

190

cruelty and terror to which it gave rise. It took long to uproot its power. Even those who began to doubt the truth of their old beliefs hesitated about publicly disowning them, because of their effectiveness in preventing crime. " Even if it isn't true that a woman's dying in childbirth is the result of unfaithfulness, don't let the women know : it keeps them from adultery," was an example of the attitude many of them wanted to adopt : they were afraid of this liberty with which Christ would set them free. It may have been that in the recesses of their minds there still lurked some fear of the consequences magically affecting them, rather than of the immorality of such an action on their wives' part.

One remembers with what misgiving in the elders' minds the admission to the Church of one elderly man was agreed to. He was an " mfwiti " (wizard) who had been turned out of three villages because death had come on each occasion soon after his taking up his abode. Now he lived in a little hamlet alone with his Christian sons, because no one else would receive him. That was all they could urge against him. That, said their missionary, could not shut the door of Christ's Church against him, and he always had a welcome for the " wizard " when he turned up with his little grandchildren, who sat on either side of him in church.

Yet he was patient with these lingering fears, so difficult to eradicate. At one time witch-doctors were very active, magically " protecting " the people against death, if well paid, but making those who could not or would not pay their price convinced that death would come to them within the year. An old headman grumbled to Fraser about the way they were taking all the goats and cattle from the village. " You should refuse ; do you believe God has put life and death into their hands ? " " No, no ! " protested the old man, " they are frauds, as you say." " Then, why, as a headman, do you not beat them and turn them out?   That would stop their practice of magic."   "And die myself in consequence?" protested the unbeliever! Then a thought struck him.   "Framo," he said, "*you* beat them and make them afraid to go on with their practice." "No, that is not my business, but yours.   Besides, it would not do any good.   Everyone knows that we white people are not afraid of them, and they will only say that their magic has no effect on us.   One of you Africans must show that he has no fear of them : then the people will lose their terror."

Two sons of the old man were Mission teachers, and they agreed that they would be willing to act for their father.   While Fraser was still in the village the witch-doctors' ulendo was seen coming along the valley towards it.   As they approached, they were caught ; a trial was held, and they were sentenced to be beaten for compelling people to part with their possessions.   They were given a lash or two, and then Donald intervened, for it was the elimination of fear in their victims that he wanted, rather than the punishment of the men.   "That's enough.   Let them go."   "Run," said the Christian teachers.   There was no need to repeat the injunction, for the men, thoroughly scared by the contemptuous indifference of these big brawny fellows, fled.   This exhibition of fear removed the last trace of it from their prospective victims, who pursued them with shouts and yells.   There was no further intimidation of the people in that neighbourhood.

It was always in times of sickness, trouble or calamity that the witch-doctors had their innings, for well they knew how to play on the fears and misgivings and credulity of the people.   Donald had watched their methods.   Coming into a village unexpectedly he once found a witch-doctor just about to start the cure of a woman patient ; and, seeing their alarm, he assured them that he was not going to interfere with the cure they had called the doctor to effect, but that he would like to watch. He has described that scene in his *Idylls*. On another occasion, when we were reproducing scenes of the past on the Mission Station for the benefit of a cinema camera, a witch-doctor was allowed to come and give a sample of his practices. It gave us the opportunity of observing the hypnotic effect of the drums on some women in the crowd of interested onlookers; seeing the hysteric twitchings of their bodies, we realised the necessity for stopping the drums abruptly.

The witch-doctors knew that there was no personal antagonism to them in the missionary's mind—only to their profession. One used to turn up unostentatiously at our back door for treatment, for he feared the smiles it would produce if he appeared in the hospital waiting-room, unable to cure himself! Coming back from the Lake shore I once met another witch-doctor with a considerable following carrying his drums, etc. He gave me a friendly greeting, and, when I asked his destination, " To the Atonga," he replied : " has not Frasara turned me out of Ngoniland ? " But he smiled, and spoke of him as one who had worsted him in a fair fight, for to a fight it had come at last, in an effort to save a psychopathic people from a recrudescence of superstitious fears. This happened in 1919. The people had seen the effects of war in the terrible mortality among their men on transport service, many never returning, others finding their way home only to die of dysentery and other diseases they had contracted. Then, after a season of famine, came a new enemy—influenza. It left the effects of its poison in weakened bodies and minds. Depression and fear were the soil out of which the witch-doctors could reap a harvest. Their power and practices had been suppressed by growing enlightenment and British rule ; now their drums began again, and with them the " smelling out " of culprits and the poison ordeal. The Boma was keen to put it all down, but what could they do when people feared to bring an accusation against these men, and witnesses refused to speak ?

The magistrate knew well the danger of this outbreak—apart from the risk of allowing defiance of the law to run unchecked—and when Fraser propounded his scheme he gladly agreed to it.   The statutes in the Government Gazette against witch-doctoring were translated into Tumbuka, and a hundred copies sent to the teachers with instructions to read them to all headmen and chiefs, emphasising not only the long terms of imprisonment for the culprits, but especially the penalties imposed on all who harboured them.   Another notice accompanied these, announcing that a period of grace had been allowed, and there would be forgiveness for those who renounced their unlawful calling before a certain date.   At Loudon, after the neighbouring chiefs had been called in, a sermon was preached on witchcraft, giving a survey beginning with the Hebraic law against it, and ending with the determination of the British Government to suppress it.   And again the period of grace was intimated.   What would happen after that expired, Fraser omitted to expound, for the excellent reason that he and the magistrate were equally vague about what could be done if the game of bluff failed.   I can well remember the afternoon when I heard him exclaim, " Hullo ! Look here, Agnes : I believe here's the first ! "   Slipping out of the house on to the veranda, I stood and watched with him the procession that came towards the house in the gathering dusk—a witch-doctor and his followers. With impressive solemnity Donald received them, reading over again the Government regulations, accepted all the paraphernalia of their craft and the assurance that they renounced their calling, and then, congratulating them that they had escaped the penalties imposed, sent them on to reiterate their vows at the Government Station. This was the first of many weird ulendos wending their way to our Station for the same purpose. He grew strangely familiar with the various items that went to complete the outfit of a witch-doctor, and, if they tried to keep back any of their stage properties, let them see that he could not be hoodwinked.

Many a time during that week did we enter the church to see the ever-growing pile of implements heaped on the platform. By the 8th of May one hundred and fifty-two registrations had been made, and in the square outside Loudon church a cheerful crowd, including children, heaped on a big bonfire the accoutrements of the vanquished.

A friend in Scotland writes how he overcame the lingering superstition in her mind. He had been staying with her, and a party of guests had been invited to supper to meet him. While he was out driving with her sister in the afternoon, one of those invited rang up to ask permission to bring an extra guest. The hospitable lady found herself obliged to say " No ! " because it would mean thirteen at table. When Dr Fraser and her sister returned, they found her rather perturbed over the incident. " Do you really believe in that ? " Dr Fraser asked. " Well, no, I can't honestly say I do, and yet death has always invaded our home immediately after we have had thirteen." He smiled and remarked : " Apparently my address last night was the very thing wanted " (he had been speaking on superstition). His hostess assured him it had fallen on stony soil in her case, and had not borne fruit. He grew graver, refused to believe that, and went on to tell how delightful was the lady whom she had refused to accept as guest. " No doubt," she admitted ; " I did feel an awful beast ; but I simply can't have thirteen. The last meal we had with A. (a sister who had died) we were thirteen, and M. (the other sister) might just go next."

" M. *is* going now, but it's to fetch Mrs ——. That's where she's going. Come," he pleaded smilingly, as she began to protest, " I can see you are very unhappy and upset about it, and I want to see you happy. I think we'll have Mrs —— ? "

She was fetched and came, and her hostess admitted the relief and happiness her decision brought her, and a gay and cheerful evening was spent; but it was only his " marvellous persuasive powers " that could have brought it about.

CHAPTER XXIV

WOMEN'S WORK

In May 1909 Fraser was hurrying down to the Lake shore to meet Miss Brown, our first worker for women and girls. It was a need that had long occupied his mind, for he had always keenly recognised the importance of the influence of women in the community and the difficulty of getting at them through the ordinary means of working. What was possible had been done, and at the Convention of the previous year there had been special meetings for them. One of his first problems when in the early years of his life he had begun to think about religion, had been why women should require the conversion whose necessity he recognised in the case of men. It was symptomatic of the reverence of his attitude towards womanhood, and, just because of it, he was the more keen that the degradation that so appalled him in Africa should be overcome, and a fight put up for the Christian ideal.

That there were fine Christian characters among the women, the older ones especially, which showed their capacity for Christ, only made it the more urgent that the rich latent contribution which they could make towards the indigenous Church should not be lost. For one of these old ladies—he wrote a sketch of her under the title " African Saint "—he had a great regard, and however busy he might be at a Communion season, preparing for the overwhelming crowds due to arrive and all the services to be held, he never forgot to ask where Gwazi was to be housed, and there was always a great welcome for the old lady who had once swum a flooded river in order to be present. A Government man was with us on one occasion when Gwazi approached, and the few words of appreciation of her real saintliness that Donald had time to say were sufficient to make the young fellow take off his hat reverently when she began to bless him.

Miss Brown, therefore, got a warm welcome, though her coming implied the going of Miss Irvine, and more school work devolving on him. A house was put in good repair for her, and girl boarders' quarters added, and she lacked no encouragement to go ahead with a women's school. He did his best, bringing her over the hills, to provide the excitement of wild beasts and snakes after which a new missionary always hankers, but she was always ahead when anything startling occurred, and he did not feel he could prolong a fight, which arose between the men and some drunken villagers who attacked them, till she could be recalled!

Recognising the amount of heavy manual labour that falls to African women and makes it harder for them to have time and energy for learning, he often spoke to the men about giving them more help. One such scene remains a vivid memory. In the early morning he had found naked shivering children trying to learn in a half-built school, and had summoned the headman and villagers. They sat in a circle, and he spoke sternly, reminding them that he had sent them a teacher on the promise that a school would be erected. Now, six months afterwards, here it was, unroofed and unplastered. What did it mean? The headman had a handy excuse: it was all due to the laziness of the women; they were too lazy to tramp mud into plaster, too lazy to bring in bundles of grass for thatching. . . . He was interrupted by Donald, and given an eloquent account of the women carrying water and firewood, pound-

ing, cooking, sweeping, out hunting for relish of various
kinds, "while you men! what do *you* do? wear clothes
while they go naked; sit in the village and snuff while
they do the work!" In the background beaming, grateful women looked at one another and nodded their heads.
The men had wanted to turn the blame on them, and here
was the white man sticking up for them. Two days later
we were passing at some distance from that village when a
carrier said, "They are shouting; they want you to wait."
A patient, we thought; but, instead, there appeared a
string of women each carrying a basket. As a token of
gratitude they had brought between forty and fifty pounds'
weight of a native fruit they had seen him enjoying in their
village!

One article that sold faster than it could be produced by
the two carpenter lads working at it, was a simple form
of sieve he had constructed, to save the labour of the
winnowing movement of the baskets in which the women
separated the husk from the flour. It was one of the few
innovations that met with immediate success.

The thought of the women had been uppermost in his
mind when he advised me to leave the Ngoni language
alone and learn Tumbuka, in spite of the indignation of a
chief who said it was a slave's language, unfit for a white
woman. At that time Tumbuka was never used on public
occasions, and all the religious services and teaching were
in Ngoni, the other being what might be termed the
"domestic" as opposed to the "State" language, and used
mainly by the wives and slaves gathered into the tribe. But
with it he felt I could make more intimate contact with the
women, and, as the years passed, it more and more sup-
planted its aristocratic rival. This courtesy to women,
and the affection he showed to their children, gave him an
influence over them that sometimes surprised him. In one

o

village he found preparations for a beer-feast going forward ;
the women were all busy over their great brewing-pots.
" What are you doing ? " he asked. " Brewing beer," was
the reply. " You are brewing more than beer, you women,"
he told them. " You are brewing trouble for yourselves,
hunger and risk of accidents for your little ones. You
know how they cry neglected, or fall into the fire, when
you are all drunk. You are brewing quarrels—perhaps
fights that may end in the breaking up of your village.
You know of these things. You have seen them happen.
Yet you go on making the beer that is responsible. If
you were wise, you would turn it all out." As he left
the village an hour or two later, and passed the place,
he inquired in surprise where the beer-pots were. They
pointed to them turned upside-down—more than a hundred
gallons of beer had been emptied on the ground.

One has many memories of his cheery way with them.
There was one tropically wet Sunday, for instance, when
only those from the immediate vicinity had turned up for
the service, and had been gathered in a group close to
the platform. A half-witted woman sitting just beneath
Donald punctuated his sermon with frequent very loud
and prolonged yawns. It would have been disconcerting
or annoying for most speakers. Donald ignored it for a
time ; finally he stopped and remarked to her with a smile,
" Granny, I am very sorry to be boring you so badly, but
I shan't be much longer." The rest of the congregation
laughed aloud at this apology, the old lady with equal
politeness disclaimed any lack of interest, and they all
settled down again in great good spirits to listen once
more.

It was not a case of his having any illusions about the
women. If he preached to them on Sunday, he employed
many of them during the week, and he knew just how

aggravating they could be, dawdling over their work, scamping when they could, trying his patience more than did the men. But they counted; they had to be won; and he would gladly have seen far more white women helping them towards Christian ideals. He impressed his views on his native leaders. They had at first protested their satisfaction so long as the women did not drink or attend bad dances, but were diligent and looked after their children and their cooking. Their standards were raised less by what he said than by what he did. They as men were ashamed to show any sign of affection for their wives, whatever they felt. The Mzungu once, when parting from his wife for some time, had kissed her in a village, creating a sensation which set him furiously blushing! They knew he shared his thoughts and plans with his wife, and was as willing to help forward her work as she his. In this, too, they learned to imitate him, till the time came when he was not the only man who was proud of his wife and inclined to boast about what she could do.

The intuition of the best of the women made them appreciate his attitude towards them. When I asked one of them one day about a case of discipline in which I was interested, she replied, " She has confessed it all to us women; we will try to help her. But we are very grateful that Frasara says the men (of the Session) need not hear all the story. He has chosen many good ways for us women." When he was in South Africa, each Sunday the Christian women had to hear any news of him that had come, and they always prayed for his work. " He's back; he's back! " this same woman elder came rushing to tell me when the distant sound of his bicycle had been heard; " and oh! Mama, my heart was welcoming him long before my ears caught the sound of his coming."

Well might they feel like that! Not only did he recognise their need and possibilities, and plan for their proper place in the community, but he took infinite trouble on their behalf.

They may have had only a faint glimmering of all he hoped and strove for in regard to them, but one thing was unmistakably evident : they were not to him a " problem," but people for whom he would do a great deal. A trip to South Africa, when he set off, leaving his wife behind, but taking under his wing a dozen Native women and children, had been ample proof of it. It happened thus. One of the facts that used to distress him was the frequency with which so many men of the district went off to work in various parts of the Union, and remained away long beyond the period they at first intended. Often it was because they found there positions offering far better opportunities of work or pay than were possible nearer home ; sometimes they were urged to stay by employers so satisfied with their work that they did not wish to lose them. Others remained because there were attractions, not always good for them, that they did not find among their own more primitive people. Economic conditions, the demand in the south for work and the absence of it locally, made such a state of affairs inevitable ; but it was not good, either socially or morally, for their wives and children at home, apart from the temptations to the men themselves, who were sometimes urged by thoughtless employers to take a local wife and settle down in their new surroundings. It was part of the Mission work to keep in touch with such men, and to receive and keep for them, or pay out for the benefit of their families, such money as they sent home ; and some remitted it regularly. But this did not remove the moral peril. Every now and then Fraser would write one or another, urging him to return ;

he had been away long enough for all concerned. Sometimes his words had the desired effect; often they wrote that their masters did not consent; they were making good where they were, and would be very glad if their wives could join them. Masters, appealed to, said the same thing, and sometimes added that they would be glad to pay the wife's passage down country rather than lose the services of the husband. But it was impossible for any unsophisticated woman to undertake such a complicated journey. Now came this chance, offered by his proposed South African mission, of letting certain women rejoin their husbands under the protection of his escort, and much correspondence had been going on to ensure that a husband and a welcome would be awaiting them.

It meant three weeks of looking after their needs, in addition to the responsibilities of the journey. The second day after setting out from Loudon, when they should have crossed the mountainous country between that place and the Lake, it dawned cold and wet, and, knowing the danger to the African on those chilly, mist-swept heights at such a season—it was during the rains—Fraser dared not risk it with the women and children, and had to put in a day in camp. Fortunately it was bright next morning, and the journey was safely accomplished. The Government steamer took them down the Lake. On it he found two of our own women missionaries going home, and his arrival on board cheered them up, for they had been feeling a lack of courtesy on a boat that only carried passengers as a favour. A lonely little girl, too, travelling with a father who was too busy playing bridge to pay her much attention, attracted his sympathy, and he told her stories, showed her how to draw, and diverted her through the next few days. At Fort Johnston he had to arrange for the safe transport of the Native women to Blantyre, and eight days later see

them on board the train there, and subsequently on the
steamer to which they were transferred to cross the
Zambezi. A short time later they were at Beira in Portuguese territory, and a safe refuge for the night had to be
found for them there.

The following evening they started on the last stage of
their journey to Southern Rhodesia—but what a journey it
was ! At midnight, part of the train still on an embank-
ment, the engine, happily across, jumped the points and
straddled across the line. For twelve hours they stuck
there, devoured by mosquitoes, while a breakdown gang
relaid the twisted rails and jacked up the engine to get
her back on the lines. Six hours later there was a wash-
away, caused by the heavy rains ahead, at the other end
of which another train was waiting. At last it passed
them, and they moved on, only to find that it had torn
out the lines that had just been laid. The breakdown gang
who had already been working without intermission for
thirty-two hours, set wearily to work once more, and at
last they passed warily, on sagging lines, over pieces of
the permanent way that were a terror, the engine leaning
over at most dangerous angles, and once lurching so that
it seemed it must go right over. Then came another
wash-away : they were now thirty-seven hours late, and had
not yet reached the Portuguese border. Fortunately his
Native charges, who were having their first taste of civilised
travel, were not unduly alarmed, trusting implicitly as
they did in their Bwana, who was coming along to their
carriage from time to time to say some encouraging words.
Fifty-two hours after they were due, they reached Salisbury,
and here he began to shed some of his responsibilities.
European friends were there to greet him, but the person
he was most glad to see was the husband of one of the
women, who had a great welcome for his wife and child

and some of the other women. From that point onward he was dropping the others from time to time, alighting to seize what little chance there was to make arrangements of any kind. Two of the women had to transfer to a side line : he was just able to accost a boy who looked like a Tonga, and ask him to see them on board. The man promised ; he knew about their husbands farther down the line, and could reassure their rather anxious protector that they were expecting the travellers. At last only one was left. She had to be dropped at a siding some time during the night, and the train, now making up for lost days, nearly left him behind. He had alighted the minute it stopped and run forward to the carriage for Native passengers, but the train started before he reached it, and he had to swing himself aboard. It worried him, for he saw there was no one there to meet the woman ; he felt alarmed till, a few hundred yards ahead, he noticed a Native Location, and knew that there would be Ngoni there to befriend her. Later on, from one or other of the Nyasaland boys who came to greet him during his time in the south, he learned that all his charges had arrived without mishap. "And the whole thing," he wrote triumphantly, "didn't leave me more than £10 out of pocket."

CHAPTER XXV

AFRICAN PENTECOST

DONALD had been in touch with the Keswick leaders about a delegate who should visit Africa, and it was decided that Mr Inwood should come to Nyasaland in 1910 in time to be present at the United Missionary Conference at Mvera, and then go north to the stations of the Livingstonia Mission. He therefore arranged that the great annual gathering at Loudon should be held after his return from Mvera with the speaker. Meantime he let the people know that this year they were to have a deputy from home, and asked that there should be much prayer in preparation for the Convention. A month or two before it met there were many little daily meetings for that purpose held all over the district, and it was in a spirit of great expectation that the people gathered. Fraser had meantime set off on a rather unfortunate journey to the central Dutch Reformed Mission Station. His cycle broke down hopelessly, and after many attempts at repairing it, he was forced to abandon it and walk on to Kasungu, arriving in a state of great exhaustion. He had missed his loadmen sent on the previous day with instructions to meet him, and had therefore gone without food or drink, and his mouth and throat were in such a condition by the time he reached Mvera that all through the Conference it was with the greatest difficulty that he could eat anything. Knowing the hard work entailed in catering for so large a company, it was like him to refrain from asking for such light diet as he could have taken without discomfort. He was therefore feeling far from fit, and unable to enjoy, as he should have done, the meeting with so many friends, for his earlier student work in the Cape had brought him into touch with many now in the Dutch Reformed mission field.

His own Station, he was embarrassed to find, had acquired what he considered an unjustified reputation, and during discussions such inquiries as " What do you do at Loudon ? How are such questions dealt with there ? " made him apologetically anxious to prove that it was nothing to boast of, till he was taken in hand by his good friend, Miss Beck of Blantyre, by whom the evil of his pessimistic attitude was pointed out to him.

At the close of the Conference quite a party travelled north through Loudon. Besides several of the Livingstonia and one of the L.M.S. men, who only stayed a night *en route*, there came as guests for the Convention not only the speaker, but also Dr Chisholm of Mwenzo and the Faithfulls from Port Herald, who had had the assistance of some of our teachers in their work there. The Louws, a couple from Mashonaland, were to arrive next day, but, after most of the party had been stowed away in some corner or other, and only one or two of the men were still chatting over their pipes, an exhausted pair of travellers came in. They had lost sight of their loadmen with tent and food-baskets, and there was nothing for it but to keep on till they reached the Station. Mr Inwood was left undisturbed, but everyone else had to take part in the " General Post " that ensued. The Faithfulls were aroused by a knock at their bedroom door, followed by the pushing in of fresh sheets when they opened it, with the request that they would make up their bed for the new arrivals, and the intimation that they themselves would be provided for later. Meantime Dr Chisholm and his host were busy in the kitchen, one trying to blow up the fire and get the kettle to boil, while the other foraged for food.   Finally, when the latest tired arrivals had been sent off to sleep in the bed which the others had vacated, ways and means were devised whereby everyone had some sort of a couch.   This kind of scramble was the way in which intimacy and friendship between the Europeans were fostered.

The gatherings began.   Mr Inwood had urged that his host rather than a Native should act as interpreter.   Always it was an anxious time for their missionary lest this great annual opportunity should be wasted and the people go away without new help and inspiration.   Interpretation seldom helps to deepen the impression, and for a day or two it seemed as if less, rather than more, was being made. Fraser felt, too, that no outsider understood just how to put things as he who had lived among them could.   By Friday he was conscious that those who had come with a great thirst and expectation were not getting what they had looked for, and now only two more days remained.   That afternoon he asked his European guests to gather for prayer that even yet the great hopes with which they had met should be fulfilled.   On the Saturday morning the church was crowded once more, and the service went on.   Personally the thing I was most conscious of was the intensity of my husband's longing.   At the end of an address on the Holy Spirit those who wished to receive that Spirit were asked to stand.   Perhaps there was some confusion in their minds as to what was asked of them.   There was a pause, and only a few seemed to be standing.   Then suddenly a wave appeared to pass over the packed congregation, a murmur of voices, then a rising volume of sound filled the place. Into one's mind instinctively came the phrase " a mighty rushing wind," and no sooner had the phenomenon been so described than it became clear what made that sound. It was 2500 people, each praying individually, apparently quite unconscious of any other. Presently one or two began to get excited, but Fraser was already down among them, passing from one to the other, laying a calming hand upon them and getting them to sit down quietly. It had all come suddenly and overwhelmingly upon people who had never before gone through any such kind of religious excitement, their teaching having been all along on the lines of Scottish Presbyterianism. Each had now found a tongue with which to utter this revelation that had come to him. To their missionary moving among them it seemed that for some it had come as a new sense of need and unworthiness; for others it was the voice of worship and praise. Fearing what the tense emotionalism of it might break into, he started a hymn. Everyone joined in, and though at first there were numerous hymns being sung, they finally blended into one. Then after the Benediction an awed crowd dispersed.

Thrilled by the emotion of it all, a little group of us stood outside one of the doors waiting for Donald to come along. When he came, he caught Dr Chisholm's shoulder and said, " Chisholm, you are a level-headed chap and a doctor. Tell me what you feel about this?" "I can only say, 'I believe in the Holy Ghost,'" was the reply, and Donald's last fear that he might be reading too much into the scene he had witnessed was dispelled. The wonder and thrill of it lasted through the remainder of the day and the Sunday that followed, and on into the weeks ahead as we travelled among the villages. That Saturday afternoon he decided that the men and women should meet separately, for fear lest the excitement become too great. The women's meeting was held in the open quadrangle of the school, and was one continuous volume of prayer, sometimes with one, sometimes with several on their feet at once, girls as well as women, but always with a strange unconsciousness of any other. Every now and then there was a verse of a hymn in which all joined, and then again the interrupted prayers were resumed without a break, among them scores from those who had never, one imagined, done more than listen as worshippers before. The elders and leaders of the Church were filled with gladness. It transpired that the movement had started with them on the Friday evening : at the same time as we Europeans, they had been meeting too, and there had been confessions and reconciliations among those who had been harbouring grudges and little animosities against one another, till a great sense of love and brotherhood had been experienced. They were warned against the danger of allowing physical expressions of emotion to arise, and these were quietly stopped when any signs of them were noticed ; but again on the Sunday there was the same spontaneous outbreak of prayer. What struck us almost more than anything was to see our cook, present on the Sunday morning for the first time—for the white visitors had entailed a heavy week of kitchen work for him—standing praying with a face that would have served as a model for Stephen's, so transfigured did it seem. The Church knew now what Pentecost meant ; but Fraser was far too wise a man to encourage them to look for such manifestations again, knowing how much easier it was to reproduce the outward signs than the spiritual movement which had brought it into being.

He had a talk about it with the Church leaders, and urged on them that not this outward expression, but the fruits of the Spirit in the lives of the Church members, were the only sure proof of its reality. And just as at the Convention of the previous year they had estimated the impression made upon the people by the new honesty with which little things lost during that week had been picked up and handed to the evangelists for identification by their owners, so in the weeks and months ahead, there were signs that showed how truly God had come among the people.

In the years that immediately followed, knowing how easily the repetition of these scenes might unconsciously be re-enacted by those who had once witnessed them, he was very careful to avoid anything that might lead to their revival. They had had what perhaps was necessary for a new-born Church—a visible demonstration of a great spiritual reality ; thereafter it should be manifested by its power to change the lives and characters of men. Meantime there was a great awe over the land, for the news of this thing that had happened had spread far and wide. Among the crowds that gathered on the Sunday morning at the great open-air service some of the heathen kept carefully aloof in the background, fearful lest this that had come upon the Christians should invade them also.

CHAPTER XXVI

BEFORE this term closed Mr Cullen Young had joined him as his colleague at Loudon, and so in 1912 Fraser was able to leave, with the knowledge that someone who knew the people and the work was there to carry on in his absence. Throwing off all responsibility, he was able to devote himself to our two older children, from whom we were to part when this furlough came to an end, and did his best to make the journey a long, happy picnic for them. It was for him an engrossing study to watch their reactions to civilised life, of which they knew as little as any Native, except in so far as they had met it in their own home. Their first night at the Boma had brought them the astonishment of being on a station where there was (then) neither hospital, dispensary, school, workshop nor church—" nothing but a prison and a courthouse." Our polite little daughter had not wished to hurt her host's feelings by reflecting on his efforts compared with Daddy's, so she had politely remarked, " After all, we have no prison at Loudon, and yours is a very nice one " : but the magistrate had realised that what struck our children might also strike the people he governed, and started discussing the question that evening.

The morning after we arrived at Zomba the family was missing when time for breakfast came. Eventually their Daddy found them in the house of a perfect stranger, whom they had accosted in her own sitting-room with the inquiry, " Have you any little children that we could play with ? " Next day their father, riding on his cycle behind the rickshaw in which the children were, discovered that the friendly look that impressed him on the faces of all

London
Ngara
26 Oct. 13

Darling Violet and George,

I have been fearfully busy this week, and have not had time to write you, but I must at least send you a short note. We have a great crowd of teachers at the teachers school: a lot of your old friends are there, and Mrs. Irvin & I are with them all day teaching

Mammy too has begun to give them lectures telling them how to keep well. But she does not allow me to hear so I hide behind the door & listen

FACSIMILE OF ONE OF DR FRASER'S LETTERS
TO HIS CHILDREN

whom he passed was the result of shouts and waves from the two little travellers ahead. Before evening a cloud darkened their happiness, and he came up to find the men trying to comfort a sobbing child. She had waved to a little girl and had been met by a cold stare in response. " Did she think we didn't look nice ? " But at Blantyre there was again friendliness everywhere, even the train waiting by special request of a small boy, who dashed down the road and asked the engine-driver not to take it away till his sister had arrived to see it. A day or two later they boarded it themselves, and Daddy showed them how we made tea with water from the waste-pipe of the engine when the train stopped. Then came the specially interesting bit, going down the Shiré and Zambezi on the steamer, with the barges carrying native passengers alongside, and white men potting at crocodiles whenever they caught sight of them on the sandbanks. At Durban, while their parents were buying a toy for the youngest, the others, reared in a spirit of African communism, had helped themselves to a pram and wheelbarrow standing at the door of the shop, and were already far down the street with their spoils before their father started in pursuit of them. When at last we landed in England we travelled up to London with three more than our own children in the compartment : Donald had taken them off the hands of a harassed father who was trying to look after luggage and them simultaneously. During that ride every truck of coal and haystack provided a fresh thrill, and it was, for them, perhaps the most exciting part of the whole journey. They dashed from side to side so as not to miss a single sight, and the haystacks solved for them the problem of " where the Natives lived."

Thanks to their father's stories about his hero, Livingstone, the first place to which they wanted to go in London was his tomb in Westminster Abbey. It was when we left this spot that we realised that we were almost as primitive as the children. We took them to the nearest Underground Station, and, with that African feeling that the start takes place when one is ready, deliberately chose our compartment. I entered with the youngest child ; then Donald got in and turned round to help the other two to enter. As he did so the door shut in his face and the train went off, leaving the small couple stranded on the platform. This was the sort of salutary lesson we had to learn every time we came home—that we had to accommodate ourselves to conditions and become nobodies again, and put up with such indignities as being jostled on the pavement, instead of having everyone step aside as we approached !

It was good to reach home in summer time and go almost immediately to a gathering of the Fraser family at Ardrishaig. This had been suggested by Donald, who had few opportunities of seeing his scattered brothers and sisters, and his sister Violet had arranged it. Here with their families came his two sisters—one over from Canada ; his brother John, so like him in appearance that Donald once tried to shake hands with himself in a mirror outside a Glasgow shop, under the impression that he had come face to face with his brother ; and also his youngest brother, on leave from India. Mrs Lochhead, his mother's only sister, was still alive and was there too, pleased to be surrounded by so many relations, even if we did let the children run about barefoot ! There were bathing and boating parties in plenty, and picnics to the Robbers' Den or across the Loch. An old student friend, Miss Ruth Rouse, came to stay with us, and in the evenings over the fire there were talks about the old student days, while Donald smoked a pipe, and tried hard to get over his shyness to the extent of calling his visitor by her Christian name !

He was to go to a Student Movement camp in September

—a prospect always alarming in anticipation till, as usual, he found on arrival that they " seemed glad to see him." Perhaps there had only been one occasion when his coming was awaited by a leader with a little apprehension. It was in 1900, when Frank Lenwood[1] was chairman and had introduced into the Movement some mild Old Testament criticism. There was some misgiving about it, and every now and then he was told, " All this sort of thing we never heard about in Donald Fraser's time, and there was power then." Lenwood had never met Donald, and felt that he was being held over him as a sort of bogey ; so when he heard he was coming home he had to ask himself if he was prepared to stick to his guns, which, believing it was the leading of God, he resolved to do, bracing himself for the conflict. Donald turned up, and beamed about upon everybody. Lenwood decided that he liked him very much ; but it was the end of the Conference before they had a private talk, and then it was something to this effect : " Look here, Lenwood, some of us abroad have been praying that the Student Movement might broaden out in just this way, but we never thought it possible, and now that we see it, we can only thank God." " You can guess," writes Mr Lenwood, " what it meant to me. It was one of the great gifts of my early life, and I've never forgotten it. He has always been like that to me ever since."

Donald was never afraid of new light after that very first little conference he ever attended at Bonskeid at the end of the 'eighties, when one of the Oxford men read a paper that startled him a little. He turned to J. H. Maclean as a senior student, expecting him to answer it ; but when Maclean told him he accepted the views expressed, he said no more, too humble to do other than be willing to learn.

[1] Then at Oxford; later, missionary at Benares and secretary of the L.M.S.; killed on the Alps, September 1934.

P

This 1912 Conference was one for the officers of the Movement and a few ex-leaders. Donald sat silently listening to all that was said on such subjects as the need for a new evangelistic approach, for interpreting the Gospel and the Movement in terms of their own nationality, for a re-statement of the doctrine of the Spirit. He did not speak unless appealed to. He had a way of waiting to see if some other would not express what he felt needed to be said. They discussed the lack of volunteers and criticised the Watchword. What struck him was their indefiniteness about everything. They must have had some feeling that he could help, for they changed the programme and told him he could have the whole Saturday evening, after Miss Rouse had spoken, to say what he liked. He shrank from it, not knowing how he could say it; but he longed to get them out of that helpless haze. So he spoke simply of what he knew—their experiences of the early days in the Movement, their personal dealings with God, their faith in the presence of the Holy Spirit, and of the experiences of others of the power there was in the Gospel message. He stopped in the middle of a profound silence. No one moved or spoke, and once more he was shy and uncomfortable, wondering what was wrong. The chairman said, " Let us pray," and they knelt in silence; but Donald was conscious of someone near him struggling with his emotion. Tatlow closed with a word of prayer, and the place emptied, most of them going straight away to their rooms.

Next morning two Oxford dons came up to him and started by saying, " Look here, Donald Fraser; we don't believe we are converted at all. We are just a couple of miserable rotters "; and for two hours they sat on the grass expressing their difficulties in such philosophic language that Donald said he had some difficulty in following their thought. " Well, by night this is where we were," he wrote, "a whole crowd of these fellows, who are the leaders of the Movement, asserting that what they wanted was a simple New Testament declaration, in the language of conviction, that Christ is able to save from sin, and that God the Spirit can possess a man. I have been asked and pressed to come to the Colleges and say what I said on Saturday night. I am horribly unfit to do it, as you know. But it is awful to see the opportunity and to have to recognise that I have something which in some mysterious way touches men. I have been asked to go to Oxford, Cambridge, London, Bristol, all the Midland, Welsh and Irish Colleges. If the Committee will recognise that this is the biggest thing I can do, and that it will react on the whole Church and Mission Field, they may let me free."

When he approached the Livingstonia Committee with this suggestion, recognising that they too had claims on him, he proposed to work in along with the College tour as much missionary speaking in Scotland as he could overtake, as well as his share—a not inconsiderable one—in the Livingstone Centenary Celebrations. It meant a strenuous programme, and necessitated long and frequent journeys ; but he found a friend willing to undertake the additional expense involved in the student work, and flung himself so whole-heartedly into the task that by January he was confessing that the strain was overwhelming and he must call a halt.

He had had two outstanding meetings in theological colleges ; another with Birmingham medicals who, he felt, had little religious background, so he captured them with the romance of his work in Africa, got in a straight word for religion, and had a most candid discussion at the close. In December he was up in London with the Senior Advisory Committee discussing the policy of the Movement. At Cambridge he had what he described as a " glorious time," crowded congregations on Sunday, to whom he enjoyed speaking, meeting South African students and others throughout every moment of the day, every meal booked up with men of every type.

" What I have been driving at," he wrote, " is the need for positive declaration of the essentials of Christianity, the wonderful power of evangelical religion to change men, and that the best way to help men to believe is not by apologetics, except the apologetic of personal experience, ' One thing I know,' etc. And I think the leaders of the Student Movement are deeply realising this. I have been greatly rejoiced to see how great increase there has been among the leaders of a fervent evangelical faith, and how more definite their work has been this year.

" I am sure I have no hand in this. But God seems to have been leading them, through deep waters, to realise how everything depends on laying hold on Christ with a great certainty.

" But what I feel most called to, is to re-emphasise the missionary call, and I must acknowledge that many times the Spirit of God seems to have made men face up to their responsibilities to other nations.

" One good thing I have just heard—viz., that while our offices have been waiting for candidates who are not appearing, last week they had six offers from men in their last year in theology."

An outstanding missionary, at that time a member of the Cambridge Inter-Collegiate Christian Union, tells what he owed to Donald at that visit, through discovering that he who had been his hero had no fear of higher criticism—that his inner religious life was too real to be disturbed by it.

In later years Fraser had further contacts with the student world. He spoke at their Glasgow Conference in 1921, and felt that he had been a dead failure. One of the senior members of their staff who visited us during her stay in Glasgow wrote me expressing the hope that he was not serious in saying he was unhappy about it. " It was one of the really great things at the Conference. It left with me a new sense of the meaning of that love which is undeterred by any obstacle, and yet is not blind to the weakness of the objects of its love. The impression that Mr Fraser knows and loves the Africans in the way in which our Lord knew and loved men and women round Him, was left in my mind."

Some of the West African students present approached him afterwards about the pictures he had drawn of Africa's need. He arranged to meet with them and talk it over. He elicited from them the fact that none of them had ever been in their own hinterland, told them that he had not spoken of anything of which he had not personal experience, and pressed upon them their own responsibility for seeking their people's rather than their personal progress; and before they broke up, good friends, one of them remarked to him that he, a white man, obviously cared far more than they did for the welfare of their land.

The Principal of Tigerkloof recalls how once at Swanwick, as they walked round the camp, Donald told him how he felt that an uncertain note was being sounded, and that there was great diffidence in making any direct appeal to men to be missionaries, and said that when his turn came he would have to say " the old things " over again. " And indeed he did so— with passionate power. We were stirred by the old fire that had brought the Student Volunteer Missionary Union into being. After his address I met a young student who poured out his heart to me. ' Well, that's done it!' he said; 'for three years now I have been to these Conferences and wondered if I ought to be a missionary. But Donald Fraser's done it for me—I've just got to be a missionary now.'" Another leader in Africa, J. W. C. Dougall of Kenya, says: " He turned the eyes of more men and women to Africa than perhaps any other man in the last thirty years, and I was one of them. How vividly one recalls his pleading for Christ and Christ's need for men and women to work for and with him in Africa ; the talks in the big tent at Swanwick, and then the walking up and down the big field or in camp, in intimate conversation with him, which always finished up with prayer on our knees in his little tent. We relied on him tremendously in the Glasgow Christian Union—in fact, we relied on him everywhere in the Student Movement. From the earliest days of the Student Movement he has been a tremendous force . . . most for the reality of Christ made plain to us by him." Dr Wilkie of the Gold Coast and Lovedale is another whose thoughts were turned to Africa by him, and on the staff of Lovedale alone six have said that they owe it to his influence that they are there. In the last year of his life he was attending the Student Conference in Edinburgh and rejoicing in the renewed emphasis on personal religion that he found in it. Characteristically he not only stopped Robert Mackie in the lobby to tell him how glad he was to recognise the old note, but he also expressed that feeling in an appreciative report to *The Glasgow Herald*. It is true that he was often critical of them—to themselves—and perhaps did not always understand what they were after—for he had not sufficiently continuous contact with them to follow the various phases of thought through which the student world was passing—but his interest and desire to help never failed, and his appreciation cheered and encouraged them.

CHAPTER XXVII

A CHAPTER OF ACCIDENTS, 1913–14

A SHORT visit to Paris in early spring helped to give Donald the complete change he needed. He had long and much-needed sleeps, and then found so much to fascinate him in the Louvre, where he started, that it was not easy to drag him away to see other parts of the city. Architecture, sculpture and pictures all had a strong appeal for him, and he enjoyed to the full the luxury of being able to carry away glorious memories to enrich another spell of work in Africa. Little did we realise how short that term was to be and how full of accident and illness—partly, no doubt, the penalty of an over-vigorous furlough.

One of the gifts he had received at home was a side-car to add to the usefulness of his motor-cycle. The day it arrived at Loudon, and was unpacked and fitted on to his motor, we had of course to sample it, and on a Saturday afternoon off we went for a spin along the road. For some miles all went well, though he was not too certain that the coupling was rightly done. Suddenly, at a badly bevelled bit of road, with a nasty tree trunk left projecting into the path, the steering went wrong and we crashed into the tree. Donald was flung off on one side of it and our little son and I out on the other. When we slowly sat up, our first concern was the child, who was lying, fortunately, on a soft heap of road scrapings : beyond profuse bleeding at the nose, which helped to add to the gory picturesqueness of our condition, he seemed to have no injuries. Donald was very badly bruised about the groin, and I had got off with a broken rib. Leaving me to look after the child, he took a branch to serve as a support, and went limping off to find a village from which he could despatch a messenger to Loudon for help. Considerable noise helped to guide him to the nearest, but he arrived to find a big beer-drink going on, and the people in such a condition that, when they saw his plight and heard that he wanted to send for a machila to carry his wife and child back home, they hastily assumed that it was our corpses that were to be conveyed, and broke into a death wail, the distant noise of which rather startled me for the moment. I little realised that it was raised on my behalf!

Finding they were too far gone to listen, he picked out the most sober man he could see and despatched him to Loudon with the message that we were to be met on the road. Meantime, carrying the child, we started to plod painfully back, expecting that at each turn of the road we would catch sight of machila bearers. But we had to tramp the whole distance without any sign of them, for the messenger had taken them by what he considered a short cut to the scene of the accident, and they found only the badly damaged machine by the roadside. That our son was not seriously injured was certain when, after being put to bed, he asked eagerly if we might have our next ride the following day. But it was many a long day before we felt so eager, even had the bicycle been in a condition to ride. Donald's injuries gave him a great deal of trouble, and he walked painfully and slowly about the Station, only too ready to lie down whenever he entered the house and could take a little rest. Before he was better I had gone down with a tick fever that kept me in bed for the greater part of two months. While the fever was at its worst, a neglected small boy essayed to climb a high bookcase, brought it down on the top of himself, and fractured his leg. A very fevered patient had to set it ! Christmas was marked by no sports or celebrations that year. Another invalid joined us—the child of a District Commissioner, whose mother brought her along for very necessary treatment, lasting over several weeks. Then for a little while all seemed to be going well, when suddenly Donald was taken ill with severe paroxysmal attacks of abdominal pain. After a day or two, fearing an operation might be necessary, I sent messages for Dr Prentice and Dr Turner ; and in the meantime the patient refused to have opiates, because he had heard me say that these masked the symptoms, and seeing the diagnosis was presenting difficulties he did not wish to make it less easy. For six days he lay suffering acutely, but between the attacks sending for those to whom he could give instructions about the carrying on of the work.

Day and night one was frequently applying hot fomentations, wrung out by two Natives who sat all the time by a small fire in the bedroom, waiting for the signal that another was required. This duty was at night undertaken by two of the elders who had had a little training in the hospital : they were terribly anxious about their Bwana, and proud to be chosen for this service. A vivid picture remains in my mind of " Smiling Joseph," his face drawn and apprehensive, tiptoeing into the room one evening, and Donald beckoning him to approach. He knelt down by the bedside, his hands clasped, to hear what was wanted of him. " Try to smile, Joseph," begged the invalid ; " you look so serious when you come into the room that it makes me feel quite melancholy." " I'll try, my father," said

Joseph, evidently feeling this was no easy thing that was asked of him. The next evening outside the door he stopped, and one saw him contorting his features into a pathetic attempt at cheerfulness before entering. It is perhaps one of the lessons that can be taught the African only through the illnesses of the European—this atmosphere of naturalness and even laughter and tender fun in a sick-room, possible because, though suffering is there, fear and suspicion are absent. Certainly in this case it was the invalid who, in the intervals free from pain, made the jokes and gently teased the troubled attendants.

When his colleagues arrived they decided that an operation was necessary; but in spite of his pleading his perfect confidence in their skill, and the reluctance he felt to waste time and money in travelling, they were equally determined that he must go home for it, realising how impossible it would be for him to get the necessary rest on his Mission Station. So, only ten months after our arrival, we once more set off for home. Mr Caird operated, and became not only Fraser's surgeon, operating on him twice subsequently, but his friend for the rest of his lifetime. Mr Caird's orders were, that he must take a year's rest at home. For the first few months this was not unwelcome, but then came the War, and, as soon as we were back from Arran, Donald was asking him if he was not fit to serve in some way. Could he not be a chaplain? Mr Caird told him firmly that all he was fit for was to try to get back his health by learning to play golf on the Braid Hills. Miss Cairns had generously lent us her house in Braidburn Crescent, so the Braids were conveniently near. But Donald only tried a game once. He came back within two hours. " How can I play golf when other men are drilling? " he asked; " if I can't work, at least I haven't the face to play." But even walking about he felt ashamed and unhappy to pass

men in training.   " What a slacker they must think me ! "
he remarked one day as we stood on the pavement watching a weary battalion march past.   Just at that moment
one of the men, catching his eye, hailed him with a cheerful
" Hullo, old Methuselah ! "—a greeting which somewhat
lessened his sensitiveness, as it proved that he did not look
the hale and hearty sort of fellow who should be in their
ranks.   He was down at the station watching his fellow
missionary, W. P. Young, leave for France.   For himself
there was nothing to do but to wait patiently till he was
allowed to return to Africa in the spring of 1915.

CHAPTER XXVIII

WAR YEARS

THE enforced rest, with its result of making Fraser feel more alive than he had done for years, was an excellent preparation for the programme he had to face in the years that followed, when the effect of the War spread into the remotest villages of Central Africa. There was a suggestion at the first Mission Council after his return to Nyasaland that he should be appointed padre at Karonga; but, when his Loudon colleague was taken on to act as interpreter, it became out of the question for Fraser to do anything but devote himself to his Mission district. It was soon made evident that his most valuable service lay there, for an incident occurred that, but for his intervention, might have led to serious consequences. It came suddenly one night, just on the eve of the annual Sacramental gathering at Loudon.

Donald had gone to bed with a bad headache, when steps were heard coming up the road. Expecting it to be a summons to a medical case, I slipped out on to the veranda to ask who was there. " It is Daniel and Andrew," was the reply. They were two of the Church leaders in training for the ministry; and they wanted to speak to Mr Fraser. Though I said he was not well and must not be disturbed, they explained that it was urgent, as they had come from the paramount chief, who was in flight from his head village. So Donald dressed, and, bringing in the little group of men whose spokesmen they were, listened to their story. The Government had sent out word to the chiefs that so

many men and so much food must be forthcoming by a
certain date for war purposes. This order had not been
complied with, the other chiefs considering it the pre-
rogative of Chimtunga to lead in the matter. Chimtunga
himself, being drunk when the Boma messenger arrived,
had replied insolently, and the man had gone straight back
and reported his words. The magistrate had sent to
Zomba for native police to come and effect his arrest,
feeling uncertain whether it could safely be entrusted to
the local police, themselves Ngoni, and men of Chimtunga ; and the Government, uncertain as to the strength
of local feeling, were sending up an armed force and a
machine gun. Chimtunga, getting word of his projected
arrest, had fled to put himself under Donald's protection.
A message was sent him to come along at daybreak, and
he arrived, sober, frightened, and very sorry for himself,
pleading that he had not meant to say what he did—he
had been under the influence of liquor. Many a time
Fraser had warned him about his drinking habits, and had
asked the Government officials to take up a less easy and
tolerant attitude to this failing of the chief's. Now he
could only point out to him that, having brought trouble
upon his people by his folly, he must take the responsibility
on his own shoulders, and, instead of fleeing—a futile
proceeding in any case—adopt the only course open to
him, that of going to the Boma and giving himself up.
Only thus could he avert the war in which he had involved
his people. It required much persuasion to get him to
accept this advice, and he asked that Donald would accompany him. While telling him that it was better to go
himself with no suggestion of coercion, Fraser promised to
go ahead, see Mr Macdonald the magistrate, and prepare
him for Chimtunga's coming. So, while people from all
quarters of the land were pouring in for the Convention,

their teacher was motoring across to the Boma, to try to make things easier for the chief. He had not a very easy task. Mr Macdonald at first refused to accept Chimtunga's voluntary surrender : now that things had gone so far he must return to his village and await his arrest there. The soldiers and the Maxim gun were nearing Ngoniland. His visitor did not argue : he accepted the offer of breakfast, and during its course began to tell of poor Chimtunga's state of mind. He knew how kind-hearted Macdonald was, and before the meal was over his host was admitting that he could not well refuse to receive a man who surrendered himself. But he had determined that the troops should march through the land and be billeted on the chiefs until all the men and food demanded were forthcoming. On his return journey Fraser met the chief, his courage once more at zero, and, dismounting and sitting with him by the roadside, braced him to go bravely and meet his fate. (He was deposed and sent down country.) Then Fraser returned to the gathering crowds at Loudon. Aware of the serious danger of having troops quartered in the vicinity while there were 2000 strangers on the Station, he carried on the programme of meetings for that day while deliberating what had best be done. The following day he laid the whole matter before the people, explaining how the disobedience of the chiefs had brought this menace. Seeing that their chiefs had not done their duty, they must save themselves by prompt action. They were all to return to their homes, the women to busy themselves in preparing the food required, the teachers to get volunteers for Government work and be themselves the first to offer.

This unexpected return of the Christians brought the urgency of the situation into every group of villages in the land and set it astir. In two days our local chief had turned up with double the quota of men demanded from him, so the magistrate promised that no soldiers should be quartered on him. So quickly and so satisfactorily did the others follow his lead that both men and food were being turned away before the troops arrived at all, and all that happened was a sort of military display at the Boma before the men marched on north. The people's loyalty was left unimpaired, and later on, at their missionary's suggestion, they contributed freely to help the Red Cross Fund at home. Fraser did all he could to bring home to them the brotherhood of the nations, and make them feel there must be no selfish isolating of themselves while others suffered.

With so many of the younger teachers away there was plenty to do in reorganising the schools. Actually their numbers did not decrease, but rather increased, till at the end of the term there were 183, with 12,800 pupils. The agents on the stations of the Livingstonia Mission sphere were reduced by almost half owing to the military demands for doctors, nurses, transport leaders, etc., so those left to carry on bore a heavy burden. Fraser was the only white man remaining to superintend a district covering something like 10,000 miles, 200 days' travelling over 2000 miles being his record for one year, when the lack of petrol finally prevented him from being able to use his motor. He was for a while without the help of any Native pastor. For a short period he was also responsible for Kasungu Station.

Although on arriving back in Africa he found among the people the restlessness and bewilderment that arose from the knowledge that Christian nations were fighting one another, before long he was feeling that he had a good grip of his work and that there were many things to encourage him. The Church life had seldom been stronger —3000 in full communion; 3800 in Catechumens' and Hearers' classes, and work generally going on well, the offerings in one year, he calculated, defraying the entire church expenses and half the cost of education. On the other hand, there were tragic disappointments. One of these was the death of his friend, Daniel Nhlane, a man full of energy and enthusiasm, but far from robust. More than once we had seen him at death's door, but this time his vitality had been undermined by the tragedy of a daughter's accidental death, and, when he contracted the dysentery that was rife in the country, the chance of saving his life was lost through the misfortune that Dr Prentice was not at Kasungu when they carried him there for medical treatment. They brought him on the long 70 miles to Loudon, but he was a dying man when he arrived, and he passed away the next morning. He had been one of our most understanding friends, and we missed him sadly.

But it was another incident that bowed Donald down with shame and sorrow—one that one almost hesitates to tell, only it shows, as nothing else can, how completely he identified himself with his people and bore the burden of their sin and shame.

He had gone up to Council in the best of spirits, looking forward to the return of a Native colleague after two years' absence in charge of a place where the War had let loose many evil forces. Within a day or two of Donald's expected return from Council there came the following letter, written on the homeward journey; in spite of its intimate nature, it is quoted to show his state of mind.

" My precious Wife,—I am sick with longing for you. I have needed you for the last week terribly, and I just wish I could fly home to you. When I lay this afternoon in the shade waiting for lunch, I had a vision of you that just made me cry out for you. I need your sympathy far more than you can know. To-day I parted with the rest of the company, who turned aside to Ekwendeni. They were awfully

kind—could not have been gentler. Now I am going to
send two boys on to Mzimba to bring my bicycle on to Hora
so that I may run back to you on Monday. This is mail day.
You may be having a big mail. I hope it is not full of sadness. How I wish I were with you when you get it. I have
been very anxious about you, Donald and you all. No news
has come through since the note on Tuesday morning telling
of Donald's fever. But Stuart had had a letter from his
wife which enclosed one you had written to Mr Macdonald, and as there was no news of domestic disaster in it
I felt a little easier. Mrs Stuart has been having fever, so
her husband did not feel happy about her either. There
were telegrams about the last great push in the War . . . It
is no use, I had better tell you, though I thought I should
keep it till I got home. But we had a terribly sad time at
Council. Poor X. resigned his ministry. Earlier in the
week he confessed to me that he had been terribly tempted
and had sinned. Poor fellow, he could not speak for weeping and for shame. It was a terrible blow to us all. I
carried the knowledge through these days, and sometimes
it overwhelmed me and I could only cry like a child. When
my colleagues knew of it, Turner, Young and Stuart, they
were so kind and tender to me and so loving to poor X.
In the Presbytery when poor X. made his broken-hearted
confession the elders wept aloud. But we tried to see the
joy of Christ in the forgiven sinner. The pain and shame
are there, but the greatest is God's love and forgiveness.
And I hope that for X. there may yet be great days when
he may preach the Gospel of love and forgiveness in a new
way. But Oh, Agnes, the pain of it ! How I have wanted
you these days. Yet it has brought us together in a wonderful way. We prayed together and talked together as we
had never done before—so much so that at the close of the
Council we stood and sang the Doxology. So may it be

Q

for the whole Church grace to us and glory to God for the greatness of His forgiveness to X. and to us.

" We travelled down the Henga in grand form, eating well and behaving like schoolboys, Young especially trying hard to keep me full of cheerful thoughts when he saw black melancholy coming near me.   He is a good soul."

On his arrival at Loudon he tried to give me fuller details of all that had happened—how he had tried to speak to the broken-hearted man of the patience and forgiveness of God ; how at a little committee, when deposition with no hope of reinstatement at any future time was suggested, he had pled for the mercy and forgiveness that Jesus would have shown, and tried to prove that nothing made sin seem so hideous as the Cross and forgiveness, and that they would be lowering no standards of conduct if they acted towards X. as Christ did to Peter or Mary.   In Council all his colleagues agreed with him.   Their sympathy, he said, was beyond words, and he never saw the greatness of their hearts as he did when this severe pain came.   On the Sunday two Native pastors were ordained, but he was overwhelmed to think of his friend lying in his house broken and weeping, unable to join them.   The confession and resignation took the Presbytery by surprise.   A terrible silence followed when X. withdrew.   A Native minister was Moderator, and Donald, clerk, so he took the matter into his own hands, trying to let the members see that this was not a tragedy any more than the return of the Prodigal, if they could only look on it as Christ did and glory in the greatness of God's forgiveness.   They agreed to accept the resignation and wait for God's leading for the future. X. was asked to return, and he came in, his friend and Native fellow-pastor on one side holding his hand, Dr Turner on the other.   As he came forward all Donald could say was, " In the name of Jesus Christ thy sins are forgiven thee," for the Natives were weeping and the Europeans not less moved.

"Perhaps," said Donald, "this is going to bring a new emphasis on the heart of the Gospel." His own terrible pain, with the tenderness of his attitude to his colleague, brought to the African Church, one cannot doubt, some further insight into the heart of God. Before he left Africa finally he had the joy of seeing his friend restored to the ministry.

However he might feel personally, he realised the need of keeping up the heart and hope of the people, and tried to make as much work as possible for them locally. The hospital had been burnt down while we were at home, so it had to be repaired and roofed. It was at the beginning of this term that the dam previously mentioned was constructed, and each rainy season he grew apprehensive about its safety. There were times when some cloud-burst raised its level perilously high, and we worked hard to enlarge the overflows, or waited anxiously to see whether the torrent pouring over the great bank that dammed the water was going to carry it away. There was one evening when messenger after messenger was sent to call him to dinner, but none returned. Finally his wife followed, in the wake of the table-boy, a guest and the cook, only to be drawn like the others into active service. It was half-past nine when we returned, a tired, disreputable, muddy crew, thankful that the danger was over. The garden was growing during these years, and when he went on ulendo he used to bring back ferns, lilies, gladioli, and anything else that he thought would add to its variety or beauty. There were other gardens in which he was equally interested. It was during those years of war that he persuaded the people to open up community plots—140 of them—in which the whole village took a share, so that there might be an

additional food supply if times of shortage came.   In those
war years the Government was more than willing to purchase all the grain that could be raised.

Medical work during that period was heavy.   There was
no inspection of the Nyasaland men called up for transport
service, beyond the magistrate's seeing that they looked fit,
but the Northern Rhodesian Government sent several of
its batches to us to have their fitness for service tested.
There was a constant stream of men coming back from the
war area debilitated by disease, and deaths were painfully
frequent ; and in addition, owing to the absence on military
service of so many of the doctors in the country, there was
many a call to distant European cases.   Three years in
succession the holiday on the hills was interrupted by
such S O S messages, and the difficulty of making hurried
journeys of 120 or 130 miles meant that the husband as well
as the doctor had to be involved.   We had one very trying
journey south of Kasungu, on a path with nasty outcrops
of ironstone, when everything that could break without
absolutely bursting up the motor-cycle did so.   For hours,
without water or food, Donald knelt in the blazing November heat, tinkering at the machine to get it to go, and we
resumed the journey with it in a very unsafe condition.   It
was almost a relief when, as civilians, we were refused any
further supplies of petrol, and I was reduced to using a
bush-car when later calls came.   Council had agreed to let
us have the services of Nurse Cole during the later war years,
and her presence meant that the hospital work was attended
to, and that, during our frequent separations, the responsibility for the children in their mother's absence did not fall
on him alone.   He was extraordinarily ungrudging about
these demands.   One of our local tragedies of the War was
the death of the magistrate's wife.   The magistrate himself was taken ill shortly after, and for the rest of his term

was lonely, and missed his wife terribly. Before finally leaving for home, he wrote to Fraser to say that he could never forget how generous he had been about sparing his wife so often to come and look after him.

Those years of war brought us into much closer contact with the Government people. We were sharing a great common interest and anxiety, and every bit of news that reached one was passed on to the other. We were learning, too, to share the responsibility for the people and the country as a whole, instead of being each engrossed in our own task. Famine and " flu " and the other after-effects of war demanded combined efforts, and personal anxieties and sorrows deepened our sympathy and mutual understanding. When Mrs Macdonald died, Donald not only took the funeral service; he had previously been up a good part of the night with our Mission carpenters helping them to make the coffin, and our little boarder boys walked across the nineteen miles to the Boma that there might be a choir to sing the hymns at the graveside.

Between the new magistrate, Mr Macdonald's successor, and Donald a very real friendship grew up. They did not think alike on every subject, but they respected each other's views and discussed points of interest at such length that the mailbag's arrival was hailed as the next session of the Debating Society. A good deal of visiting, as well as correspondence, used to take place, and there were exciting scenes when the children watched their fathers having a naval engagement on the dam, which ended in their respective crafts (two flat-bottomed boats constructed by Donald for his family's use on the lake) sinking to the bottom while their crews, after a brief immersion, reappeared and swam ashore.

When the magistrate retired, he thought it worth while to take home with him the letters that Donald had written discussing the Government attitude to beer-drinking and the question of forced labour. Donald appreciated the mental stimulus of having so keen and interested a critic of his opinions as Mr Moggridge, who in turn said that Mr Fraser's kindness, the enthusiasm and wisdom he had put into his work, and the broad-minded sympathy and helpfulness he had shown to him, were the happiest of many happy Mzimba memories.

With our Rhodesian neighbours relations were equally cordial. They were a younger set of men, and were frequently changed, but each in turn seemed to appreciate his company and often ran over for a little change. Perhaps the " fleshpots of Egypt " attracted them, for they were less fortunate as regards cattle and garden produce.

There was one famous occasion when we had a most thrilling Sports Day. The dam had made it possible to include water sports, and an old friend, a South African athlete who had once drilled our teachers in a way that spread the influence of his efforts to the remotest corner of our diocese, was back among us, invalided from the Army, and undertook to draw up the programme. The Rhodesian magistrate was keenly interested and was doing his best to stimulate the men from his side of the border to put forth their best effort against the Nyasalanders. These were officially represented by a shy young assistant who began to lose his painful self-consciousness as he grew eager to see his men win. The Tug-of-war which ended a strenuous-day's programme was most interesting for us on account of the wild shouts of the white men yelling to get their teams to put forth every ounce of strength. Their vocal encouragement and the violence of their gestures increased the excitement and din of the onlookers. At breakfast next morning their voices could not rise above a whisper, and throat lozenges were in demand. Donald was well con-

tent. Had they not unmistakably demonstrated to the
people what he was always telling them was the case—that
their Boma men were interested in them and keen on their
welfare and development, though they had necessarily at
times to undertake unpopular tasks and could not, because
of their official position, reveal how much they disliked
having to perform them? He was always carrying on
an unostentatious campaign for better relations between
black and white. Seldom or never did I hear him discuss
the colour problem with any of our Loudon guests, yet I
doubt if any who spent any time there left without a kindlier
and more human attitude to the African. Did any visitor
express his interest in any lad he had taken a fancy to,
Donald had always something to tell that made the man
feel he had shown discrimination in discovering his worth.
One of our evangelists attracted our magistrate, and what
Donald had to tell him of Daniel made him feel still more
friendly ; so that at his death it was the Government man
who was the first to propose a memorial to him and ask
to be allowed to contribute. Fraser believed supremely
in bringing people together in the bonds of a common
interest.

CHAPTER XXIX

CHAMPIRA

ONE of the stories Donald used to tell was of a missionary in China who wrote home to his Committee asking for a grant to build a wall round his house to ensure a little privacy at times. Some time later he wrote to thank them for agreeing to his request: the wall, he stated, had been so successful that for the last three months he had not seen a Chinese! The exaggeration embodied a truth. There are times when one does need to escape to solitude from Natives and colleagues alike. It was with this need in our minds that we had built on Champira, one of the summits of a ridge of hills twenty-five miles away, a little cottage where we might find coolness and refreshment for body and spirit in the last trying weeks before the rains broke. It was a great joy to fill the ox-carts with the necessary bedding and stores, send up one or two cattle for milking, and set off for our retreat. Seldom or never did we find the solitude we sought. Some invited themselves; others, perhaps more than he ever confessed, were cordially invited by the theorist on the need for getting away from everybody. On one of these holidays we counted the population on our hill-top: seven white guests, our own family, five cooks, fifteen house-boys and girls, the *kapitao*, the ox boys, four herds, water-carriers, women bringing in grass for thatching, men cleaning the roads, and numerous visitors—teachers who came for examination, women with food for sale, stray patients, oxen, donkeys, cattle, not to mention such adjuncts as push-bikes, motors, bush-cars and children's machilas.

The feeding of this patriarchal establishment depended largely on Donald's shooting, for people from the surrounding valleys would only bring produce in exchange for meat. Sometimes it was a very tired man indeed who took his gun and went wearily forth to hunt for game.

As the War went on with its drain on the able-bodied manhood of the tribe, the Native gardens suffered from lack of sufficient cultivation, and food became scarce. Then Champira began to assume the aspect of a shambles rather than a peaceful retreat. Instead of supplying what was sufficient for our wants, Donald was now out day after day shooting up to the extreme limit of his game permit, the people from the surrounding villages coming up whenever they heard the reverberations of his gun, to help in cutting up and carrying the meat to the hill-top, where the *kapitao* was kept busy bartering it for grain from the villages where the gardens had been good. What remained was made into " biltong " by being cut into pieces like large clothes-pins, which, after being sprinkled with salt, were hung up to dry in the sun.

Sometimes he was worse than tired: he was really ill; and yet the need was imperative. Once I had to help him along to a slope to which he thought the game might come later on to browse. We sat and looked over the landscape, our attention being attracted every now and then to one branch in a thicket ahead. that seemed to catch some breeze. Suddenly it dawned on us both that the moving thing was no swaying branch, but a waving tail. A few minutes later a shot sent a great eland rushing down the hill. Donald was far too weak to follow; so, taking his revolver to administer the *coup de grâce* (if necessary, and if I could summon up courage to fire), I set off after the

wounded animal, while my husband painfully made his way
back to the house.   Far down the steep hill I followed the
spoor of blood till I could trace it no farther.   I hunted
round, but failed to pick it up.   The eland had vanished,
in spite of Donald's impression that he had shot it through
the heart ; and now my concern was to find my way home
by the route I had come.   Finally a great grey boulder
which I remembered passing on the road down caught my
eye, and I made for it, hoping that from that spot I might
once again pick up the spoor.   I did better.   The apparent
boulder turned out to be the eland lying dead ; so, tying
my handkerchief to a branch to mark the spot, I went back
to look after the sick hunter and relieve his mind by assuring him that for some days to come there would be no lack
of meat.   That was the last game he shot for many weeks.
His illness increased, and he lay suffering great pain.   It
was difficult to know how to get him back to the Station
before the rains closed us in.   Finally he did the journey
lying on mattresses laid on the spring cart, and it was a
relief to have him in a comfortable house again.   For
three months his work was carried on with great discomfort,
even when there was not actual pain.   That was his personal
share of the aftermath of the War : twice during the past
years he had had to be brought home ill with dysentery
contracted in Marambo.   It was true of himself, as of the
land about which he wrote, that " it would be long before
the sore of its wounds would be healed, and longer still
before the old buoyancy would be regained."   Famine,
disease, superstition and increased violence had renewed
their grip on it, and though he was being urged to come
home and give a year to work among students, he felt
that he could not leave the people at this stage, although
he admitted that his soul burned to go to the colleges
and manses, to the doctors and teachers, and haul out

hundreds of them to the immense fields that were open for work.

When more urgent furloughs had been taken, and relief for Loudon was available, we went home, travelling down country along with Mr W. P. Livingstone, who had recently been our guest at Loudon. One result of his visit had been to make Donald set to work to destroy everything that might help to furnish material for a biography of himself, for he had detected that his guest had such an idea at the back of his mind. It was only when it was all done that he came triumphantly to tell me how he had foiled any such possibility by burning all diaries and letters which he had been keeping. Of the possibility that others were preserving *his* letters he did not seem to think.

CHAPTER XXX

CAMPAIGNING AT HOME

THE summer of 1920 found Donald once more in his beloved Argyllshire with his children, laying in fresh stores of vitality as he smoked a pipe with some neighbour on the Canal banks, lent a helping hand in opening the locks as some vessel passed through, rowed on its waters in a hired boat christened by the family *The Rosy Sausage*, climbed the hills and explored the roads, picked up the local history, went fishing on Lochfyne, picnicked on some hillside or visited old friends in his native town. He took an interest in archæology, and spent much time denuding great slabs of rock on the slopes in his search for the cup-and-circle markings that abounded in the district, or investigating mounds that might contain cysts. The local people, if they smiled a little at his enthusiasm, were ever ready to help him with the loan of spade or pick or personal assistance. On Sunday we walked in to the United Free Church, and, of course, he had to " give the minister a Sunday," holiday though it was. He never could say " No " if he was disengaged, though sometimes he got out of it by saying, " Ask my wife if I may."

Donald had a hankering to worship again in his father's old church, so one Sunday afternoon found us among the " Frees " and accidentally installed in the pew of a very kind friend who beamed to see us there and promptly handed him a supply of peppermints. He got rid of them and his embarrassment simultaneously by passing them on to me. Seeing that I was not sharing them with him, his neighbour gave him another handful. But it was only I who did " in Rome " what the " Romans " were doing, and spoke to him afterwards about catholicity in matters of ritual ! He deplored the multiplicity of churches more than most, but no divisions alienated him from those who differed. All through the rather difficult years that followed the Union of 1900, one of his African parishes was maintained by a Free Church in Inverness ; and in his years at home he was an annual guest at one of the breakfasts given during the Free Church Assembly. With the Continuing Church after the 1929 Union he kept in friendly and helpful touch, giving what advice he could with regard to their foreign mission enterprise.

While enjoying his holiday he was putting into shape some sketches of African life, and diffidently asking Mr Livingstone if he thought any use could be made of them. They were ultimately published under the title of *African Idylls*.

Another matter he was pondering was " some way of getting something done in the Church," which resulted in the conception of the Scottish Churches' Missionary Campaign. Once again he had been asked to extend his furlough to enlist fresh candidates. This was a need common to all the Churches, and it seemed to require a mission of education and enlightenment on the world situation and the tasks awaiting accomplishment. Such a mission, he felt, could be carried out more effectively and economically by combined action. To discuss this possibility a meeting was held at Dunblane of representatives of all sections of the Church in Scotland. The project was warmly received and a Council formed to see it through, he being appointed Chairman.

The method adopted was to hold a series of local Campaigns, making an intensive effort to reach all classes of the community. Representing as it did all the Churches, each Campaign was accorded a civic reception, which was

followed by meetings of all descriptions.   With hardly an
exception the Campaigners were able to obtain entrance
to the day schools, and the children carried home excited
accounts of the strangers to whom they had been listening,
thus advertising the other meetings held for women, girls,
nurses, business men, teachers, labour men, uniformed
juvenile organisations, Sabbath schools, Bible classes,
choirs.   So many were catered for that there were instances
of those who were left out feeling neglected, and demanding
that something should be got up for them, too.   In some
places discussion groups were formed.   Before the Campaign Week was over it was difficult for anyone to remain
unaware of what was doing, and patients in the hospitals
and postmen on their rounds were reported to be discussing
Missions !   And the missionaries, gathered from different
Societies and Churches, were enjoying themselves as never
before on deputation work.   Instead of being lonely
individuals addressing isolated meetings attended by the
few interested, they were part of a strong team in intimate
co-operation working in prepared ground and in an atmosphere of welcome and expectation.   The level of
speaking rose, for all had chances of listening to one another
and noticing what subjects and what points appealed to
their audiences and what failed to interest, and could cull
some very practical suggestions from an extremely modest
little booklet written by their leader, entitled *Hints to
Missionary Speakers.*

On the Sunday the churches were invaded by missionary
speakers, women finding themselves in some pulpits that
had never before been open to their sex.   The climax was
always a great united service on the Sunday evening.   It was
generally taken by " Dr Fraser," as they were trying to
get into the habit of calling him before the Campaign was
far advanced, for Glasgow University had given him his

D.D. in 1922. The biggest available hall or church was often too small for this dedication service. People crowded in long before the time of starting, and the police had sometimes to close the doors so early that on more than one occasion the speaker found difficulty in gaining admission. At Greenock there was no sign of Dr Fraser, so the opening psalm was given out and sung while he wandered round from door to door, trying to find a policeman sufficiently gracious to be willing to listen to his reason for so persistently desiring to be admitted. To the platform-room of the Caird Hall at Dundee came a policeman to tell of a man outside who kept insisting that Dr Fraser should be sent for, and refused to go away quietly. Dr Fraser went, and found Dr John A. Mackay of Lima, Peru, who was sharing the programme with him that evening. These two often spoke together, the stripling and the veteran, and how Donald enjoyed the chance, made possible by the Campaign, of introducing to wider circles of Church life a man of such outstanding ability. To Dr Mackay that time meant much. His feeling when he first met Fraser in the Campaign office was that he had found the kindliest man, with the most wonderful smile, that he had ever known, one who influenced his missionary spirit and thinking as no other single man had done.

A most loyal and efficient staff were working in the Edinburgh office in Castle Street, undeterred by an ancient and fish-like smell that too often pervaded it from the shop in the lower regions. Donald's old friend, the Rev. J. M. E. Ross, was acting as Press Secretary. The Rev. John Macbeath resigned from the Baptist Church at Cambuslang to be Organising Secretary. The Rev. R. G. Macdonald was, first, Exhibitions Secretary, and, later, was in charge of all work connected with candidates. There were two women secretaries—Miss Boyd and

Miss Genner, the latter a Wesleyan Methodist and a future colleague at Loudon, who gave her services as a voluntary worker. A typist, shared by Dr Fraser and Mr Ross, writing of the joy and inspiration of that time, was much impressed by the perfect friendship of the two men, Mr Ross always wondering if she should not be doing something for the " bishop," as they all called him, while Dr Fraser was equally concerned lest he was taking her away from John Ross. But indeed the happy relations that existed were characteristic of the spirit of the whole Movement. Two Campaigners put into verse their impressions of one of the Campaigns, and part of this effort is here quoted, though other lines expressing appreciation of the hospitality and of the arrangements made locally are omitted.

GREENOCK CAMPAIGN

28th November to 4th December 1921
(With acknowledgments to *Hiawatha*)

You shall hear how Donald Fraser
Ran the great Campaign at Greenock ;
Not by preaching only Missions,
Nor demanding men and money,
But by asking Thought and Service
" For the profit of the people,
For advantage of the nations."

First the Churches all united,
All united in a body—
Church of Scotland, also Free Church,
The Original Seceders,
The Episcopal, and Baptist,
Methodist, United Free Church,
Congregational, and others—
All united in a body
To campaign with Donald Fraser.

Then the hospitable people
Opened wide their friendly portals,

Set themselves to welcome strangers,
Five and forty wild Campaigners.
Just a few were strangely troubled,
Vexed within their kindly spirits,
" What to do with missionaries ?
How to feed the wild Campaigners ? "

Then there gathered the Campaigners.
From all regions they came flocking,
From Manchuria and Lovedale,
From Darjeeling and Kikuyu,
Calabar and Rajputana,
Livingstonia and Jamaica,
From Ichang and from the Gold Coast,
Kalimpong and Youth Committee ;
From the North, South, East, and Westward
They invaded peaceful Greenock.

Straight they made for the Headquarters,
Union Street United Free Church,
There to find the Local Leader
Had arranged for every detail,
Settled the minutest detail,
When un-settled re-arranged it,
To the end untiring, cheerful,
Ever mindful of their comfort.

Picture Greenock simply seething,
Seething wildly with Campaigners,
Who before the sun had risen
Might be found in every Day School ;
Who before the night descended
Spoke to business men, to women,
Boys and girls, and little infants,
Howling mobs of little infants ;
Who before the night was finished
Still held forth at Public Meetings,
Open Conference and Rallies,
Teachers' Classes, countless Circles.

Greatest day of all was Sunday
When they stood in every pulpit,
Spoke to Sunday Schools and Classes.
In the streets you saw them hasting,

In the cars you heard them asking
" Tell me when we reach Argyll Street,
Put me off beside Argyll Street."
You might see them wildly rushing
From the Gaelic out to Cartsburn,
From the Mid Church to St Stephen's,
Scarce a pause between their meetings :
All day long they sped through Greenock,
Bearing thermos flasks and pieces,
Till at length all Greenock gathered
To the best and finest Meeting,
To the last and greatest Meeting,
And the Great Campaign was over.

You have heard how Donald Fraser
Ran the Great Campaign at Greenock.
In our thoughts he'll stand before us,
Over-dressed in shorts and shirt-sleeves,
Speaking to the wild Ngoni,
Counting up his Church collection,
Piles of rat-tails, two a penny,
And a cow in the collection.

So he swayed and captured Greenock,
Not by preaching only Missions,
Not demanding men and money,
But by asking Thought and Service,
" For the profit of the people,
For advantage of the nations."

The climax of this work, in which, as Bishop Walpole
said, Dr Donald Fraser had, " by means of his patience,
his wisdom and his attractive personality, lined up all the
religious forces of Scotland "—a degree of brotherly
co-operation probably without parallel in the ecclesiastical history of the country—took the form of a National
Congress attended by representatives from ten sections
of the Church.   The Congress was intended to give them
a vision of what the Kingdom of God means and must
increasingly mean in the world, if humanity is to be rescued
from chaos and darkness.   The speakers were drawn from

all sections. Many came from across the Border; India and Africa were represented respectively by K. T. Paul and Dr and Mrs Moton of Tuskegee; and others came from America. Dr Moton with his party spoke at one or two other places beside Glasgow, and Dr Fraser, who travelled with them, came to the conclusion that the one insuperable difficulty of the Campaign had been to keep them adequately supplied with drinking water on their train journeys !

At that Conference he met again, and for the last time, Temple Gairdner, who on his part said his visit had helped him to solve a problem which had been puzzling him—the question why the best sales of the Bible Plays of a C.M.S. missionary had been in Presbyterian Scotland. Now he found that they had been on all the bookstalls of the Campaign, and Fraser had been unwearied in recommending them. Many in future days confessed to the inspiration they received during that week. To Fraser as Chairman, the meaning and purpose of it all was summed up in the magnificent singing of the " Hallelujah Chorus " on the closing night, by a united choir led by Mr Roberton, the famous conductor of the Glasgow Orpheus Choir.

One of the results of the Campaigns was the bringing of the local clergy into closer touch; this in many cases led to the formation of permanent groups for fellowship. Another was the founding of the Scottish Missionary Council. For this Dr Fraser was largely responsible, and, as its first Chairman, he revealed those qualities which made him so highly respected and so widely beloved, not only within his own communion, but throughout the whole Church life of Scotland, and beyond. The first years of its existence owed much to " his sagacious counsel and firm grip of affairs, his tact and courtesy, his wide vision and unfailing energy."

CHAPTER XXXI

THE MODERATOR

It was while the Campaign was being projected that Donald, coming one day into our house in Edinburgh, asked, " What would you feel about my being Moderator ? " and seemed more amused than disconcerted by the answer, " I'd hate it." But others, besides his wife, were consulted. They felt that, far from dissipating the energies he had bent on his missionary task, the office would give him greater influence in carrying through the enterprise. So he accepted—" with great fear and awe "—the high post to which he had been elected.

His Moderatorial year began rather inauspiciously with an attack of influenza followed by pneumonia. Illness always seemed his one and only way of arranging for a holiday. This time he spent it with friends in Cornwall, and convalesced so satisfactorily that he was mowing the grass and taking long walks before he left. What greatly cheered him was the good news of the Campaigns, " proving that the system flourished independently of any one man." For a little while before the Assembly he retreated to a farm in Argyllshire, kept by an old nurse, where he was " fed and coddled and loved by the dear old lady, as if I were her bairn again." There, surrounded by the great hills, with the sea breaking on the beach two hundred yards away, and a rushing mountain stream close by singing him to sleep at night, he prepared for the busy time ahead, " spending days alone on the hill-top, with the curlews and the sheep—and God."

He returned to Edinburgh with considerable trepidation,

but the way in which the Church seemed to take him to its heart made not only the Assembly, but the year which followed, an extraordinarily happy one. He delighted to make his wife confess that, after the first ten minutes in the Moderator's Gallery, she enjoyed every minute of it. One of the youngest men who had ever occupied the Moderator's Chair, he was received with enthusiastic cheers, in which the youngest of his young family heartily joined! Dr Adam Philip, the retiring Moderator, spoke of the thoughts of many in Central Africa and throughout the world being with them at that moment. The honour of Moderatorship, as in the case of the later appointment as Chaplain to the King, Fraser regarded as a recognition of the missionary service of the Church. As might be expected, he took as the subject of his opening address, " The Supreme Task of the Church," and his words were characteristic : " Our worship of the Redeemer compels us to win others for Him. If our worship produces no service, but only a smug selfishness, it is not God the Father we worship, not the Cross of Christ that has been our vision. The Cross is for the whole world, the love of the Father sweeps over the earth, is wider than nationality or race. It is a sea without bank or boundary, and he who looks into the heart of God cannot but say ' I must ; I cannot forbear ; I must live for the revelation of this message to mankind.' "

He was no ecclesiastic, as he often confessed, so he left the control of the Court to the Clerks of Assembly ; but his beautiful opening prayers were remarked on, and he contributed what was peculiarly his *forte*—the creating of a spirit of happy friendliness, extending beyond the borders of the United Free Church. One of his innovations was to invite Dr Stevenson of Gargunnock, a Church of Scotland minister, to give the address at the Communion

Service held for members of Assembly, while at the Missionary Meeting it was Dr Smellie of the Original Secession Church who led in prayer for missionaries on furlough. The Church that year had sent out thirty-nine missionaries to the foreign field, and the Missionary Meeting marked the high tide of interest in numbers and enthusiasm. On the Continental night, when sympathy would be all directed to the Reformed Churches of Europe, it was noticeable that he prayed specially for the Church of Rome, that she might be enabled to show her people Jesus Christ.

There was a happy garden party for the children of his missionary colleagues in our own garden, when the Moderator was given little attention compared with the person in charge of the ice-cream, the guests unceremoniously superintending personally the scraping out of the last remains. And, as always during Assembly meeting, he made a point of being present at Cunningham House, the Home for Missionaries' Children.

Nor was Lochgilphead forgotten by " His Reverence of Argyll," as someone dubbed him. More than once during the sitting of Assembly, visitors from there occupied an honoured seat in the Moderator's Gallery.

The usual attendance at functions demanded from a Moderator was not allowed to interfere with the work of the Campaign, for in it he felt that he was serving the truest interests of the Church. So the usual tour in the north during the summer took the form of a series of brief missions in various centres, in Lewis, Skye, Easter Ross, Sutherland and Caithness, and included speaking in Free Churches in the north. He could speak no Gaelic beyond a smattering, but he had enough of the Highlander in his composition to understand his audiences and be thrilled to the marrow by the Gaelic singing.

As always, he was a welcome visitor. Manse ladies liked

him because he was so homely and considerate ; children clustered round him like bees round a skep. An English visitor in a manse in the north remembers how his hostess gave him a peep into the spare-room to show how he had tidied it up. He was known as " the Moderator who made his own bed," for he understood just how much extra work such a visit put upon these most hospitable hostesses of his. There was but one type of woman whom he found it difficult to get on with—the uncharitable censorious type. " I found myself driven," he wrote *à propos* of one such whom he met, " to defend strongly the delightful Christian habit of making oneself pretty with paint and powder." He was always more ready to defend than to attack, and encouragement and comfort were always forthcoming for those who needed them, even when the occasion seemed trivial. For instance, one day at dinner the pudding was rather a failure. Very diffidently our hostess asked her husband if he would have some more. He refused, with perhaps unnecessary emphasis, and she flushed up and did not offer it to anyone else. After a moment, " Would you think it very greedy of me if I asked for a little more ? " inquired Donald, passing along his plate as he spoke. He was generously served by the relieved lady. An hour later he was asking his wife for soda-mint tabloids. " I suppose you realised this would happen ? " " Yes, but it was worth it. It would have left her so uncomfortable if the dinner had ended like that."

Children loved his stories, which he was always willing to tell to them. Grown-ups were equally greedy for them. At times he grew very weary of roaring, as the " lion " from Africa was expected to do. He would so gladly have listened to what others could impart, for he had a wide range of interests, and the time in Scotland gave him the only real chance of getting into fresh touch with subjects outside of his own province. Instead he had to go on interminably answering such questions as " I suppose it is very hot in Africa ? " People, he regretted plaintively at times, *would* ask friends in to supper after a tiring day of speaking ! He knew it came from a courtesy that made them feel they should share their guest with others, but during that Moderatorial year I accompanied him as much as possible, and it was an understood thing between us that if I " barged in," it was to intercept those inquiries I was as competent to answer as he. After we had retired for the night he would sometimes remark, " That is the *n*th time this week you have interestedly discussed the climate of Ngoniland," and my reply was that the interest lay in seeing for how long I could keep him out of the conversation. Few realised how this " giving " of himself so whole-heartedly took it out of him. In intense weariness he could welcome a friend and give no sign of his real condition. Even when ill he had a way—annoying to the nurse who wanted him to be seen as he really was—of pulling himself together when the doctor arrived, to give him a cheery welcome and seem much better than he really felt.

He had a habit of making the best of situations. When a number of ministers who had been invited to meet him before a Rally of the local Sabbath Schools accompanied him to a cold, gloomy church, to find that the Rally consisted of a dozen children sitting huddled in the choir seats, they were aghast at the fiasco. But he took it cheerfully, and, after the opening hymn, gathered the children round him and engrossed them with his stories ; for he went on the principle, not of scolding the people who did turn up, but of trying to make the people who didn't, regret what they had missed.

There were many happy memories of that year. The

" Celestials " (his College year) held their usual dinner during Assembly Week, and J. M. E. Ross, whose gift of writing verse had amused them in College days, produced an epic poem entitled " The Celestials in Paradise," which made fun, among others, of "Jim Moffatt " (as Donald always referred to him), as well as of the Moderator—the only member who failed to turn up at that " Celestial " re-union. In the case of the Professor, the Bard in somewhat highly-coloured language described how a copy of the well-known *Introduction to the New Testament* fared at the author's hands :

> To the gold bar of Heaven he flew,
> And out his valued work he threw
> Into the void. . . .
> We asked him why he treated thus
> A work which seemed to all of us
> So wise and timely.   Moffatt groaned :
> Then in heart-wringing accents moaned,
> The while he cursed his cruel fate :
> " My book's already out of date ;
> I met to-day the Apostle Paul,
> *And he wrote Hebrews after all.*"

Then, having searched every other where for the missing Moderator, they found him at last where they least expected him :

> By wireless phone we spoke our mind,
> Entreating him to be so kind
> As to explain his awful fix :
> Took he the wrong boat on the Styx ?
> By wireless phone we heard his voice—
> Said he, " I came of my own choice.
> Accustomed long to regions black,
> I knew that I should feel a lack,
> Dwelling with you in realms of light
> With everybody clean and white.
> And so I've settled in the pit
> To try and do some good in it."

" How fares your Mission ? " then we cried ;
And Fraser with good cheer replied,
" Not badly ; for beneath my rule
Young devils come to Sunday School."

   .   .   .   .   .   .

Long ages passed ; we got no news ;
Then we resolved once more to use
The wireless telephone to find
If our dear friend had changed his mind.
We got him.   " Come," we said, " and spend
A week or even a long week-end
With old friends in some happy star :
The joy were worth a journey far.
For old times' sake," we urged, " do try."
But Fraser answered with a sigh,
" I cannot come just now, I fear ;
They've made me Moderator here."

One hesitated whether to include this or not. He
thoroughly enjoyed it himself (a copy was found in his
desk), as during that year he enjoyed other verses from the
same pen, such as the " Hymn for little Citizens," scribbled
during a rather animated discussion of the Committee on
Church Praise,[1] to unite them in laughter.

African interests were never neglected.   This year
brought one of the occasions when he was asked to form
part of a deputation to the Colonial Office in connection
with conditions in that continent.   He spoke, apparently,
with more knowledge and a great deal more directness than
some of the others, for Lord Milner, in replying, seemed to
address himself to this missionary rather than to the more important people with whom he was associated.   But his attitude
was unsatisfactory, and as the discussion went on, Dr Fraser
had to overcome his shyness and ask leave to make further
explanations ; he felt grateful for the smile with which he

[1] The official hymn-book (up till 1927) of the Presbyterian Church of
England.   J. M. E. Ross was editor.

was encouraged to do so. He urged his points, calling things by plain names, and yet somehow, in that disarming way he had, seemed to appeal to his opponent's friendly interest, so that the interview ended by Lord Milner taking a far better position than he had occupied at the outset, assuming a much more friendly manner, and giving him at parting a far more determinate handshake. When they emerged from the building the Archbishop of Canterbury remarked that it had been well worth Dr Fraser's while coming down from Scotland to make such a contribution.

A more social function which we attended in London was the wedding of the Duke and Duchess of York. It was characteristic of Donald that he said nothing about not having received the invitation that should have come to him as Moderator. It was only at the last minute, when a friend said he hoped we would enjoy the ceremony, that the fact transpired, and the mistake, through his intervention, was set right. Never before had I seen Donald walk without embarrassment in his court suit, but the London streets so swarmed with gorgeous uniforms that day that no one troubled to look at his clothes, though one girl giggled over " the 'at." In Edinburgh he had always tried to evade observation, and the only times when he was willing to wear his finery without protest were when he was assisting at some wedding; then if the bride wished it, he was willing to dress up " any way you like." The only other people for whom he would do the same were his African folk, and it was partly to gratify them and partly because it might be wanted in South Africa, that we took out his Moderator's gown on our return. It was stolen on the way up country, and he drew a picture of a big native chief sitting over his beer-pot swathed in its voluminous folds, with the inscription beneath, *Sic transit gloria mundi !*

CHAPTER XXXII

SOUTH AFRICAN CAMPAIGN

FRASER's interest had never been confined to his own work or colony. Those who have looked at African problems as a whole always recognised that his views were those of a statesman. He studied with assiduity all that related to Africa, paying particular heed to conditions in South Africa, so closely linked to Nyasaland from the point of view of the influence it exerted on his own people. The demand for employment which could not be obtained locally—one has seen him on a Monday morning surrounded by a yelling mob of 200 applying for a two-men's job to last a week!— sent great numbers south to work in the mines and other industrial centres. Thus the work done in the Livingstonia Mission was considerably affected by the effect on mind and character of the conditions of life, and the attitude to the Native, which those men had experienced who returned home to Nyasaland after a longer or shorter period spent there.

Fraser understood the difficulties and complications of the question of race relationships, and realised that the supreme task for South Africa was to work out to its solution the problem of a stable ethical civilisation. It had been suggested, when we passed through Capetown in 1919, that he might be able after his return to help the South African Churches to get a clearer view of the Christian responsibility and attitude, for the problem lay so very close to their own doors, and personal considerations were so involved, that it was difficult for their members to take a dispassionate view of the situation.

The idea of this Campaign for better relationships was warmly received by the leaders of the Churches. It was a unique undertaking in the history of the colony, and was peculiarly timely, for serious thought on native affairs had been growing. Not only did all the Churches, apart from the Roman, combine to support it, but the leaders, including archbishop, bishops, moderators, chairmen of unions and others, appointed a Day of Prayer in preparation for it. Many apart from the Church welcomed the idea. General Smuts sent a message, telling of his interest and pleasure that they should have the guidance of an expert like Dr Fraser, coming to speak, with the authority and experience of a lifetime spent in African work, on the subject that most concerned the future of the country.

Knowing as he did that it was no abstract question with which he had to deal, but one intimately associated with critical political situations which made it peculiarly difficult to tackle, Fraser set off on his mission with some uncertainty as to the lines he should take. Of only one thing was he clearly convinced—that the solution was to be found in loyalty to Jesus Christ and the application of His principles and His spirit. Some urged him to lash out and attack abuses ; but he felt that little would be done by putting men on the defensive, so he refused to do so except by implication. He agreed with the words of Professor Brookes : " If Fraser leaves South Africa indignant, his Mission will have failed ; if he leaves it penitent, it will have been a great success." This does not mean that he did not speak out with great frankness to those whose religious professions gave him the right to rebuke their disloyalty. He told apathetic Churches that what was the matter with them was that Jesus Christ meant nothing to them ; he told Christian students that their great need was to be willing to get true views of the

Bible and to apply the spirit of Christ to racial relationships ;
he gently rebuked the lack of courtesy which, in a gathering of students, made them conduct all the service up to
the time of his speaking in Afrikaans, telling them they
had done their best to make him feel an " Uitlander " by
not enabling him to worship along with them.   He spoke
plainly about Church division and the absurdity of bringing
their historic prejudices out to Africa.

His fellow missioner throughout the tour was Arnold
Bryson from China—a singularly congenial colleague.
Thrown into constant intimate touch for four or five
months, the one thing they found to regret, as they were
having their one rest of two days on the Natal coast
together before sailing to Capetown, was that the hospitality they had enjoyed had so often separated them.
There had been disappointments and failures, and it would
have been easy to throw off depression or irritation if
they could have faced it together and together laughed
at their despondency; it would have helped so much at
nights if they had been able to talk and pray together, and
laugh off their wearinesses and discouragements.   His
" dear old Chief " completely won Bryson's heart at the
first moment of their meeting in Bloemfontein, by the
warmth of his greeting to an " unknown, untried colleague who was desperately nervous, and overawed by the
company in which he found himself."   The confidence
and friendship so quickly established lasted throughout
life.   The two missioners had one great bond in common,
—each was desperately homesick for his wife, and both
talked a great deal to each other about the wonderful
women they had married !   The fact that their wives had
been old College friends made each ready to believe that the
other's wife might approximate to her husband's estimate
of her.   At Women's Meetings they relieved their feelings

by taking their wives as their text and telling of the work they did, and the kindly ladies seem to have listened sympathetically. How much the speakers idealised their subjects one does not know, but it was sufficiently for one impressed audience to cluster round the platform at the end of the meeting demanding to see the wife's photograph. Fortunately for the husband's reputation for veracity, he had none to show ! But it indicated how the old shyness was disappearing, for as a younger man he said he could never speak about anyone he loved. Some of these South African ladies must have realised his homesickness, for they seem to have taken great care of him and mothered him. He actually submitted and allowed one of them to help him to select the clothes he required and prevent him from buying the first thing shown him, as assuredly he would have done if left to himself. At Stellenbosch they discovered when it was his birthday, and he was publicly presented with a cake by two little girls dressed in white. A very uncomfortable " lion " he must have been ; but, as long as they stopped short of trying to fit a halo on his head, he could endure it all with a tolerable grace. It was in places where they were inclined to regard him as a saint that he " squirmed," and he wrote pathetically of the hot-house piety he sometimes encountered, and of his endeavours to dispel the aura of sanctity with tobacco smoke, to dissipate any false impression. If people condemned smoking as wrong, he at least made them aware that he did smoke, though he was too thoughtful for others to do so if they simply disliked it. He was a little afraid of the intensive kind of piety which he sometimes met, especially in its effect on children, and felt very grateful to Arnold Bryson for the fun and high spirits with which he entranced the youngsters and made shouts of laughter come as a wholesome corrective after some deeply impressive evening meeting.

Not that the services were always impressive : there were times when he " made an awful mess of it," and then he blamed himself ; there were times when he thought he talked " rot," and his colleagues thought he had given a peculiarly effective message. Then in his letter to his wife he hoped that it did not sound like bragging to tell her so, for indeed he was in no mood to brag, but was fairly terrified by his own inability to say anything in face of the great opportunity that was given him. There were one or two dead places where the organisation had been neglected and little could be done. In one such place the two missioners met with a curious aloofness on the part of the ministers, and the only men who shared their ideas and gave real support were the Salvation Army officers. They preached in very thinly-attended churches, without a word of thanks from the ministers, and the opening reception was attended by a score or so of people. One meeting was cancelled by the unanimous consent of the chairman and speaker, who were the only two to turn up for it. A Ladies' Meeting was represented by one who was standing outside the closed door when the speaker came up, three minutes before it was due to start ; but eighteen had gathered before it closed. Their kindly hosts and other laymen were indignant at their treatment, and it beat the two missioners to explain what lay behind it ; but they decided that it was for the good of their souls to meet this sort of thing after all the attention they had been receiving in other places.

Their ordinary welcome was far different. Sometimes, as at Port Elizabeth, they were taken straight from the train to the reception, and stood up to speak with their heads still in a whirl. Four great meetings on the Sunday were followed on Monday by a Ministers' Fraternal, a public lunch in the Town Hall, and a large public meeting in the evening. After this "off day," three meetings apiece on the Tuesday! This programme came after the visit of the Prince of Wales the week before.

The Universities were not left out, and the students at Grahamstown gave a rather unexpected turn to the Dedication Service there. Rain having postponed their sports till the day on which a meeting for students and staff had been arranged in connection with the Campaign, Fraser sent a message to suggest that the meeting should be cancelled, and that, instead, they might come to the evening meeting. This was done. Fraser attended the sports, and in the evening, instead of the usual dance, the students marched down to the City Hall singing ragtime songs. When the platform procession, led by the Bishop, entered, the students, who filled the gallery, stood up and sang, "For he's a jolly good fellow," and gave three rousing cheers. Unconventional beginning for a Dedication Service though it was, it was yet absolutely natural. The speaker felt that it only increased the depth of the ensuing appeal, and was thrilled to have so great a part of his audience composed of that class. That friendliness of spirit was one of the features of the Mission. In the same place Fraser was to speak in the Wesleyan Church, and, by request, in full canonicals. A second D.D. hood, to replace his stolen one, had arrived from Scotland, but it was a Canon of the Cathedral who produced a black gown for the Presbyterian minister! This was typical of the brotherly relations engendered, which in themselves made the Mission worth holding. Several of the bishops had Fraser as their guest, and he wrote of the great kindness with which these High Anglicans received him. It was, however, with Bishop Karney, of Johannesburg, that he found the

S

hospitality that won his soul and made him feel at home, for here he experienced the completeness of Christian fellowship in being invited to join each morning in the celebration of the Sacrament in the private chapel, as well as in the intercourse of a very delightful family life. One little touch of thoughtfulness meant a great deal to him. In a united Service of Intercession held in the Cathedral the Bishop asked that there might be silent prayer for Dr Fraser's wife. " You can think how it thrilled me, dear lass, kneeling there, with that great congregation praying for you." Not only so, but the Bishop sat down during that busy week to write to an unknown woman a letter that made her heart glow, as he told her news which, he said, he felt sure that her husband would not write, ending by speaking of him as one of the best bits of Christian evidence it had ever been his good fortune to come across.

His host spared no pains to further the success of the Mission. When the Dutch Reformed Church invited Fraser to preach in their pulpit, it was felt to be a matter of some moment, considering the state of racial feeling. Fraser had already promised to conduct the Presbyterian service, but the Bishop took his place there in order to set him free. Driving to the Dutch Reformed Church Fraser was told that he would, of course, be interpreted into Afrikaans, not, it was admitted, because they would fail to follow him in English, but because of their sensitiveness about their own language. To his glad surprise when he entered the Session room, where the Kirk Raad were assembled, one of the old men announced that they had decided that he should speak without interpretation. He might well rejoice that, quite apart from what the missioners were saying, the Mission itself was having such practical results.

Nor was it only the religious public that he was able to

approach. There were frequent opportunities through Rotary Clubs, receptions and public lunches, to get into contact with influential laymen, including Jews and men of no religion, and on one occasion at least a delightful French Roman Catholic drove him to a meeting in his own car.

The Natives, too, were not left out. In most of the larger places meetings were arranged for them, and Fraser not only seized the opportunity of meeting some of their religious leaders in conference, but also felt it his responsibility to try to get into touch with one of their rather disturbing political leaders, who in his early days had been taught in a Livingstonia Mission school, in order to suggest to him that bitterness and exaggeration would not in the long run help the native cause.

Towards the end of the tour, in addition to some speakers belonging to the Cape, they were joined by Dr Zwemer,[1] whom Fraser hailed as a most effective speaker, saying that he himself could now edge out of all prominence, for here, to his great relief, was a man with a message who could speak it out. For a time he contented himself with addressing smaller Group Meetings ; but it was not for long. The Campaign came to a splendid finish at Capetown, where some great meetings were held. The Governor-General and Princess Alice invited the missioners to lunch, and had been prepared to preside at some of their meetings ; but General Hertzog had advised otherwise, as he confessed to Fraser, lest the Campaign might be identified with politics. Twenty-two week-day meetings were followed by four on the last Sunday of June, the final one being held in the packed City Hall. Besides the Church leaders there were on the platform

[1] Dr S. M. Zwemer, leading authority on Moslem Missions and editor of *The Moslem World.*

General Smuts, the Chief Justice, Sir Thomas Smartt, and many of the Members of Parliament. It was so expectant a crowd that he found it easy to speak to them with all the passion of which he was capable, and apparently a great impression was created, Smuts speaking of it as having been electrical, and regretting that the people had not had some opportunity of expressing their feelings. And so back to the hotel, very tired, but very thankful. He had that week sent the cable that changed the current of his life, and now he was starting back for Nyasaland the next morning, with no time to join the others in the trip to the Victoria Falls that was to be their relaxation after their strenuous labours.

CHAPTER XXXIII

THE MISSIONARY AND HIS PEOPLE

In the busy little store at Loudon a big crowd of Natives were gathered with their week's pay, all wanting to be served at once. Bewildered by their clamour, the one man in charge exclaimed, " I can't stand this ! " " Why not ? " asked one of the prospective purchasers ; " it's what you are paid to do." Donald, entering at that moment, overheard the exclamation and the reply. Often afterwards, when we thought things terribly vexatious, he would quote with a reminiscent smile about his eyes, " It's what we are paid to do."

Perhaps our people remember that, more constantly than we missionaries do. Why should they be grateful because we do not neglect our job ? It is not the faithful performance of duty that impresses them (though they are observant of failure in that respect), but the little extras, the uncalled-for bits of thoughtfulness. When the missionary, after having put in a good day's work, sits up more than half the night in hospital with his Native colleague, sharing his anxiety for a wife who is going through a critical confinement after fifteen years of childless married life, then it is that they recognise that his love and interest are deep and personal things. I shall never forget so little a thing as the glance that passed between Donald and his fellow-pastor one night when I came excitedly in to tell them a piece of good news as they sat side by side in the waiting-room. Through the open door came a feeble little wail that forestalled me. As their eyes met, their hands went

involuntarily out to clasp each other's ; one knew that
there was no consciousness whatever of race or colour at
such a time.   That was the real secret of Fraser's success
as a missionary : the people knew that he had given himself
to them ; they had his heart.

To those who do not know the African, dissimilarities
are not apparent ; intimacy is needed to bring to view the
infinite variety of character and manner, and the little
idiosyncrasies which, it has been said, sometimes more
endear a man to his fellows than his standard worth. Donald
had that kind of affectionate knowledge of those among
whom he worked, and his attitude was always human rather
than professional.   Personality did not strike him as of profound importance only, but as of profound interest, and anything that prevented its unhampered development had to
be fought against.   It was no abstract sense of justice that
made him so keen to oppose the colour bar and the racial
prejudices of the south : it was his quick realisation of the
psychological effects that these produced in men, black and
white.   Once when travelling into the Union from Nyasaland, he turned and asked, " Do you notice the difference
in the Native people here ? "   There were various differ-
ences, but the outstanding one—the saddest to him—was
that they had lost their smile.   Often he used to quote
that remark made by Crawford of Luanza when, on a visit
home, he watched in the underground trains the crowds
that went in to business each morning : " What shall it
profit a man though he gain the whole world and lose his
smile ? "

There was a good deal of St Francis of Assisi about him
in the simplicity and gladness of his friendship with all
around him, but he learned a great deal too from that other
Francis—Xavier—whose life he studied so carefully ; for
he was indeed as catholic in his admiration of the great men

of history as in his friendships with the living. Biography interested him more than any other general reading. In his library, however (the one thing he felt more than justified in spending money on), he specialised in all that related to Africa and the general problems of missions. His *New Africa* was written without his being able to consult any books of reference beyond those that were on his own bookshelves. One of the things he really did regret about coming home was the necessity of leaving so many books behind, because of the cost of transport. Neglect of reading was to him one of the most serious temptations a missionary had to fight against. He was eager to promote reading among his people by supplying them with literature in the vernacular, and for some time he edited *Makani*, the monthly paper brought out in the local dialect. It was interesting to watch him trying to stimulate a desire for books in his evangelists. Books that would teach them something they were glad to borrow, and lives of men also interested them ; but fiction made no appeal, and—this rather surprised him—they showed no desire to read about the life of their own colleague, Daniel. They knew about him already, thank you !

Fraser was always keen to see what creative or artistic powers could be discovered in his people. One year he had an exhibition of any handicraft they cared to produce. A great deal of it was sheer imitation, such as a book carved from a block of wood, and a bicycle that had all the parts and could do everything except move ; but there were also little clay figures which showed some artistic talent, and he pointed out to the exhibitors how they failed most by trying to reproduce reproductions instead of going back to a study of the original. The development of a kind of primitive art that was springing up in connection with the building of the schools, it also gratified him to notice. It took the form of rough frescoes in clay on the walls—at first mainly of animals, but tending towards the pictorial representation of events. Some were attempts to illustrate Bible stories, and when he first saw St Mark's in Venice, with its mosaic representations of Bible scenes, from Genesis to the missionary apostles, in the Baptistery, he remarked that we had the rough germ of that in Africa, and he would have liked to show his Africans this ultimate triumph of the art.

The possibilities of dramatic art as a missionary method were first brought home to him by his friend Temple Gairdner, but too late for practical exploration of their value. How greatly he could enjoy the histrionic powers of his people one had only to be with him on ulendo to realise. Over the camp-fires the men would reproduce a scene with such a wealth of tone, expression and action that, watching from a distance too great to catch the words, one could yet get a very fair impression of what it was all about, and of which European was being mimicked. Nothing gave more amusement to a village than some of the tales acted after the War by the returned carriers. Europeans who had behaved foolishly had little idea of the vivid impression of their speech and personality that was being imparted to delighted audiences by some man who had seemed scared or stupid in their presence. Once for a few days, in the interests of a cinema camera, Loudon was the scene of many incidents in the past history of the people, though it was the church beadle who administered the poison ordeal, and, as headman of a village, tried with bow and arrow to defend it against an Ngoni attack, and who lay speared as it burst into flames. So many fierce Ngoni warriors had taken possession of the Mission Station that week, that a small white child would only go about if Daddy held her hand.

One of his " Celestial " friends, Bulloch Douglas,[1] in reviewing Fraser's *African Idylls*, hailed it as a book that was free from the missionary's touch, which, to his mind, spoiled Fraser's other books as literature. Yet it was in these *Idylls* that the missionary in Fraser was more fully revealed than in anything else he wrote. The others dealt with the externals of anthropology and history ; these sketches revealed his insight into and delight in the people to whom he ministered. His deep reverence for their personality could not brook the discussion of them as " problems."

Unfortunately there was comparatively little time to give to these personal contacts, but there was an inner circle, with whom he was much more closely in touch, and on whose growth he knew much depended. He saw into their weaknesses, but he dwelt on what was best in them, and did his utmost to draw it out by trusting and encouraging them, though he could, if necessary, speak to them very straightly with no beating about the bush.

There was music, too. One of his children shrewdly remarked one day, " Daddy would like the people to like the 'Hallelujah Chorus' best, but they really like Harry Lauder." It took no knowledge of English or training in musical taste to understand and appreciate so international and contagious a thing as the great comedian's laugh. The audience gathered round—who peered into the box from which the laugh came—often roared in concert, and went away trying to reproduce what they had heard, or murmuring to themselves in their desire to acquire English, " A'm tellin' ye," or an intention to " poker up the fire and make themselves a wee cup of tea." But every now and then he would find unexpected appreciation among the listeners. His old beadle wanted nothing more than to slip away, with tears in his eyes, after hearing a *Messiah* record. The dirty,

[1] Rev. R. Bulloch Douglas, D.D., of East London, South Africa.

untidy old man had an artist's soul. It was he who grew to
value the beauty of form and colour in a sheaf of reddened
leaves and dried grasses, and felt that his church was not
ready for the service till the flowers on the platform had
been placed and gazed at by him, with his head on one side
to survey the result. On the last Sunday of all it was
he too who, helping in the vestry, said he had no eyes
to-day for flowers or aught else, sorrow and tears blotting
out everything.

After one happy evening with the evangelists, when we
had listened to Daniel telling in his inimitable way the story
of Kamzunguzeni and many another, and had heard
reminiscences of the old wars and the early mission days,
Donald slipped on to the gramophone a record of Melba
singing *Ave Maria*, and, while doing this, told them the
sums she received for a single concert. They exclaimed
incredulously, perhaps a little contemptuously, at such a
stupendous price being paid to a woman for merely singing.
But after they had listened, the profound silence was
broken by Daniel exclaiming enthusiastically, " Give her
the money ; she is worth it ! " A gleam of gladness came
into Donald's face as he thus realised that the power to
appreciate was there.

Minutes are generally formal and rather uninteresting
things, but there were some paragraphs in those of the
Loudon Session which met at the time when their missionary
was leaving them, that reveal what had attracted their
observation. In reviewing the situation he had found on
arrival in the country, and the changes that had been
wrought, they said :

" We shall not forget his hardships. He ate the ordinary
food (sima) of the country. He protected himself with
green leaves when the sun scorched him on his journeys.
This truly shows that he gave himself to us soul and body :

he denied himself to become one with us. He loved the children of Africa : we remember his tucking up black children in his own bed that they might not die of cold on the Vipya. We shall not forget how he sided with us in the case of Kanjechi, for it was he who in this case pleaded our cause when Sir Alfred Sharpe inquired into that matter.

" We remember the longing of his heart after wandering souls. Although the Ngoni country and the Marambo is extensive, there is no village where he is unknown. The chiefs and everybody knew him, for he never had a frown on his face : he was 'Chisekeseke'—(one who is always smiling).

" By showing a heart of love he drew many to Christ. He entered into smoky and bug-infected huts seeking lost souls. His house, although very fine, was a shelter for the weary and sinful in heart, and he helped many who came to his home seeking the way of salvation for their souls. He taught the evangelists and catechists and elders to be like-minded in doing this. We are ashamed that we have not caught the infection of a like heart. He was kind and gentle with old people, both men and women. He had many ways of quickening the work of the Church. We are aware that he often spent sleepless nights in think-ing of the Church in Ngoniland. By the grace of God his faith overcame many difficulties.

" On his departure for Scotland we have sore hearts ; but seeing that we are not able to keep him here, we have reluctantly agreed to his going. Knowing that it is the Will of God drawing him to Scotland, we have simply to submit. We know that his heart is still with us, and also the remembrance of his teaching and work still sustains us. Words fail us to praise him. . . . We thank the God of all grace for sending them to us. We thank the Home

Committee who sent them here. God be with them all the days till we meet again."

This grateful affection was not confined to the Christians. The Native Association of the district, which included chiefs, headmen, teachers, Government employees and other leading men in the tribe, wrote him a letter enumerating all the services he had rendered, spiritual, educational, political, economic, and summed it up by saying: " In difficult circumstances, both spiritual and physical, you have stood firm in faith and hope for brighter days. Surely you have proved yourself a real optimist, and your encouragement to us in dark times has put new life in us. We admit that on the part of the people you came to help there have been ingratitude, disappointment, sin and apostasies from the Christian faith " (there were such cases among those who signed), " but amid all these you have been found faithful to them. Hence many love you dearly, and call you a father who has begotten them through forbearance and sympathy. . . . Your coming among us indicated that you ' first loved us,' but as we became acquainted with you and found in you a true and loving friend, although your body is different from ours, we had to respond to your love by loving you in return. . . . It is a great loss to miss your encouraging and smiling face, from which Natives of this land have derived your nickname ' Chisekeseke '—one who smiles with any."

" The smiling one " may sound rather an unattractive title to anyone who did not know that smile, " all the more beautiful because of the gravity in it," as one of his friends described it. It was no chronic amiable expression, but the sudden spontaneous outbreaking of friendship, gladness or amusement, the word Chisekeseke coming from the same root as the words to laugh, rejoice or give pleasure. In the villages, when he first came among them, one heard the children, clustered behind some hut and peering out to see what the white man looked like, whisper, " He's smiling," as his eye caught theirs. It was doubtless in some such way that he first got the name, and his fun and friendship and good cheer made it stick to him.

Names given to Europeans are not all so complimentary, but they always refer to some characteristic of the owner, for he is invariably subjected to the closest scrutiny by an extraordinarily observant people who can reproduce him to the life. I never realised how ungracefully I ran till I saw a boy imitate me, unaware that he could be seen through the window. When he saw my husband emerge, looking wrathful at the impertinence of it, his running regained a speed and gracefulness that carried him out of sight in a very few seconds !

Unconsciously or consciously, every missionary is imitated in many ways. Watch a Native preaching, and it is easy to tell by whom he was trained. No one was better aware of this than Donald Fraser, and it humbled him, for he attributed to his own shortcomings those failures he saw in his flock. As we walked home one day from a service where a vigorous preacher had not given us very much to think about, Donald remarked to me, " What a humiliating picture of myself—plenty of energy to make up for the lack of real power ! " There was another side that others rather than he were aware of—the influence he contributed to the growth of those in contact with him. A letter I once received from a teacher at the Livingstonia Institution contained this query : " Why is it that the Loudon boys who come up are for the most part such a topping, lovable lot ? Of course there is ——, who is simply a goat ; but look at ——, and —— and ——, who are always bright and cheery, and ——, who is an absolute dear, and little ——, and oh ! lots of the nicest lads. Is

it simply a coincidence ?   Is the tribe naturally a finer one ?
Is it the result of contact with one Donald Fraser ?   I know
which you would agree with, and personally I like to think
there is a lot in it too."

All through life Donald had felt the handicap of teaching in a foreign tongue.   He wished often that he had not
had that barrier of language to hamper him in expressing
his Message.   But his life interpreted it better than any
words.   As an African widow put it to me : " We saw
how he put himself about for us black people.   He was
truly recognised as being like God in his dealings.   For
God did not love individuals here and there, but all.
Dr Fraser was like Him in that."

CHAPTER XXXIV

ABOUT this return to Africa there was an element of uncertainty that made Donald speak of it as "venturing back." Even before we left, numerous suggestions were abroad that his work in Africa should be given up for service at home. The very fact that the idea was so distasteful kept him from lightly dismissing it. One day I found him in talk with one of whose judgment he thought highly, and who was urging this course on him. Convinced that he had not the temperament for such a task as was proposed for him, and that his life in Africa had made him even less fit to stand its restrictions, I sought desperately for some new argument against the step, and, less selfishly than it sounded, inquired, " And what about *my* life-work ? " He immediately accused himself of being egotistical and inconsiderate, and definitely declined to discuss the matter further. Yet, the thought of the family was never absent from his mind, though they had always concealed from us their consciousness of any sacrifice, and never allowed us to realise, till we were settled in Scotland, how keenly they had longed for a home of their own. When the suggestion was mooted that their father should go back alone, they protested that he needed his wife far more than they needed their mother. " So do the Africans," added the youngest, who had spent many hours in hospital with her dear " Colie " (the nurse), and knew something of African patients. We left all four with a sorer heart than ever before, convinced though we were that ultimately they would suffer no loss on account of their sacrifice, and went back to the life and people he so loved, away from the trammels of crowded cities, walled-in spaces, time-tabled existence, and all the noise and stir of civilisation. Yet shades of the future haunted his steps, for letters began to follow him urging that he should let himself be nominated for the post left vacant by Dr Webster's death.   Into the ins and outs of this whole question there is no need to go. He had to admit that he knew he was becoming less fit to stand the African climate, but he felt neither fitness nor inclination for the type of work which he would be expected by the Committee to undertake, and wrote home frankly about his difficulties.   The reasons for staying, he said, came rushing in like a flood ; yet, because some of them should not be allowed to count, he brushed aside such considerations as the supreme attractiveness, variety, freedom and massiveness of the work in Africa, and the limitations that would be put on him at home, the humiliation of retiring from active service to the base, and the suspicion there might be that he had chosen the easier service.

His real fears were for his capacity—that he should grow stale ; that 50 per cent of any appeal he had been able to make had come from the fact that he was a missionary, and that this would now be lost ; he feared, too, the grip of officialdom with its narrowing and deadening effects, and recognised that missionaries brought home did not always prove a success in such work. He was fifty-four, and might fail to adapt himself to the change ; looked with dread on interminable committee and sub-committee meetings ; lacked the temper which made debate and fighting for one's ideas an easy or undisturbing factor, and in committee debate had too often found himself in the minority.   For remaining in his present sphere he had the qualifications of experience, adaptation, knowledge of the people and language—assets not lightly to be thrown aside when his people had come to a point of development where great amplifications in their religious and educational life were possible. Senior men were dropping out fast. Yet if he allowed himself to think of what, by God's grace, he might do for the wider service, he saw many an aim worth the best he could give.

" I should like to help some into the glory of serving a world-wide kingdom, and help the Church to recognise the unity of the Kingdom of God, to break down the departmental isolation of foreign mission work. I should like to help to make commercial and national life more contributory to evangelisation ; to help colonial life to be more sensitive of its trusteeship for native people. I should like to combat the growing menace of racial prejudices, and help to foster the spirit of brotherhood which is the only foundation of peace. I should like to help to penetrate the schools and the youth of the land with great thoughts of responsibility for the backward races ; to unite more vitally the work of the Young People's Societies and the Student Movement with the overseas work of our Church. I should like to assist the spirit of unity in the Christian Churches through service abroad and at home ; and to bring the congregations into the fuller life that comes from practical dedication to the Saviour of the whole world.

" To foster any of these would be a big service, and would not be done merely by big dramatic displays, but by patient and minute care of the details by which expression may be given to such a spirit. Money and candidates and intelligent interest would eventually and necessarily follow any success in doing these things. I may not be fit to do them, but at least the thought of such an aim stirs

T

me, when the thought of a secretaryship such as the Sub-Committee has defined creates only revulsion and a certainty that I am unfit for it. What gifts or grace God has given me are not mine, but His for His Kingdom, and if they can best be used at home I am willing to undertake the harder service, and deny myself the attractions of service here. . . ."

But there were definitions in the Minute with which he could not agree. That " The need for a more developed home organisation is primary " he could not accept. " Every ideal of my soul protests against it. *Life* is primary ; organisation is only created to allow life to express itself. . . . I believe in careful and minute organisation, but I believe, too, in the futility of organisation that is ' primary,' and it would be fatal for me to make organisation my primary concern." The main lines of work defined—to raise the presbyterial organisations to the same pitch of efficiency that the women's had reached, and to foster among men and lads an interest comparable to that of the Girls' Auxiliary—he disagreed with, pointing out that it was a matter of history that both these interests were created by voluntary effort without the concentration of an official secretary's guidance. " And, last, the Secretary is to have ' gifts of inspiration,' ' to inspire presbyteries and congregations.' I should be mad if I claimed these. And fancy inspiring a presbytery ! The angel Gabriel would shy at it !

" Such a paragraph and such definitions make me feel that the official harness is prepared and is to be slipped over me. But the shafts are too narrow, and the harness too ill-fitting. I cannot submit. I expect that the Committee wish to guard themselves and assure themselves that the work will be done. If this is their aim, I think I have made it plain in this letter that I have not the temperament or grace to undertake the work. And I am much mistaken if the Assembly would ask me to do it.

"It all sounds so bumptious and conceited. But I am certain that I do not refuse this work because I think I am too big for it, but because I know I could not do it. If the call was to relate the Church's life and service more fully to the service of the Kingdom of God, and I were left free to do this in the best way I could, with what help and advice the Committee and others would give, I believe that I could respond with my whole soul. . . . Should you and the Assembly be ready to address a call to me on the conditions I have suggested, I should think it a call of God to be obeyed. Should you on the other hand feel that I have revealed myself as impossible and not the man for the job you wish to fill, I shall be profoundly thankful that you allow me to continue in the service which I love with my whole heart."

The post he outlined was " not the secretaryship now vacant," and the friend to whom he had written cabled to say he would not propose him, feeling that he had " emphatically indicated his unwillingness for the post." We breathed freely for a little, but when the question of selecting a secretary was deferred by the Assembly to the following year, and we noticed how frequently his name was mentioned in the recommendations sent up by presbyteries, he doubted his right to resist the will of the Church, and even contemplated resignation from its membership as the only honourable alternative.

With this uncertainty hanging over his head he went off to South Africa, to carry on the Mission which had been arranged there, leaving me with some reluctance, as it meant that we would have no opportunity of discussing the question together if it again arose. But the parting was inevitable, as there was no one else on the Station with sufficient experience to take over the responsibility, although Mr Stuart promised to give all the assistance he could, consistently with the care of Ekwendeni. Famine, too, was threatening to add to local difficulties of administration.

Never had the work seemed so attractive and so necessary, and the people so needy and so lovable, as during those weeks when we were bullying half-starved men into crossing the high plateau to the Lake to bring up the bags of rice landed there ; when we were carefully distributing the food so that each might get a little, and no one more than another because he had more money to pay for it ; when the neediest were receiving enough to keep them alive, and little crowds were gathered at the kitchen door waiting for the food we handed out for the babies, and the hospital work grew more strenuous as disease seized on the ill-nourished bodies. How *could* it be right to leave them, in order to serve a Church that should be actively serving ? The letters that came to him from Loudon did not make the problem Fraser had to face any easier. " I can see," he wrote, " that all this feeding of the starving is endearing the people to you more than ever, and that you would find it even more difficult than before to contemplate leaving them." But before decision became necessary, a letter of capitulation arrived from his wife, telling how a neglected fracture of the wrist had set so badly that even intra-muscular injections for the lepers had become impossible, and that other branches of work would be still further beyond her present power. It looked as if this indicated a compulsory retiral from much of the *hospital* work, at any rate : the decision must be made without any thought of her. But her real concern was for him. " Fraser," one of his colleagues had said to him, " before you agree to go home, go and look at a caged lion in the Zoo, and say to yourself, ' That is what I'll feel like in the Church Offices ' " ; and she knew how wise that judgment was.

Yet no such object-lesson would have influenced him even if " bonds and imprisonment " were awaiting him : the question for him was to know the Will of God. He kept hoping that the problem might not have to be faced, or that he might at least have time to talk it over again with his wife ; and when he received a cable telling of his unanimous election and asking him to wire his answer before the Assembly rose, he felt that he was being stampeded into a decision before he knew all the circumstances and conditions under which he had been appointed. He cabled back, " Deeply moved by Assembly's confidence ; await fuller information," and hoped he would not be considered disrespectful. But when a longer cable followed, telling him that he had been elected on the terms of Dr Forgan's Memorandum—to which he had agreed—he could offer no objection ; there was nothing for it, he decided, but to face the prospect of going home. " This is one of the sacrifices I have to ask of you," he wrote to his wife, " to come back to Scotland, and help me not to throw away my life in failure." He accepted the call at a time when the perpetual motion and strain of the Campaign, with " so little time for reading and thinking," and the cold, wet weather, making him feel " so utterly miserable," caused him to dread the same type of life repeated in Scotland. There was only one clause in the agreement over which he laughed happily when he read it—the provision that he must retire at seventy. His own suggestion was that he should test his fitness for it for five years.

There were those in Africa who, knowing its need of the type of man he was, not only a devoted lover but a missionary statesman, deeply regretted his departure. Smuts had asked him at Capetown about the call, and begged him, when he returned to Scotland, to " remain an African and continue his services." Another, a District Commissioner in Northern Rhodesia, wrote a furious letter asking what was the matter with Christian Scotland that they must have the one man so much needed in Central Africa to speak out about the high taxation of the Natives in a way that would cost the salaried officials their posts. And it was not an altogether easy task to explain to his own folk why the Church at home required him. He could only promise that he was going to do his best to get other and younger men to carry on the work.

No sooner were the meetings at Capetown over than he was hurrying back to Loudon to make the most of the limited time that remained, for, in order to fit himself for his new post, he had decided that he must visit the mission fields of the United Free Church in South Africa, and acquaint himself with conditions there.

CHAPTER XXXV

THE SECRETARY IN OFFICE

It was well for him that those last few months at Loudon (1925) were such busy ones that there was little time for reflection. It was not that he had misgivings about the work which he was giving up. He never was tempted to think himself indispensable, because he never thought of his work as *his*; and he felt that quite possibly the best thing for Loudon might be the incoming of new life. In spite, however, of the confidence with which he could entrust the future of the Station to Dr Turner, he felt intensely the pang of cutting himself off from all that it had meant to him, from the people he had loved and for whom he had planned and toiled and suffered. We grew skilful in learning to evade the little groups of folk who came to express their sorrow at parting, for we had to keep our own feelings in check, and for once no playful teasing could turn them aside. It was no use saying lightly that we were worse off than they, for we were losing our African children for good, and they would soon have a new father and mother. "Tell me this," said an old woman; "tell me how long it takes for a stepfather or mother to take the place of the one you have lost? These new parents are for the next generation, not for us."

Coming up to breakfast one morning Donald confessed he had kissed every little girl in the Junior School. "I began with one irresistible wee thing," he said apologetically, "and then, of course, I had to go on."

Fortunately the manner of our going was exciting for

those days of less than ten years ago. On the spot where private aeroplanes can now alight, there was the unwonted spectacle of an old Humobile lorry which had been sent by a planter to take us and our baggage down to Blantyre. It had passed through many a vicissitude during the war period, and looked like a Heath Robinson invention, or a nightmare, but it was very impressive to the gathered crowd, and curiosity on their part and misgivings on ours as to what would happen if the strings with which the driver was doing repairs gave way, held emotion in check. It was only after we had rattled away on our three days' adventurous journey that the tragedy of the occasion gripped one old lady who, in Biblical language, broke into a lament that their father had been carried away from them in a chariot of fire !

On the second day, as we passed through Portuguese territory, we saw a village being built by the side of the road. Standing superintending the work was a figure warmly clad in a Jaeger dressing-gown complete but for one tassel. That missing tassel supplied the circumstantial evidence. With a smile we recognised the garment, and remembered that in this neighbourhood, two years before, our boxes on their way up country had been stolen during the night from the side of the sleeping carriers, forced open and rifled, and one tassel picked up by the side of the road had been the only thing our men had been able to retrieve. With the knowledge that there was also a Geneva gown and a D.D. hood in the vicinity, we felt entitled to believe it was no idle boast that we left behind us tangible evidence of the introduction of comfort, culture and Christianity !

Before sailing for home we visited the Mission Stations of our Church in the South African field, and it was the observations made then that so deeply impressed on Donald the great need for medical mission work in some of the native areas, and also the necessity for training men in Bible study for the sake of producing capable and educated evangelists. He was able to give valuable help in evolving the schemes that afterwards took shape to meet these two great needs. The Bible School that has been set a-going at Lovedale has had the indirect effect of bringing nine Churches into co-operation, thus helping to create that unity of aim which he considered so much more important in fostering true brotherhood than the laborious removing of barriers.

We arrived home towards the end of 1925. One of the first decisions that had to be faced was the question where we should settle. Glasgow was chosen rather than Edinburgh, for several reasons. It was the centre of the largest Presbytery in the Church, and to Dr Fraser it did not seem wholly wise that it should be controlled entirely from Edinburgh : he felt that Church interests might be fostered by having one of the secretaries in the west. Office accommodation was available there, and, as deputation work would take him all over the country, railway journeys would be inevitable in whatever centre he chose to reside. Although latterly he came to feel the heavy strain of so much daily travelling, he never regretted his choice, for he appreciated the warmth and brotherliness of the welcome Glasgow gave him, and made many firm friendships with business men, who gave loyal support and generous backing to the schemes in which they, as well as he, believed.

He always planned to work in the train when travelling to Edinburgh ; but whether people recognised him or not, they seemed to wish to talk to him, and work was impossible. In the second year of his secretarial duties, therefore, he took a first-class season ticket, in order to get less communicative companionship, and feel certain of securing a seat, for he was always last in a scramble for places and the first to give up his seat. But when finances went down in those years of increasing stress, he reverted to third class again, in spite of the added weariness it entailed. He was a hard worker, always trying to leave to-morrow a little more free by managing to get a little more into to-day's programme. Long hours spent in office and train were followed by almost daily evening meetings. Often he did not reach home till after ten o'clock, and Sundays, too, were full of engagements. The one purpose he shamefully failed to achieve throughout life was the admittedly wise one of having some time off in the week. Illness was his one chance of getting a rest, for even his summer month seemed always to be encroached on. When he had an evening at home it was seldom free : often there was business that he had not had time to cope with during the day, or some young man might have an appointment with him to consult him about mission work. Such a one was never treated just as a possible or impossible candidate for posts that required filling ; in each case Fraser looked at matters from the point of view of the future of the individual, went fully into circumstances and qualifications, and gave wise advice about the advantage of the stern discipline of adequate preparation for such a calling. It was never the immediate future and its needs, but the wide and ultimate issues of the Kingdom, for which he worked.

He had arrived home at a difficult time, and it was well for him that he *had* that far-reaching aim, for he had to admit, with a rueful smile, that the apparent result of his administration was a steady decrease in the finances. Disappointed though he might be, he did not let that discourage him. He was convinced that increased generosity would result from deepened spiritual life, and one of his methods—made possible by the financial support of one who shared

his views—was the holding of a series of gatherings of
ministers for spiritual uplift. Of the many conferences he
arranged during the time he was Secretary, very few were for
habitual attenders of such gatherings. Many who came to
them had had little or no experience of such things before,
and the happy fellowship and renewal of spirit derived from
them meant much to men from isolated country charges.
These conferences, by general testimony, did much to help
forward the cause of Union. Speakers and guests were
drawn from both the uniting Churches, and mutual appreciation resulted from close friendly contacts in an atmosphere
that was suitable for discovering how congenial and
spiritual men from the other side could be. Always a little
apprehensive beforehand lest the conference should not go
well, Dr Fraser was a genial, vicarious host on such occasions,
and for him it was the beginning of many very happy friendships with Old Kirk brethren, one of whom declared it was
worth while having the Union if only to acquire Donald
Fraser for their Church.

Thanks to the same generous backing, other conferences
were held for missionaries and for presbyterial corre-
spondents, both before and after the Union. Dr Fraser
never lacked offers of assistance, and he had the advantage
of the honorary service of two or three retired business men,
who gave valuable help in the Office in the organising and
financial departments. One of these, asked how he came
to offer his aid (which very often included that of his wife),
replied that he had " just met Fraser and felt that he was a
man with whom he would like to work." Two ministers
of the Church also became his honorary colleagues. Among
other schemes for increasing efficiency, a plan of deputation
work was organised that ensured that every church in
every presbytery should have a visit from a missionary once
in three years. Bookstalls, films, missionary exhibitions,

and many other methods of increasing knowledge and interest were thought out in the Home Organisation Sub-Committee, which was his special department.

On the General Committee Dr Fraser's long missionary service made real and deep his understanding of the business with which he was called to deal. A detailed knowledge of other mission fields than those of Africa he did not attempt to grasp—that was outside his province—but his experience and imagination made him quick to realise the vital issues that underlay many of the questions relating to them, and, if he felt these were not fully understood and were being too lightly decided, he would interpose to explain, or to protest if necessary against the summary disposal of a matter which involved a great principle or policy.

On the other hand, he was often wearied by the time spent on trivial issues. He disliked argument, and he some-times found it difficult to appreciate another's point of view. He had no love of the machinery of organisation as such, only valuing it as a means to an end : and the results were often so disappointing and meagre. Yet, with all that sense of being frustrated and impeded, he never lost his courage and his faith ; he who had begun his service in Africa full of its " intoxicating inspiration," and had " run and not been weary," learned now to " walk and not faint."

The day he had taken up work in the Offices he invited Mr R. F. Young, who worked in the Foreign Mission Department, into his room and said, " I expect you and I will be working a great deal together, so let us begin by praying together." Many a time he regretted that there was no quiet prayer-room in the building, even more so when increasing demands for extra accommodation led to his having to share a room with a colleague, although that colleague was one so congenial as his friend, the Rev. J. U. MacGregor, who gave up his church in 1926 to lend voluntary assistance in the task that confronted the new Secretary.[1]

That " gift of accessibility " which he possessed made privacy of any kind difficult to secure, for many a visitor, arriving from the country or overseas, and feeling rather chilled and lost in the " vast rabbit warren " of 121 George Street, found his way to the room of one who gave the impression that he had time for all comers. His quick glance and smile of recognition, extended to missionaries after years of absence, were grateful indeed to some who felt lonelier than they cared to admit. " He made the Offices seem homely." If many an hour seemed lost, much else was gained, for many have told of the effect, in heartening or otherwise influencing them, of some such time devoted to their affairs. One came on the very day of his dedication to withdraw his offer of service from a sense of depression and unfitness, but he chanced to meet the man he wanted most, and the talk they had together there, when Dr Fraser spoke to him of his own early days, made him see such new light that he felt that in knowing Christ as the source of all power, he had indeed something with which to go to the ends of the earth. In the years that followed Dr Fraser was an unfailing friend, and answered his letters in a way that made his correspondent wonder at the time he was willing to devote to them.

Nowhere was his courtesy more marked than in the letters he found time to write, some in answer to letters written in a somewhat different spirit. One of the most truculent he ever received was from a perfect stranger who, after hearing him broadcast, wrote to tell him of the " disgust and indignation " with which he had listened to him, the correspondent's point being that the primitive African,

[1] A prayer-room is to be included in the reconstructed Church Offices, as part of the Memorial to Dr Fraser.

living in a state of nature, was in the state in which God intended him to be, and therefore there could be no illness or trouble or serious wrong of any kind until the missionary introduced him to all the horrors of civilisation. If some of them did fight, how infinitely preferable to die of a clean spear-wound rather than of the lingering horrors of disease; and much more in the same strain. It would have been easy to write telling of the suffering and mortality among these " children of nature," and recount methods of death rather less pleasant than being speared ; but Dr Fraser's reply was a polite note in which he expressed his pleasure at finding the writer so interested in the African people, and said he felt sure that, if they could meet and discuss things at length, they would find they had much in common.

In reply to another letter wherein the writer disapproved of the Union and expressed his intention of stopping his contribution to Foreign Missions, he wrote :

" MY DEAR ――――, You were very good to write to me a few days ago about your feeling of uneasiness about the Union, and your intention of withholding your sub-scriptions to Foreign Missions. I am very sorry that you do not think the Church is being wisely led at present. I fancy that most people will agree with you that it might have been better led, for we all have a right to our private judgment and we always differ in some detail from our leaders. Yet I must say, the courtesy and desire to understand the minority's position which Principal Martin has shown have been wonderful, as Mr Barr himself has publicly acknowledged. But we Scots can never be quite unanimous about anything.

" However, I feel that the reasons for union are so strong, and the hope that a reunited Church baptised into the Spirit may do more for Scotland and the world is so well-grounded, that I should be willing to overlook a great many obstacles so that I might attain to a visible and corporate unity. If we unite, we should be able to do more for the coming of Christ's Kingdom. But does it not strike you that there is something wrong in your attitude, if it hinders you from giving the service that you used to give to Christ's Kingdom? That seems to me the strongest argument for overcoming our difficulties about union, that by refusing to join we cut ourselves off from a fellowship of service for Christ and the world, and limit the influence of ourselves and those associated with us in bringing in the Kingdom. I would beg of you, then, in face of the great need of the world for Christ, to consider well whether any liking or disliking on your part justifies you in withholding what Christ requires from you. I look with great sorrow on the prospect of having some of my best and most respected friends breaking the comradeship of service in which we have been engaged for many years, and finding themselves with hands tied. For every missionary in the field has agreed to come into the Union in spite of all the difficulties some of them have found. Yours very sincerely, ———"

Of Mary Slessor's *Life* he wrote to Mr Livingstone some words that might be applied to himself, though *he* wrote with a humbling sense of contrast: " It has stirred me to the depths. I do not remember another human document telling of such continuous toil and sacrifice, all borne with humour and gaiety and deepening quiet peace in God. It makes one feel as if the very fringe of the missionary passion had not touched one yet, and as if we were having the most indolent and self-indulgent of lives. And what a call it all is to the Church! . . . How many a great person's life is shadowed by the lack of those about them knowing that a prophet was among them."

Other letters to missionaries show how he tried to guide them through the problems they laid before him.

" I am interested in what you say about a celibate brotherhood. Almost every generation of ardent young fellows who realise the greatness of the need, and who rejoice in sacrifice, make the same proposal, but somehow it never materialises. For one thing, a vow of celibacy, or a time-limit, is peculiarly dangerous, for in spite of all one's youthful inclinations, somehow most succumb when the right person appears. And though celibacy is admirable, married life for most people means such an enrichment of personality and such an increase of efficiency that it is of vastly greater value to the service of Missions than bachelor-hood. Yet I always think that it is of great use to have some men who are quite free as bachelors ; they are more easily shifted, undertake hardships and dangerous bits of work without the same complications, and so on.

" However, my advice to you would be that you do not compromise the future by any unnecessary boat-burning. For God in His great love may put across your path just that person who will make your life so much fuller and richer and who will always be to you the example of God's love—given to one unworthy of her. But whether you find your fulness in this way or in celibacy, God help and keep and companion you through the days."

To another, thinking of resigning because of what he was up against : " You prepared yourself for this work through College days with far greater odds against you, and you triumphed over everything that you might be a missionary. Now that you *are* one, you must still stick at it though many difficult conditions are against you. Should you withdraw, who will do the work you are so fitted to do ? Are you considering the people, and considering Christ's need of you there ? Perhaps this is a cross in which you will find fuller life and opportunity, if you take it up. Try to bear with your colleagues, though you disagree with them. And believe that it is better to win what you think must be, by patience and perseverance, rather than by abandoning the service. I am sure you will always be sorry if you leave this work . . . which you love. But you will not regret sticking on in spite of everything, that you may help the Kingdom. . . . Your presence in —— can help to lift some of the suffering and to reveal Christ, and will give you opportunity for more grace and more of the Spirit, just because your work is so difficult."

"Sticking on," winning what he thought "must be, by patience and perseverance," was his own way. How real was the temptation to give up his work as an official, few suspected. It was hard on his ardent temperament to discipline himself to the slower pace which those along with whom he worked thought prudent, when he felt the forward call to be so urgent; hard to find that not all shared his measure of far-reaching vision and expectant faith. To lose these things for himself would have been fatal for his own life. Years before, as he entered the Offices one day, some one had laid his hand on his shoulder saying, "Fraser, souls have been lost here," and he never forgot the warning in that remark. Once in Africa he had been struck by a similar thought in a book he had been reading, and told me how it had made him afraid, and how he had prayed that he might never be that awful thing, "a middling man of God."

These years in Scotland were broken by two or three visits abroad. One was to Le Zoute, where he had been invited to act as Chairman of an International Conference of Government officials, educational and medical experts and missionaries, to discuss matters relating to the welfare of Africa. Another was to America, where he spoke at several Conferences at Northfield, Chatauqua and elsewhere. This was a visit crowded with kindness and overwhelming

U

hospitality, but he found the heat and the noise trying. Receptions were the one thing he did his best to avoid. There was one when, turning to speak to him as we stood shaking hands, I found his place empty, although there were still a large number of guests to meet.   Everyone asked for him, and I could only say I had not the least idea where he was, though I had a strong surmise that my exhortations to face it cheerfully had failed.   Later on a kind old lady told me she had him safely bestowed in her private sitting-room, as she could not withstand his pathetic plea to her to hide him safely somewhere.

One memory of Northfield stands out, when, instead of avoiding introductions, he introduced himself in a way that won him two friends.   There were two Negroes in clerical dress who sat by themselves, along with their womenfolk, waiting for a meeting to commence in the large Auditorium there.   I was sitting right in front of them and so overheard all that was said.   Dr Fraser appeared at a side-door, looked into the hall, and catching sight of the coloured men came straight up to them and said, " I must shake hands with two fellow-countrymen." He sat and chatted for a few minutes, learned that they had just arrived, and hoped they were going to enjoy the Conference.   When he left them they began to discuss what his opening remark had been : it had sounded like calling them " fellow-countrymen," but what could that mean ?   They could not have caught his words properly, they decided, but he was a fine gentleman !   Presently one of them was calling the other's attention to his appearance among the platform party.   A little later Dr Fraser from Africa was called upon to speak, and up rose their hitherto unknown friend—to their great excitement, for suddenly they began to realise why it was that he had described himself as a " fellow-countryman," and they chuckled over their previous bewilderment, and told themselves delightedly that " he thinks of himself as one of us ! " Two very appreciative listeners applauded him that afternoon. On the Sunday following Dr Fraser was speaking in the open air, and some joke he made was quickly seen and appreciated. He started his next sentence, but had to stop, rather puzzled because the amusement, instead of passing off, was increasing, and he could not be heard. Then he saw what had happened. Among his hearers were his Negro friends, and one of them, stout and elderly, had in his amusement thrown himself flat back on the grass and was rolling about in helpless laughter, infecting the rest of the crowd. It seemed so right somehow that not only should he make friends with these coloured men, but that he should help to make others feel more kindly towards them by sharing their laughter.

The following letter from our New York host, and old friend, who had not met my husband since student days, tells of the impression he made upon him :

" The first word I ever heard him utter was the word ' God ' ; and it is both the first and last word in the meaning of his career. It was in the post-Henry Drummond days, and at the suggestion of an aunt of mine I went to Edinburgh and to the Assembly Hall to hear a student who, she said, was somehow different. When Donald rose, he did more than ignore what had been said about him in the introduction. He had, I imagine, scarcely heard it. He didn't allow anything to interrupt the flow of his previous thought or to move him from the centre from which his thought flowed. Speaking in our presence, but as if apart from us, he began : ' God so loved the world that He ' . . . from that point he deviated from the New Testament text and said what he wanted to say. Except by the use of the word God I never could fathom the richness and depth of his mystical life, which seemed to come from something deeper than faith, some kind of inner insight that made his mind live in a world of simplicities and assurances and visions for which most of us have no capacities."

That American trip enabled him to see for the last time some of his relations in Canada, including one of his two surviving brothers, who died suddenly a few months afterwards, leaving a young family to whom "Uncle Donald" became a very good friend.

His third trip was to Buda-Pesth, to take part in the first European Conference of the World's Sunday Association. The record of what he did there is largely a pictorial one, for one means of making a little money out of visitors was the taking of endless photos on every occasion, and he was so impressed by the gnawing poverty, covered by a cloak of dignity and courtesy, that he who so hated being photographed, bought from all who approached him. The result was that he brought away abundant evidence of having hobnobbed with archbishops and bishops of the Greek and Armenian and Coptic Churches, and of leading a procession to lay wreaths on the Unknown Warrior's tomb, there to dedicate themselves—representatives of twenty-seven nations—to work for international peace and good will. Singularly indecipherable correspondence that occasionally turned up afterwards at his Glasgow address seemed to point to his having left friends behind him, and a book that arrived with his name on it we accepted as a translation of his *African Idylls*.

It had been arranged that, after leaving Buda-Pesth, he should meet our younger daughter and myself at Munich and go with us to the Tyrol before returning home. We arrived to find that he was not awaiting us at the hotel on which we had fixed. Presently came a wire asking us to join him at Innsbruck. He had started on what appeared to be the right train, but before the night was over he learnt that its destination was Innsbruck, not Munich. Having made this mistake, he did not reveal that he had had a bad moment before starting, when he made the discovery that he had apparently lost his tickets for the homeward journey. He had confided this sad fact to Mrs Smellie, one of his fellow-delegates, and she, " knowing what men are," had made him relate to her everything he had done since he had last handled them, and then suggested that he might carefully search the pockets of another coat—in which he found them.

He seemed tired when we met him, and a few days later, on returning from a shopping expedition, we found him in the tea-garden in which we had left him, quietly resting, looking white and faint, evidently having had a bad attack of some kind in our absence. We immediately decided to go on the next afternoon to a quieter spot ; but, while we were packing, he wandered out, and the time for starting arrived without his having returned. At the last minute he turned up to say he hoped we didn't mind, but having gone exploring on the small railway to Iglis he had found a place that had taken his fancy, and had engaged rooms there. He enjoyed being free to act on impulse in his holidays, so to the Pension Elizabeth we went, there to rest, stroll around, and only gradually add to the length of our wanderings as he grew more vigorous. Passing through Paris on the way home, he spent some hours at the Paris Exposition, in order to get ideas for mission-ary exhibitions in Scotland, and decided it was worth while to send one of the Forward Movement staff to take notes.

With such a passion as he possessed to see the Will of God dominant in all spheres of human life, he found it hard to keep out of sympathy and co-operation with any agency that would help towards that end. He spoke on behalf of the League of Nations, was a member of the B.B.C. Committee on Religious Broadcasting, and enthusiastically gave his support to the Livingstone National Memorial scheme. His optimism had kept the Committee going in the early days, when many difficulties had to be faced, and no one rejoiced more than he in the ultimate success which crowned Mr M'Nair's indefatigable efforts. He showed the Duchess of York round after she had opened the building, and the last time he visited it was with a large and happy party of delegates to the Troon Conference.

In the establishing of the African Churches' Mission in Liverpool, which arose out of the selfless devotion of Daniel Ekarte, a West African who had been taught by Mary Slessor, he took a considerable share, making his story public through an article in the Church *Record*. He was also a member of the Standing Committee of the Conference of British Missionary Societies, and its Chairman in 1922 and 1932. Of the impression he made there and as Chairman at the Le Zoute African Conference we can form an idea from the words of Canon Spanton, Secretary of the Universities Mission to Central Africa: "It was always easy to work with him, always a delight to meet him. Surely few people with such complete devotion to a cause have been so richly gifted with a sense of humour, and not many people since the days of St Paul have so combined the capacity to be all things to all men with an almost fierce enthusiasm for the right."

Another undertaking with which he was associated was the annual Easter Vacation School for missionaries on furlough and missionary candidates, now so firmly established and popular an institution, held in the Women's Missionary College, St Colm's, Edinburgh. To it he came whenever he could. In the last year of his life he was acting as chaplain there, and perhaps the last time he dispensed the Communion was in its little chapel.

He contributed to the *International Review of Missions* and other papers, and *All Nations*—a little monthly paper issued by the Foreign Mission Committee—was another suggestion of his for supplying to busy ministers a digest of the most interesting current missionary news. He even allowed himself to be drawn into the venture of a new religious weekly for Scotland. This gave him many an anxious hour, and the day on which it passed entirely into other hands, was one of profound relief to him. He came from that meeting of shareholders, who had lost money over the venture, unspeakably grateful for their recognition of his untiring exertions to make the paper a success. The journalists with whom it brought him into contact write of what they learnt of Christian wisdom from him—he was so lenient and yet so discerning—and of the gift of his friendship, which was a door into the Holiest of all.

For the last few years he was an elder in Wellington Church. Though he was very seldom free to take his place among the others on a Communion Sunday, he was faithful in going round his district, and felt ashamed if ever, instead of calling, he had to post their cards to the members. On the last, if not the only Communion at Wellington in which he took part as an elder, he replied to a lady who on leaving the church expressed her pleasure at seeing him there. " And I can't tell you how happy I am to be here to-day, for it is Catherine's first Communion." Now all his children were communicant members of the Church.

In 1929 he was appointed one of the King's Chaplains in Scotland. It was more appropriate, perhaps, than any realised, for the intensity of his Highland loyalty to the King had always amused me. He had instilled into our

African people a real devotion to their unknown sovereign. No gramophone entertainment was complete without their hearing the voices of " Jorodji and Mary " speaking to them. When he visited Balmoral and preached before the King, he " just gave a missionary address," and as thoroughly enjoyed the friendliness of his week-end there, as if he had been in an African village presiding over a banquet of titbits taken from some beast he had shot, as they were roasted and eaten at the evening fire by a chattering group of his dusky African folk.

CHAPTER XXXVI

THE FORWARD MOVEMENT

THE Forward Movement was Dr Fraser's last enterprise. In its ultimate form it was something far different from what he had planned and felt able to undertake. Foreseeing the danger of the long-prepared-for Union of the Churches being looked upon as a consummation rather than as a fresh opportunity for advance, he had thought out a scheme for an Overseas Forward Movement. When it finally emerged from the melting-pot of discussion, it was altered to embrace all the interests of the Church's life and work. After the first sense of dismay at the complexity of a task which he felt to be beyond him and would gladly have handed over to another, he shouldered it " with cheerful, patient, gallant endeavour." Those responsible for enlarging its scope had not relieved him of any of the financial responsibility, and his support and encouragement came more from a special band of supporters than from the official leadership of the Church.

The Movement was inaugurated by a carefully planned and successful Congress held in Glasgow in the autumn of 1931, with the object of setting before the delegates, and the congregations they represented, the Church's activities and responsibilities in the light of her resources in God. This Congress was followed up by Missions of the Kingdom in various centres, to which the missioners went only by invitation of the local ministers. These were carried on for two years, with degrees of success which varied, largely in proportion to the thoroughness and enthusiasm with which local preparations were made. But those were difficult and depressing years for the country, the atmosphere was unfavourable; and many did not hesitate to call the Movement a failure because, in such conditions, it was not accomplishing all they had hoped from it. Dr Fraser's sympathisers watched him carry on, handicapped, as few suspected, by failing health, but undaunted in spite of much that hindered and hurt him. If *Agonia* is the measure of success, he did not fail. To others in more intimate touch with it the Movement seemed to be succeeding, as one phrased it, " in the Calvary tradition; and although the foremost standard-bearer crumpled up at the very gates of the citadel, he had willingly given his body as a stepping stone for the real assault." If it came to no triumphant climax in his lifetime, men who had worked with him, men who had watched " the way he went on and on regardless of the stones," were influenced and inspired, and he was the last man to care who leads, if only the onward march begins. For the younger men in the ministry, and those who reckoned themselves " his humbler brethren," he had strong attraction. To know him, said one of them, was to see the Gospel incarnated in a form hauntingly attractive. These younger men had made him a member of the New (after the Union the Renascence) Club, and held him the most honoured and beloved of members, their very hero and intimate friend.

Only occasionally did some friend get a glimpse of the increasing hardness of these years. To one he opened his heart in a moment when his skies grew very clouded, and what his friend saw was a heart " reduced to the quality of his Lord's—tremendous in its meekness, passionate in its loyalty, unmurmuring in its affliction, and containing unfathomable wells of compassion for all who were out of the way."

Generally, however, he went cheerily on. With children he was always at his happiest, and it may be that the widening ripple of his contact with those he met as he went about, will be noticeable in the colleges and further afield in the days to come. He was so absolutely natural with them, so free of " pious " talk. Remembering how he would have hated it when he was a boy, he never pressed the missionary calling on young people, and regretted the ill-advised earnestness of those parents who did ; yet he infected them as few could do with his own enthusiasm. It is told that one mother—an Episcopalian—finding in her little boy's pocket a pamphlet entitled "Advice to Mothers," learned that the boy was reading it in preparation for being a Presbyterian missionary like Dr Fraser, who had said that everything one learned came in useful some day !

They always listened to him even if his words were not invariably so implicitly accepted. At the Orphan Homes at Bridge of Weir a " Mother " was asked by a small child if missionaries were always good men and spoke the truth. When she tried to discover what had awakened such early scepticism, the child, who had been listening to an address from Dr Fraser, replied, " Because that man *said* that in Africa his children got tired of strawberries and cream and asked for rice pudding instead ! "

Dr Fraser's active share in the Movement came to an end with the Conference at Troon in June 1933. The idea of holding it had arisen in part out of an invitation from some of the Church of England's leaders to speak at their annual Cromer Conference. He was too diffident to accept the invitation, but the conception of a Conference based on fearless thinking and unfaltering loyalty seized his imagination afresh, and made him wish for something of that nature for his own Church, especially as the ever-increasing volume of business to be dealt with by the Assembly crowded out the possibility of getting more time devoted to developing its inspirational value.

Though the attendance was not all he had hoped for, a clash of dates having prevented a number of the leaders from being present, it was a particularly happy gathering, and he enjoyed every minute of it. In the Speakers' House he had great delight in listening to and laughing at the witty sallies of Dr T. R. Glover as they were countered by the Irish humour of Mr Hamilton.[1] How he admired quick wit in others, and how often he had confessed what a blessing it was to have Mr Hamilton at hand to put a humorous complexion on something that might have depressed him otherwise. There was a fine spirit in the meetings, whether the gatherings were for prayer and devotion, or for hearing the charming talks of Dr Glover or the arresting addresses of some of the younger ministers. In the afternoons there were excursions, where everyone was so friendly and hospitable that any delegate, by merely expressing the wish, could go to them in a private car without having to own one, and the tea seemed to be mysteriously paid for.

" Wasn't that fine ? " he asked with shining eyes, after his friend, Dr Millar Patrick, had conducted the Communion Service, Donald's last on earth.

He himself gave the closing address on Christlikeness. When it was all over, he sat down, with grateful courtesy, to send, through Mr Gordon Stewart, his thanks to him and to the local Committee for all they had done to further its success. It was a happy ending to his public work to have had this time among friends so appreciative of the gathering and so affectionate towards himself.

But he " saw no future," he told me, now that this task was drawing to a close. Others had in hand and could

[1] Rev. J. E. Hamilton, Hon. Secretary of the Movement.

carry on the work that had been his before the Forward Movement had been started. He could do something in South Africa, he felt, if he were authorised to deal with the situation there. " Well, after that we'll retire, and you'll take a wee country kirk," I suggested. His answer was characteristic : " Would they have me ? "

CHAPTER XXXVII

CLOSING MONTHS : THE LAST ULENDO

Dr Fraser had long had a way of evading inquiries about his health by replying, " Oh, I'm breaking up fast ! " The cheerful smile that made the statement seem ridiculous, invited the remark, " You're a very long time about it ! " But those who saw him most closely realised latterly that truth underlay his words. When 1933 dawned he had gone to have a few days' rest at Inveraray, instead of assisting Mr Burnet at the Watchnight Service in Westbourne as he had done for some years. He had scarcely resumed work when, at the opening meeting of a Mission of the Kingdom at Carluke, he had a bad collapse, and lay for three weeks in the hospitable home of Mrs Smellie, explaining the rigors with which his illness started as " just the onset of malaria," and never mentioning the pain that accompanied them. His condition, however, was sufficiently serious to make me feel it to be wise to suggest to our younger daughter that she should return from Germany, though it was only to a German friend that I expressed the misgiving that she might not have much more of her father's company. After his return to work these attacks were liable to recur ; and, although he called them " sick turns," he always made straight for home when they came on. A proposed visit to our South Africa mission fields, to which his many friends there were eagerly looking forward, he gradually grew willing to postpone, realising that he was not then fit to face it. One noticed how he felt the stairs that led to our flat, how grey and *done* he

looked when he turned up in the evening and collapsed into
a chair, too exhausted even to smile ; and we ceased asking
any questions about his day's work, knowing that when he
felt fit he would tell us of anything that had cheered or
encouraged him, while the rest he would try to forget.
Even at his worst, if he thought he had alarmed the family,
it was wonderful how he could resume all his old brightness
and gaiety, and joke with them and with the friends he
was still glad to welcome.   Sometimes he would suggest
a cinema, and no one enjoyed more than he a really
good film, especially " something to laugh at " ; and then
one wondered what had hurt him which he wished to
forget.

He had no suggestions to offer about the summer holiday
—" just anything that the children would like "—so finally
we arranged to share a large house which friends had taken
for August on Lochfyne side.   Then, rather unexpectedly,
he bought a second-hand car, because he wanted the children
to enjoy themselves, and they and he took lessons in driving.
A wedding was calling him to London in July, and it was
decided that, instead of making a hurried journey, we
should motor up, and on the way back visit some of the
English cathedrals.   We went via the Lake District, having a roughly-sketched programme but no cut-and-dried
arrangements—leaving just that sense of freedom which
he loved and had so little chance of indulging.   How
intensely he enjoyed backing into some leafy lane for lunch,
stopping when we felt inclined ; yet it was significant that
he allowed himself to be persuaded to leave the driving to
his son.

A few days were spent near London with his only
surviving brother.   On the Sunday he preached in Tooting
Presbyterian Church, and spent a happy day, in spite of
some physical discomfort, with the M'Gregor Rosses of

Kenya. Then we set off for Canterbury and all the other cathedrals we could conveniently include during our return journey, his architectural interest making the visits to them a very real source of delight. Yet somehow one was haunted by a curious sense of finishing up, of " getting in " some of the things we had so often talked about doing, just as in Africa he would see that books were written up and odd jobs attended to, before going off on a journey. Two nights were spent at St Andrew's, Whittlesford, with newly-made friends there, and on the intervening day we drove across to Ely to visit our friend, Canon Raven. He had been one of the speakers, and our guest, at the Forward Movement Conference in Glasgow, and had at the very first meeting with him been gripped and inspired by his host and Chairman—" one of the very few in whom one felt at once the eternal quality." The same impression of impending change seems to have been conveyed to Dr Raven, for when Donald thanked him for that afternoon and said, " I wanted the children to have happy memories of this place," it was " as if he were already a bit detached from us all—just hoping that we would remember happily."

The last Sunday of our tour was spent at York. He went out in the forenoon to attend the Minster service, but found himself late and shut out from the choir in which it was held, so wandered out and into a Salvation Army meeting. He was equally happy to worship there, join in the hearty singing, and listen, impressed, to the address given by a cultured woman. Had he not wished to attend the Presbyterian service, he would have accepted their invitation to him to come back and speak to them in the evening.

The effort with which he set his face to return to his office work was obvious, and when, on our way home, we set him down at the West End in Edinburgh for what was to be his last spell of work there, we tried to cheer him by telling him to think of the holiday that lay ahead.

Before the month was over his sister and niece from Canada arrived a day early—a circumstance which enabled them to spend an evening with us in Glasgow instead of deferring our meeting till August. We drove out to Loch Lomond, and he was full of fun, teasing his niece about her Canadian accent, letting her dress up in his Geneva and D.D. gowns and his chaplain's cassock. He seemed to have cast all care aside, and the letter he sent to his son George in Africa was "very full of the joy of life, and family and friends."

On the last Saturday of July Donald was going to spend a day at Duchal,[1] and, when Lord Maclay telephoned suggesting that it might be a week-end instead of a day, we urged him to agree, saying he would be better out of the way as we would be busy preparing for our start on the Tuesday. In reality we wished him not to be at home if, as often happened, he was rung up and asked to take a service because some minister in Glasgow had been taken ill or unexpectedly called away. So he left his home with no "sadness of farewell," but in a bustle of pleasant anticipation of rest and change. Late on Sunday night the telephone bell rang, summoning me to Duchal, as he had been taken suddenly and seriously ill. A few days later he was motored in to a nursing home, and an operation was decided on for the 8th of August. On hearing the date he insisted on my going down to Argyllshire to spend the intervening week-end with the family. The day before it took place he sat up in bed, scribbling a number of notes, such as the following to Mr R. F. Young of the Church Offices. "Well, the day of adventure is to-morrow—Wednesday— and I am looking forward to it with joyful anticipation.

---

[1] Lord Maclay's house at Kilmacolm.

x

It seems absurd to call it an adventure when all I have to do is to go to sleep. That is a peculiarly easy act of trust —trust in the surgeon and in the wonderful goodness of God. I am looking forward to months of freedom from public speech, and to a new lease of life. The surgeon is to remove the gall-bladder, which is septic, apparently. It is a major operation, but not a dangerous one. I have really not suffered at all. Beyond these first two days when I had to have morphia, I have only been weak. So good-bye for the present. . . . Everyone seems to be doing something except me, and all I am doing is sending a note or two to friends."

That afternoon the family all arrived, and a gay tea-party was held in his room, he in high spirits, keen on the children enjoying themselves, and planning what they might do to entertain their relatives from Canada.

It was dry, sunny weather, his windows were wide open, and the breeze that blew in reminded him, he said, of African wind blowing over arid spaces. He laughed when his son pointed out that it came straight from the University, towards which the room faced. That night he entertained his nurse with stories of Africa.

When the operation was over, and he lay looking exhausted and so different from the cheerful host of the day before, he urged that the family should not see him again till he felt fit to talk to them. He did not wish that anything in his looks or weakness should depress them ; so Donald did not see him at all, and Violet had only one more glimpse of him when she tiptoed in to kiss him before leaving town. Catherine alone was present when he passed away.

His sick-room was always a cheerful place ; he was so uncomplaining and grateful, so considerate. One of his nurses—" my wee Miss Campbell," as he always called

her—came from Inveraray, and he liked her soft voice—
as he always did like soft voices in women—and told her
not to lose it—it was such an asset for a nurse. He told
me—so like him—that the first time I passed through
Inveraray I must call on her mother, to tell how well she
had looked after him.

No friends saw him after the operation apart from those
in medical attendance on him, except for a few of the
visiting doctors to the Home who looked in in passing.
Among these was his brother-in-law, Dr Wilson of Airdrie,
so soon and unexpectedly to follow him, and he spoke of
the smile and the " Come in, dear old chap," with which
he was welcomed.

It seemed to me that Donald had half expected that the
operation might be the end of all, but that realising the
anxiety of the surgeon and doctors, and knowing from
his own experience in medical work what it means to lose
a patient, he set himself loyally to recover. He seldom
questioned anything, accepting all that was done for him,
only asking sometimes about what I was saying to the
dear children or to my mother, the latter being ill at the
time. No suffering made him querulous, no service went
unthanked. His nurse, for instance, remarked one day,
" Now I am going to bring you your tea." " I wonder
if you'll give me a great treat first ? A sponge with cold
water." As she washed his face and hands he murmured,
" So delicious. . . . Oh thank you, thank you. That
wasn't asking too much, was it ? "

Constantly he asked for others who were ill, and kept
inquiring if messages of thanks had been sent to those who
supplied him with flowers. He remembered one engagement that had not been cancelled and asked me when
writing about it to apologise for his unreliability. And
" How kind " he pronounced everybody, adding once, " It

is a profound mistake to talk about the cynicism and
unkindness in the world ; it is just full of goodness and
sympathy." How he suffered he only revealed when he
said, " Tell H—— (who had recently undergone a similar
operation) I am sorry I had no idea how much he suffered."

As the days passed, new and trying symptoms super-
vened, and none of the remedies tried were of any real
efficacy. One evening he had a fancy that port, which
had been suggested, would help him, and late as it was, his
surgeon went out himself to procure some for him. After
drinking it he said gratefully " Blessed be the Lord for
His good gift of wine—the first thing I have retained ; "
then, glancing up at his nurse, he asked " Are you shocked,
Nurse ? Are you a teetotaller ? You see," he went on
seriously, " it means so much to me because I only taste
it at Communion " ; and one could not fail to notice,
after that, how he received and drank it, as if he were
partaking of the Sacrament.

At first I spent the days with him, but when it became
evident that he found the nights harder to get through,
I rested part of the day and sat with him through the night.
The sleeping draughts administered to him sometimes confused his mind through the curious sense of dissociation
from his body that they produced, and he said he liked
to have me there to " explain." Very often the preface to
any conversation was, " Come and help me to understand."
Frequently it puzzled him that " Brother Ass " should be
monopolising so much time and attention. " There are
things to be done. I want to get this straightened out.
Why am I lying here with my body like this ? Why can't
I get it right ? " I told him that he should not trouble
about it ; " Brother Ass " had had scant consideration for
a long time. " But there is God's Will to be done," he
interposed. " God is not asking you to *do* anything about

His Will just now—just to suffer it," I began, when he interrupted, almost reproachfully, " *Suffer* it ? Oh, my dear, His Will is adorable ! But it is never stupid or use-less. That is why I was wanting to understand." A little later he remarked, " I can't get hold of that Hebrew word that they don't know the meaning of, but think may mean a pause in the music." When I said, " Do you mean Selah ? " " Yes, that's it. I have been thinking that my time here is my Selah."

If he wished to talk he used to raise his eyebrows to inquire whether Nurse was behind the screen or we were alone. Once he informed me that since his operation he had neither read his Bible nor prayed. When I told him that it seemed to me that God was never out of his thoughts, and that the very mention of Him seemed to clear away any haziness in his mind, he acquiesced, adding, " My mind has been running tremendously on the wounds of Christ . . . wounded for our transgressions, bruised for our iniquities."

He never alluded to the possibility of dying ; so long as the doctors were fighting for his life, so long must he fight too. The nearest he came to it was one day when after a time of distressing pain, in which he must have been conscious of my misgiving, he suddenly put out his hand and calling me by a name he only used in rare moments, asked, " What is troubling you ? I am not worrying at all about you or the children." When I told him that the *only* thing that was hard was to see him suffer so, he looked relieved.

On the last Friday evening the doctor told him that his condition was better. " Do you think so ? " he replied, " Well, you should know best ; " but it sounded as if he were either a little incredulous or regretful.

Noticing how he disliked the inability to think clearly

produced by his sleeping draught, I had suggested, on the
night of Saturday, the 19th August, that the effect of
omitting it should be tried, with the result that when I
drew up the blinds at dawn on the Sunday morning his
mind was absolutely alert, and, remarking on the beauty
of the morning, he began to quote :

> " Blest morning, whose first dawning rays
>   Beheld the Son of God
> Arise triumphant from the grave
>   And leave His dark abode."

With my assistance he repeated the whole paraphrase,
for his inability to quote correctly was a family joke.   At
breakfast time I left him and went home to rest.   While
we were at lunch the telephone rang, and we were told that
the end was unexpectedly near.   Hurrying back, Catherine
and I found him propped up in bed, struggling painfully
for breath.   It was long before he could speak, but finally
he managed to whisper, " I think I am a little easier now."
A moment later he asked, " Do they say I may go now ? "
It was as if he had been waiting for permission, for when
I told him he might go any minute now, his face lighted
up and he said, " Oh, I go joyfully ! "

He seemed to want to say something more and I bent
closer and asked, " Are you sending your love to the
children ? "   " *God's* love," he amended, " and God's love
to you," turning to the surgeon who stood on the other
side of the bed.   And so, having given for the last time
the message he had preached and revealed all through his
life, he passed on.

GLOSSARY OF AFRICAN WORDS

Boma,   enclosure, Government station—synonym for European Government.

Bwana,   Chief, also given to white man.

Dambo,   little valley.

Dona,   white woman.

Framo,   a native form of Fraser.

Indaba,   lawsuit-quarrel.

Induna,   army leader.

Jorodji,   George.

Kapitao,   overseer.

Karata,   letter.

Machila,   travelling hammock.

Marambo,   Senga country in Loangwa valley.

Mfwiti,   wizard or poisoner.

Mzungu,   white man.

Poso,   food-money.

Tiyabonga,   " We give thanks."

Ulendo,   journey, file of travellers.

Ungano,   gathering, convention.

Vipya,   hills rising 5000 feet dividing Lake Nyasa from Ngoniland plateau.

BOOKS BY DR FRASER

THE FUTURE OF AFRICA, 1911. Published by the Mission Study Council of the United Free Church and the Foreign Mission Committee of the Church of Scotland.

WINNING A PRIMITIVE PEOPLE, 1914. Seeley, Service & Co.

LIVINGSTONIA, THE STORY OF OUR MISSION, 1915. Foreign Mission Committee of the United Free Church.

AFRICAN IDYLLS, 1923. Seeley, Service & Co.

AUTOBIOGRAPHY OF AN AFRICAN, 1925. Seeley, Service & Co.

THE NEW AFRICA, 1927. Edinburgh House Press.

INDEX